NEW TRENDS IN DEVELOPMENT THEORY

Essays in development and social theory

P. W. Preston

Routledge & Kegan Paul
London, Boston, Melbourne and Henley

First published in 1985
by Routledge & Kegan Paul plc

14 Leicester Square, London WC2H 7PH, England

9 Park Street, Boston, Mass. 02108, USA

464 St Kilda Road, Melbourne,
Victoria 3004, Australia and

Broadway House, Newtown Road,
Henley-on-Thames, Oxon RG9 1EN, England

Set in 10pt Linoterm Times
by Ann Buchan (Typesetters), Surrey
and printed in Great Britain
by Redwood Burn Ltd, Trowbridge, Wiltshire

Library of Congress Cataloging in Publication Data

Preston, P. W. (Peter Wallace), 1949–
New trends in development theory.
(International library of sociology)

Bibliography: p.
Includes index.
1. Economic development.   2. Sociology – Methodology.
I. Title.   II. Series.
HD75.P74   1985   338.9'001   84–15972

British Library CIP data available

ISBN 0-7102-0377-2

For Rose

Contents

Acknowledgments

This text continues work I began as a PhD student in Leeds and it reflects in diverse ways the influence of my teachers and friends of those days. My thanks to them all. I should also like to record my thanks to Edwin Thumboo and Ong Jin Hui, who rescued me a little while ago from the threat of Mrs Thatcher's dole-queues and brought me to the National University in Singapore. Living and working in Singapore has been a rewarding experience, and I offer my thanks to my colleagues and students.

'I have slowly become convinced that development presents a major challenge for the social sciences, notably sociology: perhaps its main challenge in the immediate future' C.A.O. van Niewenhuijze, *Development Begins at Home* (1982), p.2.

' . . . the heir of "classical" political theory is now sociology. It is sociology which is concerned with the understanding of that process [of becoming/being industrialised], which is now central to validating, or even conceptualizing society' E. Gellner, *Thought and Change* (1964), p.34.

'Once the limiting perspective of mainstream social science has been challenged and the biases at its foundation exposed, new questions and problems emerge. These cluster about the interpretation and understanding of political and social reality. How are we to engage in this activity? What is the relevance of empirical studies of regularities and correlations to the interpretive process? Looming in the background is the central question of how one can rationally adjudicate among competing and conflicting interpretations' R. Bernstein, *The Restructuring of Social and Political Theory* (1976), p.114.

Introduction

1.0   These essays are addressed to the exchange between issues of development and problems of social theory. They represent an attempt to present and codify some of the problems for an understanding of theorizing (and, therefore, theorizing development) which are generated from a review of the career of development studies conducted in the light of Gellner's suggestion that this post-war history reveals the nature of 'classic sociology'.[1] Elsewhere I have made a preliminary investigation of these issues,[2] and these essays represent a modest further step. In this introductory chapter I want to offer brief notes on my (developing) view of the nature of social theorizing, the character of the post-war career of development studies, and, finally, the contents of the essays that form the main substance of this book. These notes will serve, I hope, to make clear which are the principal themes which are pursued through the subsequent studies.

2.0   In a recent review of the 'present state of sociology', Giddens[3] remarks that there have been a variety of responses to the loss of surety associated with the eclipse of functionalism. These include both rejoicing and despair: in contrast to these, Giddens looks to a systematic reconstruction of social theory. My own response must, I suppose, be taken as a variety of the first noted option. I am content that there is no orthodoxy, for it seems to me that this leaves us free to consider directly the prior question(s) of what social theorists have been doing and might, in the future, usefully do. Thinking along these lines does have the effect, it seems to me, of ruling out more than a few responses to the 'loss of surety'.

It rules out libertarian rejoicing. I want to follow what has been done; that is, to pursue the classic tradition of social theorizing in presently relevant ways. The multiplication of theoretical novelties does not seem an appropriate move. It also rules out the pessimistic

1

invocation of particular creeds or specific 'Golden Ages': John Carroll's[4] suggestion that we rework the legacy of the eighteenth century does not seem to me to be especially helpful. And Giddens's project of a systematic reconstruction rather defeats my imagination: what *use* would a *new* orthodoxy be?

If we simply look at what has been proposed as 'social theory' then it is clear that we confront no single 'object' or 'project'; rather we find, to borrow an over-worked metaphor from Wittgenstein, a *family* of activities. Social theorizing comprises a *diversity* of pursuits. This 'insight' is easily gleaned from the history of social theorizing: it is a view that is also readily generated by reviewing the post-war career of development studies. There is, as far as I can see now, no reason to, or intellectual profit to be gained from attempting to, squash this diversity into a single mould. Contrariwise, and *contra* the libertarian rejoicers, there is no reason to suppose that we cannot *order* this diversity.

What I am going to propose – returning to Giddens's trio of responses – is an understated rejoicing. Social theorizing encompasses a multiplicity of strategies of making sense of the social world: unity and diversity. A general label might be useful. I am affirming a 'dis-integrated' view of social theorizing. The substance of such a view can most easily be *sketched* by offering a characterization of two views of the nature of social theorizing organized around my particular concern with making sense.

Recent work in the philosophy of social science has both cast doubt upon the intellectual status of the prevalent post-war view of the nature of social theorizing[5] and been closely bound up with discussions of the philosophy of natural science. Now this last-mentioned area of enquiry is one with which I do not, in the following chapters, concern myself, but there is one crucial aspect of the multiple and overlapping debates of these two areas that will serve as a peg upon which I can hang these introductory remarks on the nature of social theorizing. Thus, within these debates, and among other things, it has been strongly argued that the 'received model' of natural science is an inappropriate starting-point for social science work:[6] and to this I would add that it is an inappropriate starting point for *discussion about* the nature of social science.[7] We can offer a simple characterization of the whole field of social science around this matter of the affirmation or denial of the 'received model'. Thus I will distinguish, for my present introductory purposes, between social scientists who adopt some sort of 'naturalist-descriptive' stance on the one hand, and, on the other, those who adopt some sort of 'reflexive' stance.[8]

To cast the matter of my interest in social science at a very general level, I would say that my concern is with how actors, collectively, *make sense* of the social world. Now, clearly, the orthodox 'naturalist-descriptive' theorist could also affirm this as their most general interest. It would be understood as the natural science-referring description of structures: Bauman's 'Durksonian' social science.[9] For the orthodox theorists the way in which actors make sense, and the way in which this can be social-scientifically appropriated, is conceived in an essentially passive fashion. Thus social science gives a report on how sense has been made, how the world has been patterned: the social world is a reality *sui generis*. The social scientific enquiry is also, itself, cast in passive form: the provision of value-neutral reports on how things are, how the world has been patterned.

The alternative approach is to see the business of making sense as essentially an active process and enquiry itself as active. The given is the process of structuration[10] – the (re)creation of the patterned social world in and through patterned human action. Giddens discusses this under the heading of 'agency and structure': the simple point being that the terms are mutually implicative in the context of theorizing the social world. This alternative, 'reflexive', approach also denies the 'received model'. A passive engagement with the material of enquiry is seen to be unpersuasively and arbitrarily restricted. Thus the alternative seeks reflexively to lodge the community of social scientists (as one group among many) within a society which is conceived as an interplay of processes.[11]

Within this frame of possibilities the approach to theorizing/conception of the social world which I would affirm is the 'reflexive' schema. To continue, very briefly, at this rather general level, there is one important further point which I must note. My declaration of a general level interest in the business of making sense of the social world has the effect of specifying an object of enquiry that not only embraces the entirety of the social sciences and the humanities but also shows distinct signs of expanding to include the realm of the natural sciences as well. Clearly, my general level specification is in imminent danger of a rather rapid decline into meaninglessness! However, my interests are narrower, and noting them will indicate how I see the general approach/conception being usable in social theorizing. Thus my interest in making sense is expressed in the particular context of (more or less) deliberate or self-conscious efforts at what would ordinarily be recognized as social-science-type theorizing.[12] So the paradigm case of my interest is the production of ideologies: here we find the matter of the effective contribution to structuration of actively produced ideas about structures. Ideologies contribute to structuration (when they become meaningful cultural objects for large or significant social groups) while taking as their rational core the presentation of reports about how structures are and might be.

The key term for the subsequent essays, and for my own views about the nature of social theorizing – how it is to be characterized, how it embeds in the social world, how it differs from natural science work – is *ideology*. This term I use non-pejoratively and in a way that resembles Giddens's structuration – that is, to point to the interplay of various agents, variously located in various social structures – because I acknowledge the point about the intimate link between agency and structure.[13] However, my enquiries diverge sharply from those of Giddens: I am not (unlike Giddens) interested in a 'non-functionalist manifesto' (what would we? do with it?), or in a systematic reconstruction of social theory (to what end?), neither (unlike Giddens) am I going blithely to neglect the major post-war area of social scientific work, that is, development theorizing. Instead, I am going to pursue the matter of 'reflexive' theorizing by concerning myself with the production of ideologies in the area of work that Gellner has indicated; that is, studies of development. It seems to me that there is a rich, and neglected, body of social-theoretic material here from which much could be learned.

3.0 I have alluded above to the revisions presently in train of our ideas about the nature of social science. While these debates have been taking place, an analogous review of the post-war career of studies of development now seems to have been placed on the intellectual agenda of specialists in development and, as I have suggested, of social scientists more generally.[14]

The early post-war period saw the establishment of US hegemony within the First World: this extended (of course) to theories about development. Thus most (in)famously we have Walt Rostow and his schema of stages of growth. But now the overweening confidence of the heyday of 'modernization' theory has long dissolved, and the equally confident counter-view of the 'radical dependency' theorists is also clearly less than satisfactory. It is now possible to look back, over nearly forty years of effort, and to identify a series of 'schools' of development studies. Each of these can be seen, in retrospect, to have been offering circumstance-specific and problem-centred analyses of their immediate social, political and historical situations, and with reference to given intellectual situations. They were, to put the matter directly, preparing delimited-formal ideologies. Now, to be sure, this sequence of statements did not comprise a series of monolithically closed systems of thought, nor were they so conceived, and one would not expect that the replacement of declining 'schools' would proceed in any mechanical fashion. Indeed, reviewing the post-war history of development studies, it is clear that despite the dominant influence of the 'received model', which acted to suppress diversity in formulations, there were many divergent conceptualizations of the nature, and practicalities, of development. The question which might now exercise commentators is this: can we discern anything of the outlines of a rational framework appropriate to the theorizing of development in today's world?

It seems to me that there are a few points which can be made. And here, it should be noted, I am anticipating the enquiries in respect of the exchange between development and social theory to which these essays are directed. I shall present these interim conclusions and then proceed to indicate how the subsequent essays pursue aspects of the various issues adumbrated. Thus, in the light of the dual reconsideration alluded to here, I would say that the following points must be acknowledged within any rationally defensible framework for the analysis of development.[15]

(1) That the 'received model' of scientific explanation is deforming social scientific enquiry. The corollary of this would seem to be that social scientists are obliged to locate themselves in the processes of which they speak. Further, it is fairly clear that there are a multiplicity of such 'locations' available for social scientists. The key (dual) problem seems to be to map these locations and specify how they relate to the 'location' of scholarship.

(2) That the idea of development is an ethico-political one and is not technical or obvious. This is another way of invoking the idea of the unity of theory and practice. The way development 'experts' have proceeded exemplifies a view of how the world ought to be. A 'reflexive' strategy of theorizing enjoins the routine inspection of ethico-political commitments. A corollary of these views would seem to be that what is to count as 'development' in any given circumtance will have to be locally determined: there are no definitive general recipes.

(3) That social theorizing (and theorizing development) must be seen as a circumstance-sensitive and problem-specific enterprise. It is consequently presented, in concrete analyses (and indeed abstract reflections contributed thereto in the process of ideology construction), in diverse guises. Thus circumstances and problems call forth modes of engagement, each of which will have its particular appropriate manner of theorizing with its distinctive mix of conception/intent. There is an important corollary to this: theorizing development is an essentially complex business to which must be added the recognition of a wide diversity of interests in the process (of development) itself. The scientistic orthodoxy would have us squash this complexity and diversity into a single, policy-scientific, mould: this is an error.

4.0 The essays in this book address a series of issues related to the 'dis-integrated' view of social theorizing which I have sketched. I am concerned with pursuing the question of the mapping of the field of modes of social-theoretic engagement and, thereafter, with attempting to characterize some of the (more obvious) modes of engagement themselves, particularly in the context of development issues. My general strategy, to recapitulate, is to enquire into the nature of a 'reflexive' conception/approach by looking at the career of studies of development.

In chapter 1 I present a review of this post-war career of development studies. This identifies the raw material, or, to borrow a phrase from the philosophers, my stock of examples, for the succeeding enquiries. In chapter 1 I present a series of five exercises in ideology construction which can be identified in the post-war history of development studies. To these five should (or could) be added the residual position of the now evidently untenable orthodoxy, or 'bourgeois'[16] position, and the perhaps emergent 'post-neo-marxian' school. However those issues are resolved, what we have in chapter 1 are a series of circumstance- and problem-specific efforts to theorize development.

The matter of the diversity of social theorizing is pursued in chapter 2. If we adopt a 'dis-integrated' view of social theorizing then, if only to keep our own thinking and scholarly discourse minimally coherent, we need some strategy for mapping the field of possible modes of social-theoretic engagement. Two approaches are presented: the detail-sensitive specificiation of 'exemplars' and the heuristically fruitful construction of an abstract schema. These are discussed with reference to the neo-marxian approach to development and it is argued that some neo-marxists have lost track of their 'location' and that consequently errors of formulation (and criticism, by others of them) are being made. The chapter concludes by underlining the specificity of social-theoretic engagement.

In contrast to the neo-marxists, the interventionist orthodoxy positively embraces a non-reflexive mode of theorizing. But this orthodoxy finds an imaginative (and often reflexive) expression in a group that I label here the 'intelligent orthodox'. In the third chapter I consider the (latently corporatist) work of Gellner, Galbraith and Myrdal. In their industrialism/modernization/convergence theorizing we find a clear statement of the planning mode of engagement which is familiar in studies of development and also in the politics of the First World monopoly capitalist states. Drawing upon the work of Jürgen Habermas, the fatal confusion of technical and political matters is pointed to as the clue to an appreciation of just how their work contrives to be simultaneously creative, plausible, humane and strictly anti-democratic.

The business of the confusion of technical and political matters raises one question of central importance: that is, the confusion engendered in social theorizing by the 'received model'. This issue is pursued directly in chapter 4. Recent debate within the philosophy of social science has resulted in the widespread acceptance, among social scientists, of the 'importance of theory'. However, it seems to me that the discipline retains an extensive latent scientism. Looking at the career of development studies, I identify a series of strategies of invoking the 'received model' to 'secure' the status of scientificity for enquiries that are quite obviously ideological, in my sense, in character. This sort of deformation is extensive, and it occurs in the work of theorists who would otherwise wish to dissociate themselves from any orthodox position.

Having repeatedly stressed the importance of the notion of ideology for my 'dis-integrated' view of social theorizing, I turn to one element of a discussion of ideology in chapter 5. I confront the business of rationally adjudicating between competing schemes.[17] The notion of ideology has been widely discussed in social science. My usage has been introduced elsewhere,[18] and it is further adumbrated throughout these essays. It is clear that the matter of rational adjudication is but one issue: I think, however, that it is rather an important one, and that it goes to the nerve of the debate between 'naturalist-descriptive' and 'reflexive' stances in respect of conceptions/approaches to theorizing. Thus where the former would affirm the pursuit of accurate description and eschew the taint of valuation, the latter would embrace the presentation of argued cases and look askance at the purported scientificity of the former. The hinge upon which debate turns is the possibility (or otherwise) of *rationally choosing* between different argued cases, or ideologies. In chapter 5 a series of ways in which rational adjudication can be accomplished are presented.

In chapter 6 I offer a detailed argument designed to remind theorists that the term 'development' is indeed an ethico-political one. Again this follows my general injunctions about acknowledging specificity of engagement in theorizing – thus what is to count as development will have to be locally determined – and it also picks up the point made in chapter 5: thus it is clear that ethico-political discourse *is* amenable to rational discourse.

I conclude by offering a summary review of the career of development studies. Within the community of academic (in the main) social scientists there has been an attempt – in particular amongst the orthodox, but also, if rather differently, among professed marxists – to constitute an autonomous discipline. It is my view that this attempt has collapsed under the combined weight of its own inherent implausibility (*one* theory for so many interests?) and its success in refining argument, If this sounds somewhat paradoxical, then it can be seen as a signal of my admiration for much of the work produced and an identification of the basis for my attempt to pursue the suggestion of Gellner which I noted at the outset.

The failure of the project of an autonomous discipline has been a fruitful one: theorizing development is now to be seen as a complex business, one (peculiarly informative, in my view) instance of social theorizing itself now seen to be many-sided in essential character. If we understand social theorizing as being, generically, concerned with (actively) making sense of the world, then it has to be acknowledged that there are a diversity of modes of engagement: a more or less loosely associated cluster of activities. And if this seems an intellectually untidy view of social theorizing, and theorizing development, then I can only repeat that it is my present purpose to attempt to codify some of the problems attendant upon this view. This seems an appropriate task: it is certainly the central problem bequeathed to anyone who reads the history of the career of development after the suggestion of Gellner.

1   Some notes on the significance of the career of development studies

1.0   In this chapter I want to present a schematic outline of a history of the main types of theories of development produced in the post-World War II period. This will serve a dual purpose. First, it will allow me to present an overview of the 'raw material' of the subsequent essays. Second, it will introduce this material as being quite clearly, and quite properly, *ideological* in character. This is important as, in the following chapters, I want to look at some of the problems which typically attach to a conception of social theorizing which starts from this position.

2.0   With regard to the general approach adopted in this chapter, I would say that I take social theorizing to be concerned with *making sense* of the social world. This means both that the term 'social theorizing' must be taken as generic, and that the examples and instances of social theorizing are many and diverse.

To order my own work I follow one particular line of thought within social science and make *ideology construction* the paradigm case of social theorizing. (The term 'ideology' is used in a *non*-pejorative sense.) Roughly speaking, this is the humanist marxian tradition.

The idea that social theorizing is, in its central and most unequivocal guise, concerned with the construction of ideological schemas whereby action in the world might be ordered and legitimated is readily available within recent discussions of the nature of social theory.[1] Simplifying matters, it can be said that these theorists are concerned with the nature of already constructed efforts. On the other hand, Dobb[2] has something to say about the *process* of construction and this is of particular interest for my present purpose.

Dobb, writing about economics, observes that the history of

economic thought reveals that 'history conditions theories', and asks how this is so. Dobb proposes an answer in terms of a dialectic between current practice and presently accepted theory – both having their own dynamic. Current practice throws up 'problems'[3] and these are shaped by their own social context, of which it is noted that 'this context itself is a complex mixture and interaction of accepted ideas and systems of thought . . . and the problems presented by current events and practical situations'.[4] Contrariwise, 'thought' is not to be taken as the passive recipient of problems presented to it: 'current problems are something created as much by thought-inspired human action upon an existing situation as by the given objective (but changing) situation itself'.[5] The source of the medium of criticism, theoretical discourse, is the corpus of existing theory reworked as seems appropriate. Consequently: 'new ideas are necessarily shaped in part by the antithetical relation in which they stand to the old'.[6]

This presents the exchange of theorist and circumstances in a relatively simple sociology-of-knowledge fashion, and I shall make use of this scheme by presenting substantive analyses in line with it. Thus a theorist is taken to fashion his product in given circumstances, out of particular resources, in response to specific demands. A simpler version of this scheme treats the exchange of theorist/circumstance in terms of the dialectic of the dynamic of society and the dynamic of theory.

In regard to 'history', I would want to claim that the theorist bestows coherence upon the period selected by virtue of the questions he is moved to raise. This being so, it seems clear that this constitution of an 'object of enquiry' is itself a *process*. The particular interests of the theorist are lodged within the frame of his discipline, itself lodged within history. The 'object' is a distillate of particular interests, disciplinary constraints and the common sense of the society of which the scholar is a member. I am interested in reviewing the history of 'development studies' to see if something of general interest about social theorizing itself can be spelt out. My interest centres upon *argument-strategies* and it is the matter of the *changes in approach* to theorizing development that can be discerned in the post-war career of 'development studies' that is the key to the construction of my 'object of enquiry'. It is a key that lets my enquiry begin with the ideas of the practitioners themselves.

So if we ask to what extent it is legitimate to pick out theories of development as a discrete realm of discourse, or how much is it a new separate discipline and when did it start and why, then three general sorts of answers can be identified. The three views are as follows. First, it can be said that it is not correct to single out an area of enquiry called 'development studies' because the whole enterprise properly belongs to a positive science of economics. Second, it can be argued that it is proper to single out 'development studies' and that, moreover, there is good reason for this scheme of enquiry to be regarded as the basis of the first genuinely adequate and generally relevant economics. Third, it can be said that it is an error to single out 'development studies', as its concerns and questions should be subsumed within the study of the historical development of the world capitalist system.

3.0 I shall now construct a history of the post-war career of 'development studies, in line with this tripartite scheme. And in a series of concluding remarks, in section 4, I shall indicate those broad lessons for our ideas about social theorizing (both generally, and in respect of matters of the Third World) which might be drawn from this history.

3.1 So, first, it may be argued that it is an error to single out 'development studies' as being anything other than a sub-specialism of positive economic science. The purist Bauer[7] adopts such a position, and seems to want to deny that 'development studies', and the theories proposed, are especially novel in the light of: (a) the efforts of colonial governments, which he takes to have been pursuing development for many years; and (b) the corresponding intellectual reflection upon these matters.[8] Any novelty development theories might have is that of being wrongheaded and generally mistaken in diagnosis and prescriptions.

That economics is to be taken as a science and that the proper exchange of economics with the problems of the Third World is one of the extension and application of the established, proved tools of the former to the circumstances of the latter, is generally taken for granted by those who can be identified as taking this line on the matter of the status of 'development studies'. Yet those who take this line do not, in the main, adopt Bauer's purism. The conventional wisdom of development studies, established in the immediate post-war period, is, as we shall see, in its initial presentation quite clearly Keynesian. It is this that Bauer rails against. Thus it is characteristic of the work of this early period, of those who would follow the general theoretical line indicated, that it pursues what I would call an interventionist strategy. The notion of development was taken to be essentially technical and, further, it was also assumed that the experts of the present developed nations had access to the requisite technical expertise. A relationship of super- and sub-ordination was thus legitimated and responsibility for the future reserved for the technical experts of the developed nations and their agents.

This scheme can be taken to present itself in two broad versions, the first of which I call 'growth theory': an ideology of *authoritative intervention.* And the second, which is characterized by the relative emancipation of the general body of the social sciences from the restrictive domination of economics, and which I call 'modernization theory': an ideology of *elaborated authoritative intervention.* This second scheme is distinctly American, in contrast to 'growth theory'. We can now look at the occasion and character of these two versions in turn (though I shall concentrate on 'growth theory' which, in the literature, has been neglected in comparison with 'modernization').

3.11 I use the term 'growth theory' to specify those schemes that treat matters of the development of the Third World. The way these theories of growth in general were used in respect of economic growth in the developed areas is not my concern, though both matters should be seen in the context of the more general *doctrines* of growth which emerge in the wake of World War II.

The background to development work, the dynamic of society, comprises the three elements of Keynesian economics, Depression and war, and the model of Western European recovery. These elements together determine the 'structure of the possible' for the post-war theorists. Simplifying matters, we can say that the possibilities opened up by the theoretical work of Keynes are squeezed between the twin pressures of popular (left) demand and US determination to hold the line against change. Ordered reconstruction and development (growth) is now taken to be within the grasp of governments. But the ruling factor in any such efforts is the overwhelming economic and military power of the USA. Interventionist activity aims to restrict change and is subsumed, paradoxically, under the imposed rhetoric of economic liberalism.

The way in which work treating matters of the development of the Third World was lodged within this framework of possibility, and emerged from it, is detailed by Streeten.[9] He argues that the subject, 'development studies', has its origins in two general sets of thoughts. First, problems of resources and people are taken to be urgent in view of the population explosion and soluble in the light of the success of post-war European recovery. Second, political change in the form of the rise of new states in the Third World, and the 'cold war', increases the concern of the 'West' for the 'proper' development of these areas. Out of the set of descriptions and explanations available to the theorists in the wake of Depression, war, and 'cold war' the demands for the reform and defence of Western capitalism bring out three theoretical novelties which can be deployed in the context of 'development'. Thus the explanatory theory, the *legitimating* construction that permits and guides action oriented to development problems, is found in 'growth theory'. The *organization* of intervention is effected by notions of planning; and the *implementation* of schemes is a matter of aid.

The explanatory core of the effort revolves round the Keynesian-informed scheme known now as the Harrod-Domar model. (Here we focus on Harrod's contribution.) Harrod's work is of interest in the history of 'development studies' for several reasons. Not only does the 'H–D' model inform the first statements of the orthodox line in 'development studies', and clearly reveal the Keynesian interventionist line of thinking, but most crucially it presents a particular notion of social-theoretic engagement with the social world. In terms which I take from Fay,[10] the effort is essentially 'policy science'.

Fay uses the term 'policy science' to designate the assumed product of mainstream social science. Thus it is said, in response to the question, Why have a social science?, the answer is given that it permits the rational ordering of decisions in a complex modern society. Or, more bluntly, it 'will enable men to control their social environment'.[11] The intervention made by the policy scientist in his social world aims to be (or, conceives itself as) knowing and authoritative manipulation: consequently its theorems are typically of the causal-descriptive sort. In common sense parlance, what is sought is a 'theory', but it is not that simple, of course. Harrod I take to be working within an essentially empiricist-positivist tradition of economic theorizing and what this tradition presents as a central explanatory or methodological device is the idea of a *model*.

Harrod's work is in the style of Keynes; he uses his terminology, assumptions and techniques. His seminal essay[12] focuses upon 'the necessary conditions for equilibrium between aggregate saving and investment in a dynamic economy'.[13] His basic proposition is that $Ga = s/v$, where Ga is the actual rate of growth of National Income, s is the marginal propensity to save, and v is the marginal capital-output ratio. This fundamental relation can define a growth path for an economy.[14] Now if it is true that Harrod's work underlay much post-war enquiry, it is also true that this work becomes rather impenetrable for the non-specialist. Yet the centrality of this work for this episode in the career of 'development studies' is clear. Brookfield records that: 'The economic planners of the post-war era hoped to find in capital investment something like a development-vending machine: you put in the money, press the button and get growth'.[15]

So what is the status of Harrod's scheme, taken as a model? Hindess[16] points out that in mathematics a 'model' is a precisely specified set of rules relating one area of mathematical discourse to another. This is a 'paradigm case of a theory in which the concept of model has a definite and rigorously defined function'.[17] From here on, thinks Hindess, if I have understood him rightly, things get steadily worse. Thus in positivist philosophy of science this intra-theoretic relation is altered; a model now details the relations between theoretical machineries and the real world – a set of observations. Hindess takes this to be the substitution of analogies for models. Claims to the use of models in natural science are taken to be few and implausible.

But it is in the realm of the social sciences that, according to Hindess, the use of the notion of model reaches its intellectual nadir. Bauman (1972) and Lévi-Strauss (1968) are cited. Bauman is quoted as saying 'theorizing consists in modelling reality. Theories *are* models'.[18] Hindess comments: 'In these lines we have a concise statement of what might be called the epistemology of model building. Knowledge of the world is to be obtained through the construction and manipulation of models'.[19] The precision of mathematics or the rigour of positivist schemes are abandoned; so far as Hindess is concerned this social scientific sense of modelling reduces to the status of persuasive metaphor. The supposed process of abstraction, simplifying and experimental manipulation is epistemologically ill founded and practically unhelpful. The theorist begins from some formalized element of common sense, be it the common sense of society or the narrower disciplinary common sense, and thither he eventually returns.

The attempt to model the circumstances of the Third World as a basis for authoritative prescriptive action, and the assumption, by theorists, of the role of the expert (the social-science-attempted analogue of the privileged position of the natural scientist in regard to his objects) are probably the two most immediately distinct characteristics of this mode of engagement, as evidenced by the present case. Both traits are present in the works which, arguably, best exemplify the work of the immediate post-war period. These are Lewis *et al*. (1951)[20] and Lewis (1955).[21]

Of the first of these works it has been observed that 'The U.N. 1951 publication . . . was an eloquent testimony to the new, post-war, post-Keynesian hope of raising the living standards of economically backward countries through deliberate action . . .',[22] and this judgment seems to me to be entirely apposite. I have argued that the work of Lewis *et al*.(1951) can be taken to be the seminal statement of the post-war orthodoxy of 'development studies'.[23]

This orthodox stance is codified, so to say, in Lewis (1955). Here we have an attempt to invoke the classical nineteenth-century tradition of economics; though it is the perhaps ambiguous figure of J.S. Mill that Lewis specifies. In this work Lewis pursues an explanation for 'growth'. Enunciating the three 'basic principles' or 'proximate causes of growth': 'the effort to economize'; 'the increase and application of knowledge'; and 'the dependency of growth on capital', he then attempts to move closer to history and to discover why these 'proximate causes' operate in some societies more strongly than in others. Around the Keynesian-inspired central role of capital in generating economic growth, matters of the social and cultural character of the underdeveloped are ranged. They are taken as being more or less conducive to economic growth. Here we have an early version of the distinction between 'economic' and 'non-economic' factors.

Recalling the criticisms presented with Fay and Hindess, it can be seen that the argument-strategy adopted by Lewis is somewhat unsatisfactory. He begins with assumptions of a superficially formal kind, adds in aggregated empirical notions characterizing social types and builds abstract models. The return to the practical is effected by the removal of simplifying assumptions. But this procedure admits of a wide variety of treatments of any particular problem. Assumptions may be varied, aggregated notions varied, and procedures for stepping down to reality varied. The amount of intrinsic 'slack' in the procedure permits the investigation of a practical problem to be so ordered as to produce a favoured 'sort' of answer for the theoretician's 'client'. Clearly this is not science, however loosely that is defined. From Fay, the empiricist-positivist conception of engagement is, strictly, incoherent. From Hindess the strategy of modelling is hopelessly imprecise.

None the less, to conclude, it should not be thought that these early efforts to theorize the circumstances of the underdeveloped were either monolithically similar or entirely fruitless. Though I want to present Lewis as a central figure of this period, it is true that there was a wide variety of work being followed. Equally I think it would be wrong to dismiss out of hand the efforts and insights of these theorists. They were evidently alive to the complexity of the problems they addressed and sensitive to the difficulties of shifting established intellectual tools to the novel situations of the Third World. That their effort was misconceived in intent and miscast theoretically are judgments made easy with the benefit of hindsight. The problem for 'development studies' is perhaps to be found in the extent to which this approach lingers on today.

3.12 Turning to 'modernization theory', I shall offer only a brief set of remarks, as this scheme has been extensively treated. Moreover much of the detailed criticism offered by those on the left seems to me to be correct.[24] As far as my history of the career of 'development studies' is concerned, what is at issue is a *revision of the legitimating theorem of intervention*. Thus 'modernization theory' replaces 'growth theory' as the orthodoxy of 'development studies', and does so in the context of 'cold war' competition between super-powers for influence in the Third World.

It is my contention that 'modernization theory' is the ideological child of the 'cold war'. The US theorists operating within the ambit of the notion of 'containment' seek to secure allies for the US within the Third World. Competition with the USSR necessitates that self-interest be disguised; thus, in reply to offers of 'socialism', the US presents 'modernization' and membership of the 'free world'. This I take to be the moral core of 'modernization theory'.

The more straightforwardly intellectual story at this point involves reference to two elements: an emasculated Keynesianism and structural-functionalism. Centrally it involves a reply, in the realm of economics, to the novelties of Keynes, and in particular it involves virtually standing Harrod on his head. Harrod's conclusions about the growth path of an economy were typically Keynesian in two obvious respects. He thought the growth path was unstable (difficult to find and harder to keep to), and he also stressed the role to be taken by the government. The neo-classical orthodoxy in economics replied with a modified scheme that simply struck out the unacceptable parts of Harrod. Growth was made simple in achievement and dependent upon a free market.[25] To this revised economics is added the work of the wider group of the social sciences, and now they are relatively emancipated from the restrictive dominance of economics.

It is here that we can observe the elaboration of the theory of 'modernization'. The deployment of a series of dichotomous constructs purports to explain the fundamental dichotomy between 'traditional' and 'modern'. These theorists pursued the goal of a descriptive-general policy science. This, it was supposed, would permit the production of general models which descriptively characterized the societies in question in such a way as to permit manipulative, corrective, interventions; these being governed by authoritative, objective knowledge. This, as far as I can see, is the effort's strategic error; thereafter it is liable to the criticisms which attach to the use of 'residual categories', 'skewed arguments', 'collapsing dualisms' and so on, all of which have been brought against it.[26] The fundamental argument-strategy of 'modernization theory' is clearly grasped by Hilal:[27] first define 'modern', then, in opposition, 'non-modern'; 'modernization' is the route between the two. But this is a nonsense, and the rest is just detail, which may or may not be intrinsically interesting. For my part the continuing interest of 'modernization' resides precisely in the transparency of its ideological character.

3.2   The second view on matters of the disciplinary status and proper mode of enquiry of 'development studies' is evidenced in the work of a fairly diverse group of scholars. In general I would suggest that they would take it to be right to single out 'development studies' as a discrete realm of discourse within the social sciences. But there would be differences in the strengths of their respective claims. The representatives of this line of thinking can be most conveniently presented as three groupings. Together they encompass a range of work from the fringe of the economic 'conventional wisdom', detailed above, through to work on the edges of marxian schemes.

3.21 The first of these three groupings can be introduced by recalling the celebrated article published by Seers in 1963.[28] In it he denies that the orthodoxy of economics is of any use when treating the economies of the Third World. Attention must be paid, he argues, to the institutional and social context of the economies in question, and to their position in the world economy. This emphasis on 'situating' analysis is taken up by Paul Streeten.[29] Streeten, who is to my mind the most theoretically subtle member of this group, can also usefully be taken as Myrdal's exegetist. It is Myrdal who is the pre-eminent figure of this group: the neo-institutionalists.

The particular occasion for their efforts is to be found in the late 1950s and early 1960s as the European colonial powers withdrew from Africa south of the Sahara.[30] I take 'neo-institutionalism' to be an interventionist scheme, of a sort, but in this case the political context of calls for 'intervention' has shifted. The 'neo-institutionalists' are not immediately concerned with confronting a supposedly expansionist communism, as was the case with 'modernization', or with a rather general commitment to development as was the case with 'growth theory'. But they are concerned, rather, with the project of reworking long-established colonial relationships. The resources invoked by the 'neo-institutionalists' include the actual experience of the colonial episode, a distinct European tradition of social thought and a relationship with government which disposes them to practical policy-making rather than the elaboration of formal schemes of great generality. Their product, 'neo-institutional social theory', is typically problem-centred, piecemeal and sceptical. I label it an ideology of '*co-operative (revised authoritative) interventionism*,' and this is its mode of engagement with the social world. This claim, and the scheme's general character, can be elucidated by considering its argument-strategy. In particular it is Myrdal, *via* the work of his exegetist, that I consider.

If we ask after the intellectual roots of 'neo-institutionalism' then we find Veblen and a particular tradition of dissenting economics in the US. This school centres its work on the attempt to manage mature capitalist society/economy through schemes of *planning*. Briefly, it is the intellectual counterpart to the New Deal.[31] Myrdal's version is straightforwardly European and he advances the idea of 'world welfareism' and makes the planner the agent of change. In terms of argument-strategy used, three areas of interest present themselves.

The first is the matter of the use made of the resources of social science. The 'neo-institutionalist' scheme is, as I have noted, typically piecemeal, sceptical and empiricist. It pursues *realism* in modelling as a means to order planned social change, and the key notion in respect of the construction of such models is that a concept has an ecology, so to say. That is, concepts are seen as working only in particular circumstances. So, for example, if the familiar economist's term 'unemployment' is used, then it is pointed out that far from this being an abstract, generally applicable notion, as the orthodox would be obliged to claim, it is, as a matter of fact, only usable in a particular context. Indeed, when an economist uses the term, he *thereby supposes* all the social and institutional arrangements of mature capitalist society. The corollary is clear: in the case of any non-developed economy a detailed knowledge of the society is a prerequisite of concept formation. But not only do social science data enable the 'neo-institutionalists' ' epistemology of concept formation to function, they also provide the general conceptual framework for analysing social systems.

The second point about their argument-strategy concerns their effort to offer a general solution to the problem of 'values'. Myrdal's solution, in addition to a reflexive effort to extirpate bias, is to invoke the notion of 'crisis politics' such that, in periods of 'crisis', value issues are rendered 'obvious' and therefore unproblematical. This is evidently a simple accommodation with the orthodox distinction between fact/value and is a non-solution to the 'problem of values'.

Finally there is the 'neo-institutionalists' ' scheme of agency, the mechanism which will effect social change. Here Myrdal presents the view that the state machine run by reasonable men will order and implement programmes of social change. What Myrdal does is to reduce *politics to planning*. Thus he remarks: 'What a state needs, and what politics is about, is precisely a macro-plan for inducing changes . . . This may, in popular terms, be a definition of what we should mean by planning.'[32] Clearly this scheme is absurd, and indeed it seems to me that Myrdal recognizes this, if only latently, in his notion of the 'soft state'. The character of the 'soft state' explains why his scheme is not yet ready to go.

In the end, it seems to me, 'neo-institutionalism' can be regarded as the most plausible of the policy scientific efforts of the post-war period. The general methodological dictum of 'neo-institutionalism' is the pursuit of problem-specific formulations and not general theories. Its analytical machineries are subtle in contrast to 'modernization' and 'growth' theories, and the claim to the 'obviousness' of the stance that the (liberal Western) theorist should take to matters of the development of the Third World may well be a part of the common sense of most of those working in this area. However, to accord them the status of 'most plausible' policy science is a deeply ambiguous judgment: the interventionist mode of engagement is, in the end, incoherent; and the empiricist approach to analysis, in particular modelling, is unsatisfactory,[33] no matter how it is hedged about with injunctions to be sceptical of over-general formulations and claims.

3.22 The second strand to be picked out is largely inspired by Latin American work. Here it is Prebisch who makes the first break with the orthodoxy of economics when (in the early 1950s) he rejects the Ricardian notion of international specialization. It was this idea which had justified Latin America's role in the world economy being restricted to that of primary product exporter. Prebisch advocated industrialization behind protective tariff barriers. The policy change is mirrored in theoretical revision, and the equilibrium model of the orthodox is set aside in favour of a 'structuralist' analysis. This approach takes the putative 'national' economy to be a concatenation of 'residues', 'enclaves' and 'parasitic forms'. The gradual failure of ECLA reformism occasions a reworking of their views. In the middle and late 1960s, the notions used were 'institutional' and 'structural' economics. According to Girvan,[34] the revision entailed adding a historical aspect to structural and institutional method, and giving the resulting synthesis the empirical content necessary to generate a full theory of underdevelopment and dependency.

From Furtado, whom I take to exemplify this line, Girvan[35] draws an interesting point about economics. Furtado comes to see the Latin American debate as resolving the issue of whether one or two economics are required to treat respectively 'rich' and 'poor'.[36] The answer is that we are treating a 'world historical system', and that consequently one economics is needed: it is to be found in the tradition exemplified in Furtado's own work. That the school of dependency economics began as a reaction against the economic orthodoxy was due to the inapplicability of that orthodoxy to the circumstances of the economies of the Third World. But now it transpires that the orthodoxy is inapplicable in the circumstances of the 'rich', and it should be replaced by the new economics of the world system. Clearly this is a bold claim.

It is with 'dependency' that we find the strongest claims to the status of an independent and autonomous discipline. For my part I think the pursuit of independence/autonomy is, in general, an unfortunate by-product of the affirmation of the priority of the model of the natural sciences.

If the pursuit of this status were restricted to the institutional realm – if it were claimed that 'development studies' was independent of economics in particular and the established social sciences in general – then there would be less of interest to note. However, using the analogy of natural science, independence/autonomy is conceived as established by virtue of the discipline's having its own *objects* and *methods appropriate thereto*. That is, an extra-social guarantor, so to speak, is invoked. The 'dependency theorists', to take the present case, take their work to be constituting a new scientific area of study, whereas I see them erecting a new ideology. The fruitless debate occasioned by such a misconstrual is evidenced in the arguments of Girvan and Cumper.[37]

Circumstances result in this unhappy borrowing from natural science appearing in various guises: the 'role of the expert' adopted by 'growth' and 'modernization' theorists is a case in point. With Furtado, particular political circumstances reinforce his early intellectual dispositions.

Furtado's work resembles that of Myrdal. There is a pursuit of realistic models, though in his early work Furtado stresses the idea of a *general set* of models. There is a similarity in methods of analysis and agreement in granting the centrality of the role of the state in any underdeveloped country's pursuit of development. The matter of the agent-of-theory-execution will serve to point up the differences between the two schemes.

The natural agent of a stance like Furtado's is the body of 'reasonable men' in control of the state, as is the case with Myrdal's schemes. However, Myrdal confronts the implausibility of his agent by invoking the notion of the 'soft state'; his agent is required to 'pull itself together'. With Furtado this entire approach seems less plausible; typically in Latin American states we have right-wing military dictatorships and not, as with Myrdal's work, democratic (India) societies. Furtado retreats into a more non-committal stance. His apparently politically unfavourable situation results in him detaching himself from any direct identification with the 'reasonable men'. Recognizing the precarious position of the 'reasonable men', he couches his analysis in more neutral terms: he affects to illuminate the nature of Latin American economies *generally*.

Furtado's political circumstances and intellectual dispositions combine to issue in a distinct view of the mode of engagement of the theorist. In his early work we find yet another version of authoritative interventionism. The national economy is seen as integrated into the world economy and as operating at less than its full potential. The solution is the pursuit of an autonomous and efficient economic development. This position is unpacked as a series of reform proposals. In his latter work, while there is much more appreciation of the political circumstances, this essentially empiricist frame is not changed, though it is subtly altered. Throughout his work there is an intellectual tension between the demand for generality of formulation (seen as 'scientific') and the demand for specific, practical, analysis. When this is coupled with his awareness of being politically blocked, so to say, then the whole effort changes and takes on an *interpretive* aspect. We can catch this in the Preface to the post-1964 coup *Diagnosis of the Brazilian Crisis*. Here we find he propounds the thesis of the supra-rationality of the intellectual who is thereby morally obliged to present analyses which are free of particular group or class loyalties. This looks, at first glance, like an extension of the Myrdalian position, viz. 'Fabianism gone mad'. But it can more fruitfully be regarded as flowing from the particular circumstances of Brazil, and of Latin America generally. This non-class-specific theorizing I take to be nationalist, in so far as the entire effort is a reaction to the theoretical and practical dominance of the 'West', and latently populist in that in its developed form it both presents a general non-class-specific recipe for national progress and calls for the removal of present élite groups. I label it an ideology of *'reactive (populist interpretive) interventionism'*.

3.23 The third group of those who would affirm the novelty of 'development studies' can be taken to be represented by the early work of A.G. Frank, though in this context their views are somewhat insubstantial. They appear as a 'transitional' group, or as anticipators of a revived marxian tradition. I will offer only a brief note on their work as the issues it throws up are more easily dealt with along with the marxian line proper.

In brief, to the above-noted 'dependency' line, there is to be added an influx of marxian notions which serves to produce what Leys[38] calls a 'left UDT/dependency'. The phrasing is deliberate and serves to indicate that the theoretical realm of UDT/dependency is not abandoned; rather, a political reorientation takes place. However, in contrast to the two above-noted groupings, each of which would grant 'development studies' a measure of autonomy, the marxian-informed radical line is, in a sense, self-annihilating. There is a shift from a political radicalization of common themes to a renunciation of its own perspective as being ultimately bourgeois, in theoretical character, and liable therefore to 're-absorption'. The final messages of this group commend the adoption of a thoroughgoing 'marxist' standpoint. Their ideology, in so far as it is useful or correct to treat it separately from marxian schemes, is probably best regarded as *'reactive-interpretive critical'*.

3.3 The third view on the matter of the independence and theoretical novelty of 'development studies' adopts the strategy of sub-suming its concerns and questions within the very much broader framework of the analysis of the historical development of the world capitalist system. This view is exemplified, paradigmatically, in the work of those who regard themselves as either marxists or as working within a tradition of social theory which counts Marx as its most distinguished figure.

The renaissance of marxian scholarship is recent. In particular it is closely associated with the rise of the New Left. The initial involvement of the renewed line of marxian work with matters of the Third World was, so far as I can see, *via* the co-option of 'liberation struggles' into the efforts of the New Left through the 1960s and early 1970s. The subsequent exchange between this circumstance-specific renewal and the established traditions of theorizing within marxism, coupled with a dawning appreciation of the complexity of the issues raised in connection with 'develop-ment', has produced, if not a theoretical babel, then at least a highly complex debate. One centre of this discussion is the matter of the precise nature of a properly marxian analysis of the Third World. This debate can be taken to revolve round the work of Baran, and his notion of dependent capitalism, where this denotes the deform-ing subordinate incorporation of the peripheral areas in the world economy. The complexity of this debate is such as to make any attempt at a simple summary virtually impossible. It should be noted that what follows is inevitably rather cursory.

There are, so far as I can see, three general areas of criticism of Baran-inspired 'neo-marxian' schemes. Thus the effort is taken to be a moralistic, non-marxian, mechanical inversion of the orthodox view.

Baran is taken by several critics to present an essentially *moral critique*. The notion of 'potential surplus' – that which could be generated in a rational, socialist, society – is taken as an idealist, humanist, standard against which irrational mature capitalist societies and deformed peripheral societies diverge. Culley observes: 'The Utopian nature of this concept is quite clear. It allows Baran and his followers to launch an attack upon capitalism as an irrational phenomenon with respect to his own ethical position.'[39] Now it is clear that Baran's notion of 'surplus' has, crucially, a moral aspect. It centres upon the idea of the quality of life available to the inhabitants of particular societies – what they do have and what they might have. But, as far as I am concerned, the charge of moralism rather misses the point: valuation in matters of social theorizing is central. So what is at issue is not whether or not Baran's work is tainted by valuation, because there will necessarily be an aspect of valuation; rather, the question concerns the character of the judgments made and the manner of their insertion into social-theoretic efforts.

Baran's work has been charged with being redolent of Keynesian reformism[40] and it seems that this may well be true. If so, then Baran is guilty of surreptitious borrowing from the stances he would attack. Against Culley and like-minded critics[41] it is, however, fair to invite them to recall the circumstances of the production of Baran's effort and to compare the richness of Baran's moral critique with the then available (and subsequent) work. Baran's work was produced in the USA of the late 1950s. Against that background and in contrast to 'modernization', then being constructed, Baran's work appears as hugely sophisticated.

Generally, against Culley, if we read her as objecting to 'surreptitious borrowing' then – excepting the point above about circumstances of production – her attack has considerable force. However, if she is objecting to all and any evaluative moral stance towards matters social, then I would take her to be pursuing the chimera of a non-engaged theory.

The second area of objection is with regard to the particular notions used by Baran and followers: especially the term 'surplus', which Baran himself announces is crucial to his analysis. Two points: first, that it is an aggregative notion in the style of Keynesian work; and second, that, despite its resemblance to the notion of 'surplus value', it is not marxian. Now these criticisms both seem to be valid, so far as I can presently see. None the less I rather doubt that these attacks actually uncover the real issue here, though the first point does gesture to it. Should we not concern ourselves less with the *textual* question of whether or not Baran (*et al.*) have *changed* the conceptual machineries of Marx's economic analyses and more with the practical question of whether or not Baran's analysis is *good or bad political economy*? I shall offer an indication of what a political economic analysis might be following a note on the last typical area of criticism.

This focuses upon the concept of capitalism and its historical development. Brenner[42] argues that the entire 'neo-marxian' line in this area of debate reduces to an *inversion of Adam Smith*. In a very detailed enquiry, it is argued that the 'neo-marxists' follow Smith by equating capitalism with a trade-based division of labour where innovation, and thus growth and expansion, is determined by market pressure. Class relations are taken merely to follow on. Brenner speaks of 'historical functionalism' and 'a classical form of economic determinism' and takes this to be wrongheaded. Rather, he wants to reduce economics to social (class) relations. The core of the matter is the conjugation of class circumstances that trigger and sustain the innovative dynamic of capitalism.

25

Of the 'neo-marxists' ' method of enquiry, Brenner argues that their failure 'to discard the underlying individualistic presuppositions'[43] of Smith's model has resulted in their erecting a mirror version of it. Palma would echo this view. Of the work of Frank, he argues that he builds 'a mechanico-formal model which is no more than a set of equations of general equilibrium (static and unhistorical), in which the extraction of the surplus takes place through a series of satellite–metropolis relationships'.[44] The 'neo-marxian' scheme of Baran, Frank and Wallerstein is, perhaps, best given the ideology label, *'interpretive (initial) critical'*.

It is *interpretive* because it aims generally to illuminate, or render comprehensible, the circumstances of the Third World. It is *critical* because it looks for change. But it is *initial critical* because it rests content with a relatively simple analytic frame plus many persuasive examples. It does not produce a fully extended political economic analysis, which is, arguably, the most appropriate argument form for treating the broad sweep of Third World development problems. A Cardoso-type enquiry (if it is good political economy) which is involved directly might be called *'practical-specific (developed) criticism'*.

Palma advocates that we look at the work of Cardoso, whose work is problem- and situation-specific. It invokes the tradition of political economy, and Marx is seen as exemplar.

Political economy I take to be the broadest and richest intellectual tradition available for those who would treat 'development'. It entails, as a way of building an ideology, the deployment of a morally informed categorial frame. This argument-strategy differs from that of the (empiricist) orthodox. There is no pursuit of abstract general descriptions. Marx here speaks of 'logical synthesis', the 'intellectual reconstruction of the real', oriented to the display of the possibilities for the future lodged in the present.

Two elements are of immediate note: this style of enquiry involves a catholicity of intellectual interest and a thoroughgoing practical intent. The explicit contrast is often drawn with the restricted, partial, institutionalized discourses of the various orthodoxies of social science. Cardoso and Faletto speak of 'a comprehensive social science . . . following the 19th century tradition of treating economy as political economy . . . its highest expression in Marx'.[45]

The key to a fruitful enquiry on Palma's exegesis is specificity of engagement: 'It is thus through concrete studies of specific situations, and in particular class relations and class structure. . . that Cardoso formulated the essential aspects of the dependency analysis.'[46]

The implications of Palma's critique of 'neo-marxism', if I read him correctly, serve to reinforce my above-noted preferences for seeing social theorizing as essentially practical. If this is true, then we are obliged to grant that what it makes sense for the theorist to say will depend crucially upon the situation he inhabits. In the work of the 'neo-marxists', given the shift from New Left activism to recent more scholarly work, there seems to be a drift toward disengagement, towards generality of formulation. This, in the context of a rather scientistic social science common sense, results in the apparent pursuit of a general theory of dependent capitalism. This seems to me to be a dubious goal – doubtless debate will continue in this area.

4.0 This history of the post-war career of 'development studies' can be taken, it seems to me, to establish the following.

(a) It establishes that this career can be taken to comprise the production of a series of ideologies. This history offers a series of supporting cases which illustrate my contention that social theorizing is about 'making sense'. The history presents a series of theoretical departures which are quite clearly extensive and elaborated ideological schemas. A detailed examination of *how* each of these schemas is *assembled*[47] (which procedure I have here sketched rather than executed) reveals how conception and intent mutually interact. By conception I mean the theorist's ideas of what constitutes a proper and fruitful analysis; and by intent I mean the objectives the theorist seeks to secure. So these *illustrative* sociology of knowledge informed enquiries are simultaneously *investigative*; they revise the ideas from which they originally spring.

(b) This history can be read as involving a progressive broadening of the conceptions of social theorizing and a moral deepening of theorists' intent. In the case of the positivistic schemes we have policy scientific work where the theorists take on the role of the expert. Typically these schemes understand development, or progress, as a *technical* term, to be established and secured by the experts. Progress is equated with growth. In the case of the theorists who took 'development studies' to be independent of economics in particular and the wider group of the social sciences in general, we find a different view. These theorists typically present a softened orthodoxy. The 'experts' operate co-operatively to manage ordered social reform oriented to the crisis resolving goal of world welfarism. Progress is taken to be ordered social reform. In the case of the last grouping identified, that is, the 'neo-marxists', we find an effort that aspires to practical-critical involvement oriented to the goal of a thoroughgoing democratic polity. (Yet arguably they fall short and produce rather more interpretive general efforts treating the future of the world economy.) This is the richest analytical scheme and the ethically richest approach.[48]

(c) This history shows that the efforts of the radicals, our middle group, to establish a discipline independent of narrow economics and of social science generally, with specified problem areas and methods appropriate thereto, is a failure. Their misconceived effort collapses under the combined impact of events, on the one hand, and their own success in occasioning refinement in argument on the other. In a similar way the comparatively understated efforts of the orthodox to take 'development studies' as autonomous and so on, *in so far* as it was an integral element of a positive economic science, also collapse.

At the end of this history it seems to me that we can see 'development studies' as being lodged in the mainstream of the interests of our social-theoretic tradition. 'Development studies' is neither peripheral to, nor a derivative of, the mainstream of social theorizing or academic social science. Indeed, this history, in so far as it does present a series of 'raw' examples of social-theoretic engagement and if they are correctly interpreted here, serves to recall attention to the heart of the matter of social-theoretic/scientific work.

(d) Most generally, the lesson of this history of the career of 'development studies' for our ideas about the nature of social theorizing is that the business must be seen to be *practical*. This central characteristic of social theorizing is revealed in the substantive areas considered. Each 'school' has been shown to have been producing situation-sensitive and problem-specific efforts. I have taken this situation/problem-specificity *both* to be the key to displaying the nature of the practicality of the various efforts *and* as requiring discussion and legitimation in its own appropriate terms and *not* in terms borrowed from the natural sciences.

After reviewing the career of 'development studies', it seems quite clear that social theorizing is practical. In general I want to say that circumstances and problems call forth engagements and that particular sorts of engagements have corresponding forms of enquiry. Social-theoretic efforts needs must be sensitive to what it makes sense to say.

Addendum

One rather obvious problem associated with the attempt to appropriate the historical/intellectual career of an area of enquiry for purposes of theoretical reflection is that the real world processes of action and theorizing do not stop neatly at the point at which the commentator makes his observations or offers his interpretive characterizations. Thus the scheme I have presented has a twofold limitation. I have focused upon the business of the *construction* of ideological positions. This is quite proper, given my declared interest in the active process of making sense. I have neglected to treat the rather more passive (it would seem) business of the subsequent decline and dissipation of ideological positions. In so far as this paper hints at a *history* of the career of development studies, then arguably I have hinted at only half of that history. The other half, the matter of the process of decline, is pursued in the final chapter, where I discuss the extent to which we can speak of a 'residual common sense' of development studies. This *sketches* the history of decline (by implication), and this is the second limitation I would note.

Following Hoogevelt (1982), I adopt the simplifying strategy of distinguishing bourgeois and marxian lines of enquiry into issues of development. This allows me to appropriate recently-produced work in a fashion compatible with my characterization of the postwar career of development studies. Thus the pattern of decline, as I would see it, of bourgeois theorizing entails a repetitious insistence upon the efficacy of interventionist strategies. There seem to be two main areas of insistence. The first is the focus upon adjusting the 'rules of the game' so as to enhance the chances of the Third World. This is the concern for a New International Economic Order (NIEO), and it is the latest of a long series of Third World political initiatives. The second area where the orthodox line is continued, or partially reworked, is to be found in the ideas of the basic needs approach. I do not intend to pursue either of these two arguments at this point, and for the moment I will rest content with simply noting that this is how the orthodox theorists have pursued their enquiries. It does not seem to me to constitute a *new* ideological scheme in the making.[49]

As regards the grouping labelled marxists, there is an analogous, though for my part potentially more fruitful, state of affairs. Here the process of the re-presentation of the intellectual claims of the marxian tradition, so closely associated with the 1960s and 1970s, has, arguably, entered a 'second phase'. The polemical edge of much early marxian work has now become unnecessary: the general cogency of marxian analysis is granted and the problem, for commentators, is now one of refinement.

In this collection I am interested in the lessons that the 'discovery' of the Third World by (primarily) First World theorists has had for our thinking about social theorizing *per se*. In this context the relative neglect of the decline of the ideologies I use as raw material for reflection is, I think, not too important. However it must also be noted that the process of decline – the supersession, discarding and reworking of ideas – is in itself of interest. In the last chapter I present a few notes which can be taken as preparatory to such an enquiry.

2 The specificity of social-theoretic engagement: some lessons for 'neo-marxian' studies of development

1.0 In this essay I want to argue a relatively simple case. It is that what it makes sense for a social theorist to say (or do) depends crucially upon the particular circumstances of the theorist and the nature of the problems addressed. It seems to me both that this point – which is virtually a truism – is sometimes forgotten, and that this failure of memory has unfortunate effects upon theorizing.[1] It also seems to me that there have been some 'failures of memory' in the recent work of the 'neo-marxists' on development, and this is the substantive area which I shall treat below. First, however, I need to say something about how this essay is to proceed: assumptions and methods.

I take social-theoretic engagement with the social world to be centrally concerned with the business of *making sense*. The notion of 'social theorizing' is thus generic, and the examples and instances of social-theoretic engagement are seen to be many and diverse. Confronted with this diversity of engagement, the question of how the field is to be mapped arises. For even if we do not want an elaborated 'theory of modes of engagement' (whatever that might be), a schema which will let us order scholarly discourse, and our own thinking, seems to be indispensable. Two ways in which such an organizing schema might be prepared present themselves. First, by invoking exemplars. Second, by constructing a systematic framework. I will turn to this in a moment.

The schema I present here attemps to be, in its dual aspect, both coherent and adequate. That is to say I hope that the schema both expresses my interests (the focus on ideology-making), and links my discourse with the 'classic tradition' in social theorizing. My approach here, then, is fairly pragmatic in the ordinary sense that I follow my line of interest. What else could I have done? Two answers present themselves.

31

First, I could have reviewed the literature in order to discover what else has been done in the way of 'sociologies of sociology with particular reference to ideology-making'. There are two obvious places to begin looking: in marxist discussions of the role of the intellectual, the humanist line in particular, and in the general social scientific literature. As regards the former, these essays follow in that line, so what is said there is supposed here. A detailed review, it seems to me, would have disturbed my present intentions.[2] As regards the latter area, again there are one or two obvious starting-points. Peter Worsley[3] cites Mills and Gouldner as having represented, for sociology, the idea of theorizing as embedded in society and history, and it is this 'reflexive' view that opens up the problem of who is doing the theorizing. Both of these theorists are useful, as is Worsley's paper. What I want with my systematic 'map' is a way of grasping the diversity of the family of games called social theorizing, but while there must be numerous texts which touch on precisely this issue, once again, it seems to me, a review of these is not my present business – it remains a 'technical' matter outstanding.

The second alternative strategy open to me was to eschew systematicness and rest content with *ad hoc* remarks. One example of such a strategy is to be found in John Carroll's *Sceptical Sociology* (1980). In an essay entitled 'In Spite of Intellectuals' he lists seven types of intellectual, the list being both conjured out of his imagination and essentially arbitrary in number (*enough* to make it clear that there *are* varieties). Carroll's essay is entertaining, but his approach is useless given that I am looking at theorizing (a) set against theories of *development* – an *ad hoc* list of intellectual engagements with issues of development would have the effect of dissolving all coherence leaving either a babel of voices or a uselessly general set of typifications; and (b) with a view to relocating extant debate (economistic and technical in tendency) within a reflexive classic tradition. Carroll is happy for social theorizing to disintegrate radically: the burden of his apparently conservative evocation of the eighteenth-century UK intellectuals (Hume, Burke, Adam Smith *et al.*) is that the illiberal pursuit of social control (power) has, since Rousseau's day (!), deformed social science. In the last chapter I look at the issue of the extent to which intervention is plausible/tenable, and my conclusions are not those of Carroll.

Thus, having rejected these two alternatives, I am left with the strategy presented here: an attempt to be 'relevantly systematic': to link up with the 'classic tradition' and thereby contrive a view of theorizing that will enable the diversity of the business, both itself and with reference to development, to be safely acknowledged. I shall now look at my 'exemplars' and present my 'systematic frame'.

1.1 Proceeding by offering exemplars, or standards, entails pick-ing out particular figures and analysing the way in which they make, or made, sense of their social worlds. Such figures I take to exem-plify particular, historically located, modes of engagement with the social world. This 'engagement' I treat using an essentially socio-logy of knowledge approach and a procedure which I have taken from the work of a noted marxian thinker.[4] I range particular examples of social-theoretic engagement against my set of exemplars. And which set do I use? The key is a humanist marxian line of thinking, and I centre my enquiries into 'modes of engage-ment' upon the notion of ideology.

Thus, for my part, if the question – just how do we produce a social-theoretic analysis of some set of circumstances or other? – is posed, then I would offer the provisional answer that it involves the deployment of a morally-informed categorial frame, whose product might properly (and non-pejoratively) be regarded as an ideological schema serving to order and legitimate action in the world. And this slogan in respect of ideology construction I take (borrowing freely) from Rockmore's[5] analysis of the general structure of the work of Marx. It designates the procedure of 'logical synthesis': the intellec-tual 'reconstruction of the real' oriented to displaying the possibi-lities for the future lodged in the present.

In the case of Marx, his major substantive theorizing was pre-sented in the language of political economy, and there are two points about the character of political economic enquiry which can usefully be made at this juncture. On the one hand there is an unfamiliar (for orthodox social science) catholicity of intellectual interest, and, on the other (again unfamiliar to the orthodox), a thoroughgoing practical intent.[6] This mode of engagement, and form of enquiry, I take to have been appropriate to Marx's circum-stances. Now this contention can be illuminated by citing Gellner, who has remarked that social theorizing (though he does not use this expression) is the attempt to make sense of novel and disturbing social situations. Sociology is seen as a nineteenth-century inven-tion in the face of the rise of the 'modern world'. The 'transition' (to the modern world – a continuing and pervasive phenomenon for Gellner) is marked by a loss of identity: this is, 'the very paradigm of a moral problem. Interesting moral crises are . . . those in which the aims or criteria, the identity of the solution, are themselves in serious doubt.'[7]

In general with social theorizing I would want to claim that circumstances and problems call forth engagements, and that parti-cular sorts of engagements have corresponding forms of enquiry. That being so, and recalling our search for exemplars, the prime case of social theorizing, originally given by the nineteenth-century political economists (where Marx is the dominant figure in this group), is the production of an ideological schema oriented to legitimating and organizing action in the world. Now this pitches the business of making sense at a very general level: that of constructing elaborated, 'formal' ideologies in the syntax of political economic enquiry. However, I do not want to restrict the 'ideological' to this realm, neither do I want to rest content with one exemplar (with attendent argument strategy/mode of engagement with the social world).

In a recent discussion of the notion of ideology, Giddens remarks: 'In the approach I wish to suggest . . . there is strictly speaking, no such thing as *an* ideology: there are only ideological aspects of symbol-systems . . . any type of idea-system may be ideological.'[8] This points to a distinction which I want to use between, on the one hand, a *delimited-formal* notion of ideology (which attaches to those efforts of political economy which I have instanced as paradigmatically social-theoretic engagements) and, on the other hand, a *pervasive-informal* notion (which permits the ideological aspects of diverse language games within society to be uncovered).

In the marxian line which comes down to the present in the work of the Frankfurt School, and Habermas in particular, the critique of ideology ('pervasive-informal') is taken as a prerequisite of social change where hegemonic culture is repressive (or repressive-tolerant) and the economic form advanced. In this school the ideas of democracy, critique, and ideology ranking, come together in that the latter pair suppose an 'ideal speech situation' which in turn supposes a democratic society. My second exemplar is thus the Frankfurt School and its argument-strategy/mode of engagement is *critique*.

In summary: I take the production of formal and delimited ideological schemes to be the prime case of social-theoretic engagement. The works of the nineteenth-century political economists are taken as the best examples, with Marx pre-eminent. This gives one reference point. The idea of ideology construction readily calls forth the idea of criticism. In the Frankfurt-School-inspired scheme of Critical Theory we have an intellectual departure which may be taken to be both a circumstance-specific extension of Marx and the establishment of a sophisticated scheme of critique. This serves as a second reference point. So, generally, I take social theorizing to be concerned with the construction, and thereafter the criticism and comparative ranking of ideologies.[9]

1.2 Presenting a systematic framework is the second way of mapping the field of modes of engagement. This idea is obvious at one level: that is, the ordinary grammar of language makes it readily available. Confronted with apparently randomly selected exemplars, the idea of a systematic framework, into which the random examples might be slotted, is easily called forth. Yet it might be asked, at this point: just what is the difference between the two schemes which makes this second line worth pursuing?

It seems to be this. Mapping the field of modes of engagement *via* exemplars requires a detailed historical knowledge of the location *from which* the exemplars are 'taken' and *to which* they (the modes of enquiry discovered in the exemplars) are 'applied'. On the other hand an abstract, systematic, scheme might offer a useful and more straightforwardly heuristic device for treating, albeit in a preliminary (or even cursory) fashion, relatively unfamiliar areas of social-theoretic engagement. The 'general systematic scheme' can be seen as a set of rules of thumb (derived from detailed enquiries previously undertaken on the one hand, and, on the other, familiar problems of coming to grips with new areas) for ordering unfamiliar material, be it a theorist's work, or a 'school', or whatever.

Evidently these two approaches are intertwined, and not sharply distinct or opposed. The 'trade-off', as we lean one way or the other, would seem to be between historical accuracy and analytical sensitivity (to the text), on the one hand, and simplicity of use and richness of interpretive suggestion (for the situation), on the other.

Now the bracketed distinction, just made, introduces one significant extension to my argument. I want to suggest that it is useful to distinguish between a *wide* and a *restricted sense* of 'social-theoretic engagement'. Taking the restricted sense first, we have the line which has been used above (in section 1.1). Social-theoretic engagement is (putting it crudely) a matter of ideas: the construction, criticism and ranking of ideologies. So my restricted sense grants some sort of distinction between theory and practice. I do not take this to be an actual difference; rather, it is a convenient distinction; and, having made it, social theorizing presents itself as the production of texts. In contrast the wide sense simply over-rides any such split. Thus, for example, Castro – making revolutions – is taken to be presenting a particular mode of social-theoretic engagement: making sense of a particular social world, where this was characterized by the presence of a corrupt ruling group and a degraded society. My 'general systematic scheme' uses the wide sense of social-theoretic engagement (into which, of course, the restricted sense can be fitted).

I shall now try to sketch this systematic scheme of mapping the field of modes of engagement with the social world.

Regarding the business of social theoretic engagement abstractly, it can be seen that, while it is concerned in the end with 'making sense', there is no reason to suppose that there is only one way of making this sense. The remarks of section 1.1 focused upon the intellectual production of ideologies. Such a procedure for making sense can be characterized as having theorists operate 'before the fact' (of social change): that is, naively, the theorist produces an analysis which is then acted upon to achieve a desired state of affairs. This temporal relationship of intellection and event in the business of making sense can present itself in several ways. Considering the process of social-theoretic engagement (wide sense), we can identify three modes of engagement: (a) practitioner, (b) theorist, and (c) interpreter.[10] I shall characterize each of these modes in turn and shall add a series of *illustrative* examples. The illustrative examples, to my schema, are presented in implicit contrast to orthodox scientism, where making sense would be construed in terms of intellectual descriptive-general accommodations to the world taken (more or less) for granted. These illustrative examples are generated by recalling my remarks (section 1.1) that social-theoretic engagement is to be regarded as circumstance/problem-specific.

(a) The nature of the engagement of the *'practitioner'* can be characterized as *immediate*. The 'practitioner' can be taken to be one who engages in successful emancipatory activity, thereby requiring changes in established theorems. For example Mao, Ho, Castro and Lenin might all be taken to be 'practitioners'.[11] The legacy of the 'practitioner' is the task of assimilating the proffered lessons. The successful 'practitioner's' behaviours are taken to exemplify an appreciation of the circumstances surrounding action. Events thus precede delimited-formal theorizing. (It seems that this scheme leaves a space where historical chance and opportunism can be accommodated in a notion of social theoretic engagement.)

Illustratively, it could be said of Castro that, given his circumstances, the appropriate course was revolutionary guerrilla warfare. Again, given Guevara and the attempt to ferment revolution in Bolivia, it would seem that his effort was neither circumstance-sensitive nor problem-specific. It has been suggested, rather, that his effort was a romantic celebration of the Cuban experience. However, the matter is equivocal;[12] there were at least resemblances in the two situations. That this is so is made clear if Guevara/Bolivia is compared with Weathermen/USA. The calls of the latter to violent revolution might have had some distant connection with the problems of black Americans, but it seems as if their proposals were altogether detached from their circumstances.

(b) The nature of the engagement of the *'theorist'* can be characterized as *prospective*. The 'theorist' constructs a 'model' of the world so as to be able to order action in it: this I have taken to be the business of ideology construction. The 'theorist' operates 'before the fact' – the changes which theorizing is oriented to realizing.

Illustratively I should, consistent with my presentation of nineteenth-century political economy as the prime case of theorizing, cite some figure of that period. Marx I have mentioned: so, resting on the work of others in this area, I can note that Ricardo has been described as the theorist of the rising industrial bourgeoisie. Clairmonte, in his analysis of the present relevance of 'economic liberalism' to matters of the development of UDCs, remarks that liberalism was a 'militant body of doctrine aimed at mercantilism and the remnants of the aristocratic order'.[13] Against the present 'scientific' conventional wisdom, he argues that 'it should not be forgotten that all the great representatives of economics were inspired propagandists for militant social groups'.[14]

(c) The nature of the engagement of the *interpreter* can be seen to be *retrospective*: that is, concerned with the identification of agents/mechanisms/permissive conditions, and so on, of noted changes and/or efforts of theorizing. This particular role can be subdivided into the tasks of 'spokesman' and 'commentator', depending upon the relationship of the 'interpreter' to those interpreted. For example Debray can be taken to be a 'spokesman' for the Cuban revolution as he presents the theory of the *'foco'*. Responding to the implicit questions attaching to the role of 'interpreter' – that is, of what, for whom and why now? – Debray interprets the Cuban revolutionary experience to all other (Latin American) revolutionaries, because change in the peripheral areas of world capitalism is taken to be more likely than change in the centres. Similarly Fanon can be seen to have been the 'spokesman' for the Algerian revolution.

The role of 'commentator' can be taken to have been adopted by those thinkers who have chosen to reflect upon, and write about, particular events or theorists. (It might be added here that the role of 'scholar' seems to belong with the notion of 'interpreter' and, in orthodox self-conceptions, would tend to the passivity of the 'commentator' rather than the activism of the 'spokesman'.) Recalling the above notes on the political economists, it can be noted that the proponents of the 'marginalist revolution' have been seen as the interpreters of the social and economic world of a settled and successful bourgeoisie. So argues Pollard,[15] when he says that the 'marginalist revolution' (otherwise 'astounding') 'made social conservatism orthodox': advocating structural social change was made to be inevitably 'economically nonsensical'. Commentary, then, is not to be seen as *necessarily detached* from social struggle.

Finally, as regards 'commentators', my interests in this chapter are with a particular group; that is, 'Western scholars', and these we will come to below. What it makes sense for them to say is the matter which will exercise us.

We now have two ways in which the field of modes of engagement with the social world can be mapped. I shall now turn to the recent history of 'neo-marxian' attempts to say something about the Third World, and attempt to plot (a) the unacknowledged shifts of role and (b) the unremarked changes in circumstances and problems which mark the emergence and establishment of 'neo-marxist' views on matters of development. I shall, finally, (c) try to indicate some of the confusions which these 'failures of memory' have engendered.

2.0 It seems to me that the work of the 'neo-marxists' treating matters of development owes much of its original impetus to the rise of the New Left. The New Left (here, for convenience, I lump together the US and Western European variants and ignore the rest) had its roots in three areas of contemporary experience. These were: (a) the Civil Rights Movement and spin-off 'poverty pro-grammes'; (b) the pressures for university reform; and (c) the surge of revolutionary activity in the Third World. The New Left, I would argue, co-opted the 'liberation struggles' of the Third World into their own emancipatory efforts. But the question of whether or not this was a good idea has been the subject of debate. Unfortunately, in treating this issue, justifiable criticism of Third World*ism* has rather spilled over into blanket dismissals of the plausibility of the analogies between New Left activity and the liberation struggles which the New Left invoked. Young, for example, speaks of 'an imagery compounded of romanticism, guilt, compassion and pure misunderstanding . . . superficial identifications'.[16] I think Young's dismissal of the New Left's co-option of Third World liberation struggles is wrong – but the nature of the exchange is problematical.

However, notwithstanding doubts about the precise status of this exchange, it can be safely asserted that figures centrally important to the development of a marxian analysis of the situation of the Third World were, simultaneously, key figures for the New Left. In particular I am thinking of Fanon and Debray. These two figures instance the issues of: (a) the co-option by the New Left of Third World liberation struggles; and (b) the business of creatively revi-sing marxian theorems to fit new situations. These two men provide a hinge upon which the history of 'neo-marxism' turns. I will look at their work – leaving aside issue (a) and concentrating upon (b) – and then go on to consider the 'neo-marxian' work that follows on from it.

Of the work of Fanon and Debray it can be noted that both are reporting on the lessons of experience: in particular revolutionary guerrilla warfare. Beginning with Debray, it can be noted that Blackburn reports that: 'Debray left France in the early 'sixties partly because of the hopelessness and corruption of the French Communist Party during the Algerian war. In the event he has contributed significantly to the rebirth of a revolutionary left in Europe and North America by making available to them the experience of the Latin American guerrillas.'[17]

Any brief treatment of Debray's work must begin by taking note of his thoroughgoing practical intent. He is concerned to interpret and learn the lessons of the Cuban revolution, and to present the actions/theories of the revolutionaries as practical activity. Blackburn takes note of this when he speaks of Debray's 'technics' – a detailed concern for the nuts and bolts of insurrection. But the matter is also slightly broader. Debray is concerned to interpret the Cuban experience to us, so the 'history', as it were, is central and thereafter links are made to established areas of debate. It seems to me that Debray is to be understood as taking the role of the 'interpreter' (or, more specifically, 'spokesman') and as attempting to render intelligible to us the experience of the Cuban revolution. He is not, so far as I can see, proposing some set of conceptual revisions which are to be taken thereafter as of general applicability. Both Fanon and Debray have been criticized as wrongly having generalized from particular circumstances to new general theory: but this line of criticism (as exemplified here by Minogue) misconstrues their treatment of the 'lessons of experience', in terms of both the procedure's logic and its point.

Minogue,[18] having correctly picked out the novelty of the Guevara/Debray line (its practical nature), goes on to claim that those who generalize from the case of Cuba (using, he argues, 'inductive reasoning') produce false theories as a result. Minogue argues as follows. If marxism is seen as a social phenomenon, then its history is marked by its heretics, for it is they who have disregarded dogma and broken new ground. This is seen as presenting the problem of theoretical interpretation: 'each change has been followed by a development of theory which purports to learn the lessons of the new experience'.[19] Now clearly this is a real task, yet Minogue hints that it is a problem of adapting dogma (where this is intended pejoratively).

Minogue fails to distinguish, as I am suggesting it is helpful to do, between the roles of theorist and commentator: he also offers a wrong criticism. Thus, he claims: 'The Russians, the Chinese, the Yugoslavs and the Cubans have all indulged in this exercise. Its logic is of course inductive. It consists in transposing the most striking facts of the successful experience into abstract terms and generating theory from them.'[20] This is wrong. If the 'learning' is done crudely then the format may well look as though it is inductive, but the logic will not be. A general objection to inductive reasoning will not invalidate the lessons drawn from experience simply because the elements of the experience picked out will be selected in the light of established theorizing. The 'learning' is not simply inductive; indeed, returning to Minogue's 'adapting dogma' jibe, we can discomfit Minogue by suggesting – raising the stake, as it were – that it might be better to see this sort of exercise as casuistry. Doubtless Minogue would take this as wholly condemning; but a strategy for 'learning the lessons of experience' is thereby hinted at. It is an accommodating revision and not any simple process of the elaboration of a revised set of generalizations. This accommodation, in the case of Debray, is couched in Althusserian terms, and the latter is quoted as saying: 'Marxists know that no tactic is possible which does not rest on some strategy and no strategy which does not rest on some theory.'[21] This format of re-integration is followed by Debray, and I think we can grant the general strategy and the importance of Debray's 'message' while rejecting the rigidity of the Althusserian scheme, which, incidentally, hardly fits with the Castroist stress on spontaneity.

Debray reports on his own work in these terms:[22]

> We are never completely contemporaneous with our present. History advances in disguise; it appears on stage wearing the mask of the preceding scene and we tend to lose the meaning of the play. Each time the curtain rises, continuity has to be re-established. The blame, of course, is not history's, but lies in our vision, encumbered with memory and images learned in the past. We see the past superimposed on the present, even when the present is a revolution.

If we compare this with our note on the 'theorist' prospectively plundering established resources, then clearly Debray is emphasizing the retrospective aspect of theorizing – the use of established resources. Indeed Debray tends to stress the idea of a conventional wisdom. (Of the radical intellectual as potential guerrilla, Debray presents Castro's view: 'the intellectual will try to grasp the present through pre-conceived ideological constructs . . . Thinking he already knows he will learn more slowly, display less flexibility'.[23]) Distinguishing between the 'roles' of 'practitioner' and 'commentator' allows us to grasp clearly just what Debray is up to: his efforts are interpretive.

This brief consideration of Debray points up two issues. First, that of 'learning the lessons of experience' which – recalling our 'general systematic framework' – is the business of the 'commentator' operating after the fact. Second, that of the business of 'creatively responding to novel situations', where this clearly cannot be the task of the 'commentator' and thus falls to either the 'theorist' or the 'practitioner'. With Debray's exegesis of the Cuban revolution it is a 'practitioner's' role he seeks to interpret to us. Debray takes the Cuban revolution to have been a 'creative revision' of established nostrums, and he is concerned to discover its lessons. These two issues are thoroughly tangled up and I shall not attempt to separate them. I now turn to consider the heart of Debray's interpretation, and this will lead into a linked note on the central aspects of Fanon's schemes.

Debray and Fanon have, it seems, been frequently misunderstood: in contrast to the criticism of wrongful theory generation, which we have just looked at, they have also been accused of having abandoned theory altogether. Thus Roxborough argues: 'The final abandonment of revolutionary theory conceived as an analysis of the dynamic of the social structure which could serve as a guide for revolutionary action came in the aftermath of the Cuban Revolution and the Algerian independence movement. It was the task of theorists like Franz Fanon and Régis Debray to divorce revolutionary practice totally from revolutionary theory.'[24] The role of 'commentator' is not available to Roxborough and consequently his model of social-theoretic engagement cannot encompass discovery in activity – theorizing just has to come first. This is the reason why Roxborough can condemn Fanon/Debray as divorcing theory from practice. But the practice which they sought to interpret was successful. The successful practice of Cuban and Algerian revolutionaries *required* revision of theorems: complaining that the revolutionists did not really know what they were doing is bizarre. Debray and Fanon did not occasion an abandonment of theorizing; it is rather that the 'role' of 'theorist' was not the appropriate one for them.

Debray's interpretive intent is clear in his discussions of violence and voluntarism. In the case of violence he argues: 'In semi-colonial countries, even more than in developed capitalist countries, the State poses the decisive political problem.'[25] Before this, it is reported, the problem has been approached *via* the coup d'état, or by mass insurrectionary activity. Debray reads Castroism as having solved the problem of the appropriate strategy of active revolutionary activity in Latin America. The solution is presented as the theory of the guerrilla *foco*. Debray summarizes as follows: 'the entire apparatus of organised violence belongs to the enemy. The violence with which the people can strike back, "mass action", is easily dismantled by the enemy's organised violence. A military coup can overnight pulverise democratic parties, trade unions, the combativity of the masses and their hope: the Brazilian example [1964 coup] is valid for the whole continent. What then is to be done?'[26] If this presents Debray's report of the Fidelist appreciation of the particular circumstances of Cuba, and arguably of Latin America generally, then it poses the crucial question of an appropriate response. Debray continues: 'To Lenin's question, Fidelism replies in terms which are similar . . . Under an autocratic regime only a minority organisation of professional revolutionaries theoretically conscious and practically trained in all the skills of their profession can prepare a successful outcome for the revolutionary struggle of the masses. In Fidelist terms this is the theory of the *foco*, of the insurrectionary centre.'[27] The permissive conditions for revolution are assumed, and the role of the *foco* is to ignite the tinder.

If we now turn and look at the work of Fanon, we find that the general occasion of theorizing is similar. His famous book *The Wretched of the Earth* grows directly out of the experience of the revolutionary war of Algerian independence. David Caute reports that: 'Algeria had belonged to France since 1820 and it was colonized in depth',[28] and when, in 1957, the socialist premier Mollet gave way to nationalist (French) pressure, 'the scene was set for total war . . . which spread from Algeria to France itself, decimated the Algerian people, brought down the Fourth Republic and raised the spectre of military rule or fascism in France.'[29]

In his book Fanon offers a general treatment of the Third World that is didactic, allusive, exhortative or 'diagnostic',[30] as Worsley puts it. It is also, as Caute points out, steeped in Sartrean existentialism. 'The wide canvas of the Third World is filled in with sweeping strokes of a brush exclusively dipped in African paint . . . The Algerian revolution is implicitly treated as a model for all of Africa.'[31] The character of the effort, in terms of its appreciation of its circumstances and its response thereto, revolves round three elements, as far as I can see.

First, Fanon treats the colonial scene in terms of a radical bifurcation of society; he speaks of 'This world divided into compartments, this world cut in two is inhabited by two different species.'[32] Second, significant change is taken to be a zero-sum game. It extends to the notions of 'truth' and 'goodness'. Fanon argues that 'Truth is that which hurries on the break-up of the colonialist regime . . . In this colonialist context there is no truthful behaviour: and the good is quite simply that which is evil for "them".'[33] Third, Fanon proposes that action be ordered around the revolutionary potential of the rural peasantry and the urban poor.

The reasons behind the affirmation of the need for violent revolution are twofold. First, this bifurcation of society leaves all weapons in the hands of the colonial power. There is a straightforwardly repressive government facing the mass of the people – there is, it might be said, no 'civil society'. Second, Fanon notes that the ease of co-option of elite nationalists by the colonial regime implies that, if there is to be progress, it needs must be achieved by violent means. Thus while granting familiar Leninist requirements *vis-à-vis* the state, Fanon lays heavy stress on the unsatisfactory character of the indigenous nationalist parties. The requirement of violence is derived, it would seem, from the experience of radicals becoming absorbed by the colonial ruling groups and from his appreciation of the character of colonial Africa. Thereafter, it seems, violence is embraced as redemptive.

Fanon's views resemble Debray's with regard to the discovery in action of the revolutionary path:[34]

> The nationalist militant. . . discovers in real action a new form
> of political activity . . . Violence alone, violence committed by
> the people, violence organised and educated by its leaders,
> makes it possible for the masses to understand social truths . . .
> Without that struggle, without that knowledge of the practice of
> action, there's nothing but a fancy dress parade.

Both Fanon and Debray concern themselves wholly with the pursuit of socialism. The circumstances giving rise to their work are such that the process can be taken as a zero-sum game – hence the 'black and white' style of their work. The corollary of this is their practicality: both are absorbed in the circumstances of their respective struggles and the issues of the general conditions of successful action. The realm of the orthodoxy of the left, the pursuit of a marxian science of the social, is in their work muted. That the Cuban and Algerian revolutions in fact represent 'creative responses' is taken as evident from their success. Explanations of the conditions for success of insurrections do not go far beyond a description of the circumstances of which they treat the histories.

Fanon and Debray I take to be presenting circumstance-particular efforts of interpretive writing. Though both shade off into presenting work that is of the practitioner, perhaps this is a matter partly of their own involvement and partly of their reception by wider Western audiences. Neither Fanon, nor Debray, offers any systematic revision of marxian theory.

3.0 Subsequent work has attempted a more systematic and coherent revision of Marx. Given that the New Left did regenerate interest in Marx, the scholarly efforts at revision/exposition/co-option/plunder have been widespread in the social sciences. These general and wide-ranging debates I shall not attempt to review. Rather, my area of interest narrows to the field of 'development studies'. That my focus has become rather more 'technical' is borne out in the material to be considered. Whereas Fanon and Debray were both anticipators of 'neo-marxian' studies of development and acknowledged influences on the New Left generally (being closely linked to active revolutionary episodes), the figures of Baran (and Sweezy), Frank, Wallerstein (to indicate the key figures) are probably better (or only) known to the members of the specialist disciplines which treat development matters.[35] Briefly, there is a shift from treating widely-known *activists* to comparatively unknown *scholars*. I am not concerned here with the various theorems of these scholars; I want, rather, to consider the implications of these noted changes in 'roles' and circumstances.

Diagramatically, these shifts can be presented as in Figure 2.1. It seems to me that the confusion engendered by the failure (of neo-marxian scholars) properly to appreciate these shifts in circumstances and roles manifests itself in what might be termed a 'slide to the general'. There are a number of ways in which this happens.

		New Left		Neo-marxism
Role shifts:	from	'practitioners', (guerrillas and spokesmen)	to	'commentators/ theorists' (neo-marxists)
Circumstance changes:	from	emancipatory, activism	to	reflective/prospective scholarship

Direction of change ⎯⎯⎯⎯⎯⎯⎯⎯⎯⟶

Figure 2.1

(a) The scholar adopts a prospective ('theorist') role, which in itself is unobjectionable, but goes on to evaluate his own work and that of others against the model of the 'one revolutionary mode'. It seems as though the generalizing (scientistic) common sense of (academic) social theorizing results in prospective theorizing taking on the guise of a pursuit of general formulations. Additionally, deference is paid, so it seems, to some (usually implicit) model of 'properly marxian behaviour', where this tends to collapse all radical activity into the one mould of 'marxian revolution-making'. It seems to me that this must have the effect of further diminishing reflexivity of theorizing.

It is fairly clear that this 'slide to the general', with consequent deleterious effect, is happening in the case of some woodenly orthodox marxists – for example Jack Woddis's[36] treatment of New Left figures – but it can also be found in otherwise thoroughly subtle efforts. Consider, for example, Brenner's paper, 'The Origins of

Capitalist Development'.[37] There seems to be a disjunction between behaviour, praxis, which in Brenner's case is the pursuit of scholarly exegesis, and prescriptions for action, politics, which in the case of those affirming a model of 'properly marxian behaviour' (which Brenner rather seems to do) looks very much like a generalized schema of class warfare.

Reflexivity in theorizing, which I take as an injunction for the theorist to locate himself and argue accordingly, would seem to entail granting that there can properly be a diversity of contributions to the pursuit of democracy (a term I use in its broad sense). The corollary, it appears to me, is that the 'liberal academic' should centre his engagement on critical scholarship, because that is what is appropriate to academic practice. I return to this point below.[38]

(b) There is a confusion closely related to that detailed immediately above, and this I call the 'exemplification-denial manoeuvre'. (Whether these two should be separated, I am not quite sure. What I am doing is to pick out two ways in which the 'slide to the general' can *start* – the end point, once the slide starts, is the same: that is, general formulations. I have not, with my present examples, pursued these two processes in enough detail to separate them out any more clearly.) The 'exemplification-denial manoeuvre' involves a vacillation between claims to the role of 'activist' and claims to the role of 'scholar'. Symptomatically we find detailed scholarship collapsing into crude politics. Rather than the prospective role wrongly conceived (Woddis), we have no coherent decision as to 'role' made at all, and there is a resultant slide to the general in default of any clear idea of an alternative. Again, prescriptions for action are couched in general terms. Brenner's article will serve as an instance of 'exemplification-denial'. Thus we find an academic exemplifying his circumstances (so Brenner offers a detailed critique of Baran *et al.*) and then presenting conclusions that seem to involve fudging the role distinctions which I have pointed up (so Brenner seems to want his effort judged against the 'one revolutionary mode' model).

These closely related errors are to be found in the work of Taylor.[39] In another example of the 'slide to the general', he presents a plea for a left-scientism. He conducts a detailed critique of Foster-Carter,[40] and this is perhaps best regarded as 'second order analysis', internal to the discipline. The concern which Taylor displays for precision in formulation of claims – if I can so encapsulate his material – exemplifies his circumstances as an academic. Yet his conception of the contribution he is making to the pursuit of socialism vitiates this self-exemplification. Foster-Carter[41] picks out Taylor's view that he (Taylor) is helping to provide Third World revolutionaries with the best possible, most advanced, conceptual

45

equipment. So we find a subtle and complex analysis linked to practice in a crude mechanical fashion, and one which implicitly both grants the model of the 'one revolutionary mode' and accepts the 'received model' in so far as it offers a scientistic marxism.[42]

(c) I would like to offer a final example of my use of this notion of a 'slide to the general'. It concerns the case of A.G. Frank, and the general point in respect of his work which I make has been dubbed the 'two Franks thesis'.[43]

The change in the character of the material in this general area from activists to scholars can be seen in the work of Frank. The 'early' and the 'late' Frank may be compared as he rejigs his efforts in a fashion which can be read as moving to render them compatible with his circumstances. In terms of my scheme of 'roles', Frank moves from (tending to) the roles of spokesman/theorist to (tending to) the roles of commentator/theorist. The task presents itself, in his work, as the pursuit of an autonomous theoretical base: the attempt to ground a 'dependency/UDT' scheme in a Marx-derived framework.

In the case of the circumstances of production of the 'early' work, I follow Booth[44] in taking Frank to have been abruptly won over to the radical left view following exposure to Latin American conditions. Frank can be seen to present a polemical critique of an orthodoxy that encompassed neo-classical economics, the dependency line associated with ECLA and traditional Latin American communist party views.

Affirming the principles of historical and structural analysis, Frank followed Baran[45] in regarding the circumstances of the presently underdeveloped as flowing from the debilitating metropolitan extraction of surplus from these long integrated peripheries. The solution was the revolutionary removal of a historically incapable bourgeoisie and the socialist-governed pursuit of an autonomous national development.

In his recent work,[46] Frank recalls that he has contributed to the formation of the 'dependency school' and that his earlier efforts have been heavily criticized for tending to the economistic and lacking any genuinely dialectical analysis. Of the 1978 work, Frank reports that it represents 'an attempt to transcend the "dependence" approach, but without yet abandoning it or the focus on underdevelopment, and to proceed on towards the integration of dependence and underdevelopment within the world process of accumulation.'[47] The book tackles a set of particular questions of analysis; issues occasioned by the criticisms of the earlier work though not flowing directly from them. These criticisms are treated in an introductory chapter that indicates Frank's line of research interest: 'This book and these introductory questions to it are an attempt to break out of the vicious circle of "development-theory".[48] The hoped-for replacement is characterized in three ways. First, by reference to method: 'To free ourselves from the irrelevance of narrowly limited neo-classical theory . . . we may take the global historical vision of Adam Smith and the dialectical analysis of Karl Marx as points of departure in an attempt to advance toward a whole world encompassing holistic, real world historical, socially structured (and therefore in fact theoretically dialectical) theory of development and underdevelopment.'[49] Second, as regards procedure, 'This will require the scientific examination of the historical evidence and record of capitalist development and the better reading (in the sense of Althusser) of Smith and Marx in the light of this evidence.'[50] Frank then indicates the expected manner of emergence of the product: 'With this purpose and in this spirit we review the participation of Asia, Africa and Latin America in this world wide historical process; and we emphasize the sub-ordinate *dependence* of these areas within the process of world capitalist development as the cause of their development of underdevelopment.'[51]

If, in order to fix the position of the 'late' Frank in relation to the 'early' one, we consider the nature of the procedures noted above, what do they reveal? Clearly there is no general reconstruction being undertaken; there is no abstract and general consideration of the categorial frame deployed in enquiry. Rather he continues to use the syntax of the natural sciences. Thus he seeks to revise his theories with a closer, more detailed, reading of history in the light of concepts that are already established in his work, yet liable (he seems to be claiming) to relocation within a subtler frame derived from Smith and Marx.

Frank's recent work seems to represent an intellectual-political relocation. That which is characteristically Frankian is not so much removed, or lost, as partially submerged. To put this another way: where Frank's earlier work grasped in one simplifying and synthesizing effort the 'answer' in respect of Latin America, he now seems to be trying (working backwards, as it were) to discover those arguments which establish his 'answer'. Yet the change of context introduces a subtle shift of emphasis. Frank seeks not to uncover the arguments specific to his 'answer' in respect of Latin America, but rather to uncover a set of arguments productive of a *general* 'answer'. In Frank's case, the 'slide to the general' is made all the more easily because of his use of the syntax of natural science.

I want now to summarize the concerns of this section 3 and to add a comment upon another, related, way of making my point. Thus section 3 has dealt with the confusion that can be fostered within neo-marxian work, as my particular specimen of social theorizing, by the failure to pay sufficiently close attention to the 'roles' being adopted by the various social theorists. Criticisms of a specific effort which misconstrue the nature of that work will, inevitably, cloud the issues. So, for example, lodging objections to the 'early' work of Frank – 'political pamphleteering' (loosely speaking, but of a very high quality) – on the grounds that it fails to be an adequate academic social scientific exercise is simply beside the point: Frank's enterprise is misconstrued and criticism does not engage with it. In respect of the 'late' Frank I would argue that *he* misconstrues (or miscasts, more properly speaking) his own work. Thus he addresses the abstract issue of the basis of a properly marxian analysis as though it were a matter of revising the framework of an essentially empiricist, and politically established, framework. These points about A.G. Frank are encapsulated in my text as the 'early' (tending to the roles of spokesman/theorist) and 'late' (tending to the roles of commentator/theorist) Frank. Thus we see that the misconstrual of role is a problem that can arise 'within' the work of a theorist just as easily as 'without' – in the work of critics.

There is another way of approaching the business of the problems attendant upon the misconstrual of social-theoretic roles. Instead of looking at the 'role-shifts' of particular theorists, or groups of theorists, we can look instead at the track through time of the issue/problematic/paradigm (or whatever) in question. In regard to my present specimen, neo-marxism, Figure 2.2 serves to bring out its recent track. Now my general point is this: if we accept that issues/problematics/paradigms and so on have a track through time (as they are successively theorized, represented, debated, adjusted, etc.), and this seems to me to be a simple corollary of a 'reflexive' view of social theorizing, then it has to be granted that we must *expect* changes in conception and intent in theorizing. In the case of the natural sciences, resting for the moment on a naive view of them, we have a process of simple improvement through time. But within the realm of social sciences, conceived reflexively, we have to see changes in formulations as being related to, or occasioned by, the double dynamic of theory and society. Formulations change as theorists rework their views in the light of changes within the discipline and change in the world. Consequently, either in discussing these issues or in commenting upon the work of others who are so doing, care has to be taken in keeping track of the various 'locations' of the various participants.

4.0 In the light of the above, what recommendations might be made for social-theoretic treatments of development? The general line I would affirm – following on from my introductory remarks about 'social theorizing' being a generic expression – is that there are a variety of modes of social-theoretic engagement. I tried to

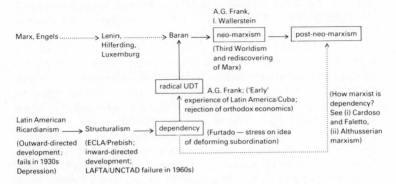

Figure 2.2

illustrate this point's validity and usefulness in looking at Fanon and Debray. This is to use the notion to survey the field: but it can also be used, reflexively, as an injunction in respect of our own work. Thus it could be said that while it is a familiar injunction in marxian writing to remember that theorizing should be concrete and historically specific, it is rather less obviously remembered that theorizing must be both a concrete and a historically specific activity. What it makes sense for a theorist to say (or do) will depend crucially upon his circumstances and the problems addressed: upon, that is, his location in his social world. This diversity of modes of engagement, and their situation/problem-specificity, results in the idea that reflexivity in theorizing is a necessary condition of saying anything sensible.

More particularly, returning to matters of development, if we recall the earlier noted distinction between two senses in which the notion of ideology might be used, then we can distinguish two broad areas of enquiry which would seem appropriate to (academic) Western discourse on development.

The notion of ideology, in the light of the extension of Marx effected by Critical Theory, can be taken as pervasive and informal: it is thus a means to analysing the ideological aspects of un-reflective common sense. This opens up the possibility of a locally engaged area of enquiry for the (Western) scholar: that is, how do notions of 'aid', 'underdevelopment', 'backwardness', and so on, present themselves in the unconsidered common sense of the peoples of the developed areas? It could be asked, whence come 'popular' notions of the exchange of rich and poor, and how are these images maintained? This role of critical scholarship seems to shade off not only into other areas of concern, such as 'racialism', but also into the activist areas of, say, counter-information and agit-prop. Clearly

49

there is much more to be said on the problems and prospects of such 'local engagement', but instead of pursuing this I shall move back to rather more familiarly mainstream concerns.

Here the more usual notion of ideology can be used. I take it to designate those more or less formal and delimited schemes of political and social explanation/legitimation. The career of development studies, since the end of World War II, can be seen as comprising the production of a series of delimited-formal ideologies. Now discussion and analysis of these various departures would seem to be a perfectly proper exercise for the (academic) commentator. In terms of judging what is good and bad analysis of the Third World, the familiar notions of ideology (and ideology critique) seem to be appropriate. This, then, is an essentially formal, interpretive, role.

However, on this question of the role of the commentator and its proper extent, there is one major difficulty, it seems to me, that the attempt to produce a political economic analysis of the Third World will find if it is attempted by Western (academic) scholars. I now introduce a distinction between 'agents' and 'allies'.

Cardoso and Faletto produce a political economic analysis of the circumstances of Latin American economies. Finding that their present dependent incorporation offers little scope for the future, they turn to the spontaneous organizations of the mass of the populace and ask how these might aid (and be themselves aided in) the movement towards socialist change. So, who can take on the particular role, this engagement? That Cardoso and Faletto's effort is engaged has to be granted, and if this engagement is taken to be circumstance-sensitive and problem-specific, it is difficult to see a theorist based in the 'West' being engaged in quite the same way. This is true even if all share an interest in political economic analysis oriented to the active pursuit of democracy. In terms of the 'roles' sketched out above ('theorist', 'practitioner', 'interpreter'), the work of Cardoso and Faletto entails taking the first two roles, whereas it is at least plausible to suggest that the thinker based in the 'West' will tend to have open only the role of 'interpreter'. Even if both pursue the 'political economy of Latin America', they must do so in different ways. At this point the notion of 'allies' might be introduced.

As the multi-nationals have local 'agents', might not the locally based political economists have international 'allies'? The notion of 'agents', presented in dependency analysis, serves to point out an important coincidence of interests on the part of the two groups: on the one hand the managements of major multi-nationals and, on the other, those members of Third World industrial and commercial bourgeoisies with whom they deal. The coincidence of interest admits of a general description based on resemblance, but the crucial point is that this mutuality of interest is occasioned by, and cemented in, their routine business practice.

With regard to the notion of 'allies' it can be asked, following the above, how might this relationship be occasioned and cemented in routine practice? (If this relationship could be secured, then the Western academic could join Cardoso and Faletto in the role of 'theorist'.) One reply might be to invoke the notion of an international community of scholarship. But this seems to be very problematic. It might be granted that there is a single world economy, and that the developed form of capitalism presents the opportunity for establishing intellectual tools of general applicability (this follows Marx), but we are, none the less, fixed in specific situations. Invoking such general and abstract coincidences of circumstance runs the risk, it seems to me, of turning into an excuse for academicism. The ease with which the 'slide to the general' can occur in this area of work we have already noted.

The pursuit of political economic enquiry actively oriented to the achievement of socialist change must be conditioned by an insistence upon circumstance-sensitivity and problem-specificity if the tempting errors of the 'slide to the general' are to be avoided. This rather suggests that for all the international traffic in ideas (that undoubtedly exists), general statements to the effect that 'we are all victims of/concerned with world capitalism' must be regarded as declarations of solidarity rather than the basis of a potentially unified programme of enquiry and action.

To attempt to reduce all the various modes of social-theoretic engagement to one model (or restricted set of models), or to allow this to happen by default, would seem to me to entail missing the point of the whole effort. Social theorizing is *practical*, first and last.

3 Becoming industrialized, being industrial: a brief analysis of a particular planning mode of engagement

1.0 In chapter 2 of his *Thought and Change* (1964), Gellner presents a sketch of a politics appropriate to the present. I shall summarize his argument, as I am interested in analysing the particular mode of social-theoretic engagement exemplified in this book. This text offers a clear statement of a position which is prevalent within First World political discourse, utterly familiar within studies of development (as I argue in the last chapter) and, I believe, fundamentally in error in respect of the nature of social theorizing generally and professional (or academic most centrally) social science in particular. Attached to this erroneous conception of social science is a thoroughly unfortunate politics.

Gellner's 'politics for the present' is introduced with the observation that a social order is legitimate for its citizens if it is both industrial (or industrializing) and nationalist.[1] This position is seen both to 'underlie. . . and dominate most. . . actual contemporary politics' (claim to fact) and to be 'correct' (claim to moral relevance).[2] It is the business of sociology, it is reported, to elucidate the nature of the process of becoming and being industrial. It is for this reason that this discipline has inherited the mantle once worn by classical political philosophy – it asks the right questions in the right sort of way. Thus Gellner reports: 'There are now very nearly only two kinds of politics. . . there are the politics of getting industrialized, and there are the politics of affluence.'[3] The rise of concern for development, the surge of decolonization, and, it seems, for Gellner the success of drives toward development, combine to present commentators (my term, not his) with a valuable learning experience: about the 'real world' and about theorizing itself. But whereas orthodox economists, who are seemingly as 'out of touch' as political philosophy or 'textbook sociology', have swept aside the crucial questions into *ceteris paribus* clauses surrounding their formal equations, some (and only some) social theorists have held fast to the central problems: 'the work of Myrdal on *becoming* (industrialized), or of . . . Galbraith on *being*, consist in the main of showing that what really matters are those features which used to be swept under the carpet.'[4]

The 'politics for the present', on Gellner's view, centres upon work, or questions, that are, and have been, of predominant interest to sociologists. I would make this a little more specific, in line, I think, with Gellner's views, and speak of the 'classical tradition of sociology'. The role of the sociologist in this new politics is to provide authoritative knowledge of the processes of industrial society and their patterns of historical change. Gellner acknowledges, with a residual discomfort and no little ambiguity as regards the precise extent of the applicability of his notions, that politics is the rule of those who understand the new societies, those who can grasp the dynamic of industrial(izing) societies. Thus we have, and the chosen labels signal the writer's unease, rule by the 'Graduate-Student-Kings'[5] or by the 'Wise'.[6] What Gellner offers, what much of the First World and development studies has taken for granted (although in development studies there are now some signs of change, as I argue in the last chapter), is a version of an authoritative interventionism: what has otherwise been called a 'technocratic politics'.[7] Only an elite are properly fitted, by virtue of their expert knowledge, to participate in discussion about the future of modern society.

In this essay I want to bring out the main characteristics of this quite distinctive planning mode of engagement. I will proceed by considering the work of Myrdal, Galbraith and Gellner. What I shall attempt to do is to indicate how such thoroughly sophisticated and liberal thinkers can end up presenting a scheme which is so flawed, albeit subtly and instructively, in conception and so untenably non-democratic in intention.

2.0 Myrdal and Galbraith have both been claimed[8] for the neo-institutionalist school of social theorists and I have elsewhere[9] used that label in respect of Myrdal. However such labels are not to be taken too seriously; they are aids to enquiry, not fixed rules. What is common, most obviously, to the work of both theorists is their appreciation of social theorizing as a creative effort to make practical, and thus ethico-politically informed, sense of complex societal problems. They do not, most importantly, attempt to reduce their work to a narrowly technical mode of engagement. However, they do, and this too is an important point, maintain a strong commitment to a fairly familiar type of understanding of the notion of expertise. Social theorizing is intellectually creative, very difficult (hence Galbraith's famous term 'the conventional wisdom' – a vested interest in *hard gained* knowledge), and consequently the province of the expert. Flowing from this conception of the social world, and the nature of enquiry in respect of it, we find their characteristic politics: reformist state planning. Both theorists offer, to put the matter in its plainest terms, a total scheme which characterizes the social world, the possibility of knowing it, and the appropriate pattern of ordering action: they offer closely similar ideologies. I shall look first at Galbraith, then add a brief note on Myrdal (whom I have treated elsewhere, as noted) and finally turn to the work of Gellner whom I introduced above. This last-noted theorist's work is of particular interest in that he attempts to offer a philosophically and sociologically well grounded theory, or framework for understanding, of what he calls the 'transition' (to the modern world). The available notions of capitalism and socialism are to be discarded in favour of a scheme which revolves, as we have seen, round the idea of *industrial* society – the theorems of industrial society and modernization, both centrally important terms in the lexicon of orthodox social theorizing in the early 1960s, are to be given intellectual coherence and respectability.

2.1   I shall consider here the trio of books which present Galbraith's general analysis of modern society. They are *The Affluent Society* (1970), *The New Industrial State* (1967) and *Economics and the Public Purpose* (1975). The first book, whose title gave common language a new phrase, is a polemical piece directed against, on the one hand, the proponents of a revival of the market and, on the other, those somewhat unimaginative Keynesians who are content to let economic growth be the sovereign remedy against the ills of inequality. The second book extends Galbraith's argument by setting out the general explanatory frame within which the first rested. Here we find the theory of industrial society and the identification of the technostructure. Finally, in the last of the trio, we have a refined representation of the over-all position *via*, first, a critique of orthodox economics and, second, a political programme for action.

In *The Affluent Society* it is argued that increased production is not the final test of social achievement. On Galbraith's account this view challenges both the neo-classical theorists of the market, whose scheme is predicated upon the continuing existence of scarcity, and those Keynesians who had, either by design or default, caused the reformist elements of the original to disappear by the process of reducing the position to a rather simplistic affirmation of the possibility and desirability of economic growth. The ancient preoccupations of economics – privation, inequality and insecurity – have been narrowed down: privation or a concern for production is now central. Galbraith asks why, and offers a twofold answer: a focus on production enables awkward political and social questions to be ignored, and it also enables economists to avoid certain troublesome theoretical issues. The economists are shown to be unable to resolve the dilemma whereby they both affirm the sovereignty of the consumer and take little note of oligopoly and the advertising industry. Galbraith argues that the conventional wisdom is ignoring the realities of the modern industrial society, which is oligopolistic, consumerist and self-moving.[10] It is time, urges Galbraith, to restore the radicalism of Keynes[11] and ask about the *sort* of production that the industrial system is actually geared to. At this point we meet the start of Galbraith's critique of spending patterns which rests upon his distinction between 'public squalor' and 'private affluence'. It is here that economics is to be brought up to date – the fact of affluence has to be acknowledged.

The Affluent Society is a landmark in post-World War II social theorizing. It has been variously criticized: both 'left' and 'right' have rather tended to put down the author as an East Coast liberal who could well afford his wittily displayed, and rather unfocused, unease about the 'state of the world'. Setting these lines aside, what we find is an analysis which neatly picks out both the irrationality of monopoly capitalism and the self- (and system-)serving incoherence of orthodox economics. And it does so with a wholly pleasing *directness* of language and purpose. The book surely deserved its lengthy stay at the top of the best-seller lists.

The reconstruction of economics around the realization that 'affluence', not 'scarcity', is the central experience of the modern world is pursued in *The New Industrial State*. The argument takes off from the identification of oligopolistic consumerism made in *The Affluent Society*. Enquiry is centred upon the large industrial-commercial corporation: the rise of these institutions, over the last seventy years, is noted and so are certain changes in its character.[12] Galbraith points, in particular, to the rise, in influence and power, of what he calls 'the technostructure' – this is the important body of functionaries and planners who staff these large corporate systems.

At a macro economic-social scale it is this corporate, planned, sector (in both its public and private forms) that is dominant. In contrast the market sector is a residual, if extensive, collection of suppliers, service industries and so on. To this identification of the character of the modern corporation and its predominance in the modern economy and society is added an appreciation of its relationship to the state. In contrast to the restricted, rule-sustaining, role of the state postulated by the economic orthodoxy, Galbraith identifies an obvious alliance between corporate technostructure and state apparatus: to put it simply, what Galbraith is worrying about is the apparent rise of a corporate, that is, fascistic, state.[13] Galbraith is a liberal (as well as a Keynesian) and this nascent corporate state is not to his taste.[14] There seem to be two choices: first, one can acquiesce in the consumerist ideology and do nothing or, second, one can attempt to alert the increasingly large group in society who have been through higher education and thus bring the trend under control; 'the future of what is called modern society depends on how willingly and effectively the intellectual community in general, and the educational and scientific estate in particular, assume responsibilites for political action and leadership.'[15] Our author, like the reformist liberal he is, is appealing to the reasonable men – they are the agents of change to whom his material is addressed.

We find a further development of Galbraith's political programme in his *Economics and the Public Purpose,* and I shall focus on this element. In a section entitled 'A General Theory of Reform' we find the scheme presented explicitly. It contains, to simplify, two elements. First there is the matter of the 'emancipation of belief', whereby the common sense equation of the good life with the consumption of the goods produced by the corporate economy is denied. The theme of public squalor/private affluence is here re-presented. Second we have the 'emancipation of the state': the link between state and business must be broken. This is the key point of Galbraith's enquiry and programme. Unfortunately he has virtually nothing to say about how this link is to be broken in practice. The only mechanism that seems to be alluded to is the systemic disposition to reform which flows from the systems having an ever larger body of (potentially critically minded) intelligent functionaries (graduates – liberals after Galbraith's own image). In government agencies, in society generally, and in the big corporations there are increasing accumulations of intelligent potential reformers – they will generate a constituency for legislative reform. Thereafter we are presented with a reform package of state actions and these, let's note, are easy to write. Almost effortlessly a major part of the problem is thus transformed into the principal vehicle of the solution.

The vision of the future proposed is redolent of Keynes, and the US tradition, going back to Veblen, that Galbraith inherits: a rational and humane capitalism ordered by the reasonable men in control of the state machine. As an image it has much to commend it. But there seems to be little intellectual warrant for the shift from 'capitalism' to 'industrialism', or political plausibility in the reform strategy. Indeed Galbraith is offering a corporatist solution to his concern with corporatism.[16]

2.2 The other theorist cited by Gellner, Myrdal, is similarly confident about the powers of the 'reasonable state'; indeed he equates politics with planning. An outline of Myrdal's scheme can now be sketched, although this will be done cursorily as I have discussed him elsewhere and at several points in these essays.[17]

Myrdal's ethic involves reading the notion of progress, or, in the context of talk about the Third World, development, as ordered social reform. Most generally we have the pursuit of 'World Welfareism', and it must be entirely clear that this is an expression of the coincidence of his biography with the historical juncture of the systemic crisis of liberal capitalism. In the 1930s Myrdal 'solves' his intellectual problems of engagement (to use my terms) by affirming the crisis-dictated centrality of the planned stabilization and ordering of the capitalist system. This intention is complemented by a conception of enquiry which has been adequately characterized as a 'sociologized economics'. Myrdal, like Galbraith, rejects both the intellectual machineries and ideological baggage of orthodox neo-classical economics. Conception and intent are fused in the promulgation of an ideology of authoritative (co-operative revised) interventionism: the LDCs with their debilitating social inertia and world economically disadvantaged position are to be moved to a new upwardly dynamic historical track. And the agent of this change? The state planning machine in the hands of the reasonable men.

To recap: my point in thus introducing Galbraith and Myrdal is to call attention to the breadth of influence of the industrialism/ modernization/convergence thinking of the 1960s and 1970s. This work represents, it seems to me, a quite distinctive planning mode of social-theoretic engagement. With Gellner the position is theorized at a high level of argumentative sophistication, and it is to this material that I now turn. In contrast to the foregoing, Gellner's work is distinctly bleaker in tone – problems are identified and commitments alluded to that would make Galbraith and Myrdal, on the evidence of their texts, flinch somewhat.

3.0 Thus far I have looked at work which refers to economics and sociology, and does so with a political end in mind. To the foregoing, Gellner adds a concern for political philosophy. Writing in the mid-1960s he attempts to redraw the boundaries of political philosophy so as to accommodate to what he takes as the demands of the present; that is, he attempts to provide an intellectually coherent, and well grounded, general statement of the positions found in the theorems of industrialism, modernization and convergence. This is not taken as a narrowly technical task: Gellner declares his goal, openly reviews and plunders the resources available, explicitly considers how to theorize his problem and then, finally, goes on to review a few obvious consequences of his newly constructed position. Summarily, it can be seen that Gellner's effort is that of an intellectual craftsman addressing complex and urgent practical problems – he is in the business of making sense.

At the centre of his concerns is the promulgation of a science (natural and social)-based politics of 'the transition', a pervasive and continuing phenomenon. The process of industrializing – or, for the First World, coming, it seems, to a slightly later 'stage' of the 'transition', being industrialized – *can be understood* (as a species of scientific problem), and *can be ordered* (as a species of social scientifically informed practical work). Power must rest with those able to command the requisite science-based expertise: this elitist stance is explicitly advocated for the Third World, muted for the First. The overall vision is revealed in Gellner's expectations of the future of ideology: an emergent dual system comprising broad, vague, legitimating slogans for the consumption of the masses, and detailed scientific knowledge (natural and social) as the actual basis for creating and ordering society. This, let us note, is my summary: in Gellner, the treatment of the issues of expert knowledge, ruling groups, relevance of stages in transition to extant politics and democracy are jumbled up, and in particular I think he elides the central non-democratic and elitist character of his position.

The text comprises, as I noted above, a specification of the problem, a discussion of how to theorize it, and a note on a few 'matters arising'.[18] I shall review the work with this structure in mind as it will recall attention to what is for my present purposes the major point; that is, that Gellner is presenting an argued case for a quite distinct mode of social-theoretic engagement. It is easy to lose sight of this among the wealth of scholarly detail.

Gellner begins with the claim that any society has, and inevitably needs, an explanatory scheme (ideology, or myth, at a *very* general level) which will render that society's form and apparent historical direction both coherent and legitimate in the eyes of its members. In the First World, it is reported, this has typically been an idea of progress. But rather than trace the history of the varieties of this idea, Gellner adopts a more ruthless strategy: he appropriates these available intellectual resources *via* a simple schematic reconstruction. Thus there are two main sorts of idea of progress, each has benefits/disbenefits, and, appropriately reworked, they generate a third idea which is appropriate to the task in hand.

Gellner identifies an 'episodic' view of progress, essentially eighteenth century, which posits one move from a bad state of affairs (barbarism) to a good one (civilization): here we find theories of society which make use of the myth of the social contract. Then we have 'evolutionist' schemes, essentially nineteenth century, which posit an all-embracing process of cumulative progress. The former scheme is deemed to be sociologically impoverished, while the latter suffers from the defects of pseudo-explanation, moral incoherence and simple factual inadequacy to the experience of the Third World. Discarding the disbenefits and acknowledging the strengths (from the first the idea of *an event*, from the second the idea of *pervasive continuity*) leads Gellner to the presentation of his preferred motif; the neo-episodic view of change. The coming of the modern world is an event in world history, and thus intellectually (scientifically) manageable; and it is also a pervasive and continuing phenomenon, and thus cognitively and morally demanding. Gellner takes this to be a plausible and usable conception of the rise of the modern world: this 'transition' requires its own politics.[19]

Having thus far described the general character of the required new myth, or legitimating theorem, Gellner now proceeds to consider how to theorize this new scheme. There are two areas of concern: 'method' and 'ethic'.

Enquiry in respect of the first element is introduced through a consideration of the nature of a moral problem. Such a problem is characterized as being a dilemma where the appropriate rules of judgment are problematic. We know neither what to think nor how to think. This characterization is then used as an analogy to illuminate the business of theorizing the 'transition'. The shift to the modern world entails pervasive social change; it enfolds the theorist; thus the shift can be grasped only from the inside. And how? Gellner answers by claiming that scientific thinking is the key because it is a qualitatively different type of thought from all others in that it is routinely self-critical: it considers its own rules of procedure as well as offering detailed substantive claims.

What are we to make of this argument? I think we have to distinguish between: (a) his strategy of intellectual craftsmanship, as I have called it; (b) his particular treatment of the transition by using the metaphor of a moral problem; and (c) his particular understanding of (natural) science. As regards the first point I think we cannot but applaud Gellner: elsewhere[20] I have contrasted his material with some of the 'jejune'[21] textbook sociology (of modernization) against which, in part, he contrasts his own work, and its general superiority is manifest. Gellner is, in my view, right to stress that social theorizing conjoins the creative anticipation of the future with a rigorous attention to the detail of disciplined argument. As regards the second point, the particular orienting metaphor deployed, again I have elsewhere[22] expressed approval at least in so far as a necessary linkage between theorist and theory – an element of the identity of the theorist, his 'ethic', gets built into the theory – is indicated. Further than this we find a preference for doubting over pre-judging as an intellectual strategy for a 'being-in-transition', and if this were another celebration of what I have called reflexivity then I would have no quarrel with the material. Yet, and here I anticipate point three, Gellner seems to slide from/between a (wholly acceptable) stress on reflexivity in argument to a (rather dubious) equation of reflexivity with scientificity[23] to a (wholly dubious) identification of critical rationalism, or a variant upon that scheme, as the appropriate stance (on philosophy of science and social substantive issues) to be adopted at the present. Finally a note on my third point. At the outset it can be noted that Gellner actually devotes an entire chapter to a discussion of his understanding of science (chapter 5) in addition to the present material (which is to be found in chapter 3). I shall refer to both parts of his text here, although I shall not have that much to say, as to engage with Gellner in any detail upon the philosophy of science is beyond my present scope.[24] Once again we find a mixture of plausible (usually philosophically informed) detail taken implausibly to be amenable to straightforward, more or less, extension in the realm of the social (usually characterized in simple sociological terms). It is easy to lose the argument in the detail. However, in this case we can use a helpful, ready-made, label to fix Gellner in place. Thus, I would suggest, his scheme of science *cum* substantive politics is a Popperian-inspired critical rationalism. It is not a slavish borrowing – Gellner is at pains to soften some of Popper's more ludicrous social theorizing – but it is none the less, essentially, a critical rationalist reading of the nature of science and its social deployment. It is a scheme that has been subject to heavy criticism both within the ambit of the philosophy of science and within sociology. I cannot here review these debates. It will have to suffice that I report that I find the position at best unsatisfactory (Gellner) and at worst tendentious (Popper). If Passmore is right, then the position is best regarded as a seventeenth-century-style celebration of 'scientific method': it is inherently implausible and it will not carry the social theoretic weight placed upon it.[25]

Intermediate between the above concern for 'method' and the matter of the 'ethic' to which I now want to turn, there is dangling on the end of chapter 5, a most revealing note on ideology. Gellner sees social-theoretic modes of cognition in the 'post-transition'[26] stage as comprising two sorts of thinking. There will be very general and vague, contentless, legitimating ideas on the one hand and, on the other, scientific thinking. Technical rationality will encompass the natural and social worlds. The model of Gellner's future industrial world is of rational order; ordered by whom is none too clear, but recalling his earlier remarks on the rule of the 'Wise', his central celebration of critical rationalism, and the curious abolition of the humanist 'man of letters' accomplished in his final chapter, it is difficult to avoid seeing the implication of a technocratic politics here.[27]

Turning to the second element of Gellner's discussion of how to theorize the new politics, we find, as noted, the business of an appropriate ethic. Much of this has been, as it is in Gellner's text, anticipated in the material covered so far. Gellner's elitist ethic of (piecemeal) social reform is, in outline, clear. In chapter 4, however, he presents a systematic review of available ethical theories. The strategy adopted resembles that of the construction of a new metaphor of change, yet here the procedure has a mechanical and predictable feel to it. Gellner seeks to identify an ethical model appropriate to his politics of transition; a secure grounding for those commitments already in place as a result of earlier thoughts on task and method.

The available theories are identified – the platonic, hidden prince, dream of the bureaucrat, way of residue, supreme target, and the rail – and characterized, and their respective strengths and weaknesses assessed. Now Gellner's model of the 'transition' entails an ethic of industrialism: in the short term we can discern the nature of the future and recognize that future as better than the present. The future is an industrial society and a diminution of unmet human wants. Thus Gellner compliments the scheme of the 'supreme target', reading utilitarianism as a variant which specifies an end state and identifies intermediate steps. Similarly the scheme of the 'rail' is seen to be useful – freedom is the recognition of necessity, thus the future is evidently going to be industrial. Quite what is added to Gellner's liberal ethic by this apparently bizarre running together of utilitarianism with Hegelian type schemes I do not know. Yet, with these discussions of 'method' and 'ethic', Gellner accomplishes the task of indicating how the politics of the transition are to be theorized. The last part of his text treats a few 'matters arising'.

The first of this trio of 'matters arising' is marxism: thus Gellner acknowledges that there is one social philosophy that actually does look at the transition. The general approach taken, the focus upon social structure and conflict in the process of change in the division of labour, is taken, by Gellner, to be correct. However, the particular concepts deployed are unhelpful and should be replaced by those which centre on the notion of industrialism. To this jejune summary is appended the observation that marxism is now the creed of Third World industrializers, as Calvin served the bourgeoisie, and their efforts are instructive for the First World, a mirror for understanding. This last point is probably the only one of note here.

The second 'matter arising' is nationalism, and we are presented with a fairly straightforward reading. Thus nationalism is a functional requisite of modernization and, in particular, of the construction from disparate groups of functioning elements of the world capitalist system.

Finally we have a thoroughly confusing endpiece to all this. The humanist model of man will have to be replaced by a scientific model (whatever that means). The scientist displaces the man of letters; indeed there is a conflict between the 'sophisticated common sense' of humanist culture and the non-obvious technical knowledge of science. And at this point, to finish on a minor note, one has to ask just how does Gellner regard his *own* text?

4.0 Galbraith, Myrdal and Gellner present us with a position which we can summarize as a scheme of 'industrialism/convergence/modernization'. The positions they individually present are varieties of affirmations of the central role of planned social change. It seems to me that social progress is conceived, over the short and medium term at least, as ordered social reform. They all offer ideologies which centre, crucially, upon the idea of authoritative and manipulative interventions in the social world to secure change.

This view can plausibly be regarded as the product of a particular set of historical, political and intellectual circumstances; a particular historical juncture. However, we ought to take care to disentangle: (a) transient intellectual fashions and political circumstances; (b) more deep seated changes in the nature of the political and economic system, and the associated shifts in ideas; (c) the extent to which the view here discussed represents a particular presentation of ideas relating to significant changes within an essentially enduring system.

In regard to the first point it is probably fairly clear that the trio of theorists cited were responding to, or interpreting (for the elite of the First World), the circumstances of the post-World War II period. At this time a mixture of concern for the disadvantaged of the Third World, confidence in the potency of social-science-informed expert planning, and concern to combat the attractions of socialism within the expanding group of the non-aligned, nationalist developmentalist, new nations, the products of decolonization, ran together to produce schemes of modernization/convergence/industrialism. In this sense the cited trio represent a now defunct position. Thus we find the work of the trio seems 'dated' or otherwise inconsonant with present circumstances. Myrdal is still writing the same book and his exegetist Streeten is apparently locked in a compulsive intellectual habit revolving round 'helping those who cannot help themselves'; it sometimes looks like a hankering after colonial days. Galbraith has both witnessed the political and imaginative exhaustion of reformist Keynesianism – 'social democracy' in the First World is now in a very sorry state and seems unable even to conceive of renewal, much less to execute it – and has seen the rise of the 'New Right' (though here, as the depression continues/ deepens, he remains optimistic that his opponents' views will be clearly tried, and found wanting). As for Gellner, the sophisticated scheme he adumbrated never was developed.

With regard to studies of development, in particular, I have alluded to just such a reading at several points in these essays, centring my remarks on the idea of interventionism, and it is discussed directly in the last chapter. There I argue that the position, within studies of development, is both weakening and yet is still a clearly discernible element of the residual common sense of development studies and, moreover, an element that serves only to inhibit the production of useful work.

Moving to the second point, we have to see that the trio of theorists cited represent a particular reading of, or effort to theorize, recent major changes in the capitalist system. The twentieth century has seen, arguably, three interlinked major changes in the fundamental make-up of the system. These are, first, the extent to which the world as described by theorems of liberal capitalism has given way to a new alignment, or pattern, of economic forces which is essentially one of monopoly power. The capitalist market is now a market in which giant corporations operate routinely on a world scale. Any idea of a self-regulating system of (necessarily) small elements is now untenable. Related to this is the second change: the capitalist system is now a regulated one. Within corporations, within governments, within international agencies, the system and its large component parts is subject to routine control. Familiarly we associate this regulation with the rise of Keynesianism: liberal reformism, shading into corporatism, designed to secure stability. The final change of note relates to both the foregoing: science and technology have become routinely integrated into the mode of monopoly capitalist production. Complex products require extensive research and development; they also have large outlays to recoup. The integration in the system of the routine pursuit of technical advance reinforces, and indeed requires, the tendency to regulation.

Now changes one and two are, I think, familiar. The matter of the routine integration of science and technology is perhaps slightly less familiar. This point can also be extended. Thus as the system itself now crucially involves routinized technical scientific inputs, so too can the system's legitimating theorem, which must address, crucially, the issue of regulation, invoke science. The system is complex and depends upon technical scientific knowledge, and ruling the system, ordering and regulating it, is similarly complex and – and here is the pernicious slide – inevitably and appropriately technical. Ordering the operation of industrial society is a matter of the deployment of scientific (natural and social) knowledge.

This ready acceptance of the role of the expert, the ready granting of credence to the claims lodged for authoritative manipulative intervention, this slide into corporatism, are surely familiar and powerful elements of the political culture of the First World. This matter has been a prime concern for Habermas, whom I shall introduce below. For the moment we can conclude that our second point – deep-seated change – bids us to acknowledge pressing and difficult issues.

The third point is simpler, at least on the face of it. It is that, notwithstanding the changes in the capitalist system to which I have alluded, the system is still a *capitalist* system.

This last point is the pivot round which the discussion of modern society, as presented by those theorists I have mentioned, can be turned. Whereas my cited trio have all urged, in various ways, the substitution of the notion of 'industrialism' for that of 'capitalism', the thinker to whom I now turn has not sought to effect such a break with the patterns of enquiry established by the 'founding fathers'. It is true that Habermas's revisions to Marx are extensive. Indeed it is a moot point as to how much of Marx's thought remains after Habermas's analyses – the body of Marx's thought seems to suffer a medical check-up so rigorous as to lead to the conclusion that at least his heart, critique, was in the right place even if, regretfully, the rest of the body must now be discarded.[28] None the less what concerns Habermas is an examination of modern capitalist society, and I think it is important to keep in mind this element as it is the clue to grasping the extensive differences between Habermas and the trio of bourgeois interventionists discussed above.

The matter of what I have called authoritative interventionism has been a major concern of Habermas, whose over-all intellectual project was, in his early work, specified as the construction of a politics adequate to the modern world. Thus, most generally, his project *coincides* with that declared by Gellner in the text I have looked at here. However, Habermas offers a very different answer. This can now be summarily presented. It will enable me to return to my starting-point – a concern for *how* such subtle theorists as Gellner, Galbraith and Myrdal could contrive such an unfortunate product – and underline what has been the theme of this treatment; that is, that the clue to their error resides in their confusion of the technical and the political.

Habermas's project involves the construction of a politics adequate to the modern world. It must combine the classical idea of politics, a practical knowledge of the world, with the rigour of scientific enquiry. The conception of such a politics involves the rejection of positivistic social theorizing and the elucidation of the tri-une scheme of human cognitive interests which results in the representation of the idea of critique, the 'heart' of the marxian project. The direction of force, of intention, of such a remade politics is radical democratic, and in this Habermas inherits the legacy of the Frankfurt School. The proper contribution of the social theorist at the present historical juncture, which is characterized, roughly, as noted above, is the critical theoretic fracturing of the taken-for-granted experience of monopoly capitalism. Acquiescence in the common sense of the system is to be challenged. Habermas's attention is focused on the political sphere, and the present political order is characterized as involving a 'technocratic politics' where this involves, crucially, the confusion of the practical with the technical. This false consciousness is a prime target: the emancipatory intent of the critical social theorist looks for the reconstruction of the public sphere: societal decision-making must seek to centre itself on discursive will formation. The heart of Habermas's scheme is a commitment to an idea of rational language-use as that which transmits truth; it is here that his scheme is grounded. The process of critical theorizing is characterized with reference to the analogy of the therapeutic exchange: to the extent that the particular addressee of an effort of critical theorizing responds in a manner which affirms the project of reconstructing the sphere of the public, by engaging in dialogue, then the effort was correct, so to say, and the shift from validation to authentication has been accomplished.[29]

The scheme presented by Habermas is distinctly 'open' in character: both in intellectual texture and in terms of the lack of any clear programme of political action. Such programme as there is, so far as I can see, and there are adumbrations to be found in *Towards a Rational Society* (1971b) particularly, centres upon the dissolution of the monopoly decision power of the established corporate bureaux of the monopoly capitalist system *via* the extension of the sphere of public discussion and control. Put in sloganistic, and perhaps rather atavistic, terms: whereas Gellner *et al.* wish to capture state power, Habermas wants to smash it. It is easy to see how this reluctance to specify familiar style political programmes reflects the intellectually open texture of his schemes – though here I am noting this at the level of analogous form only, I am not tackling the logic of his work – in that in both related areas he eschews the familiar orthodox concern for possession. Rejecting the pursuit of possessive knowledge of social life entails rejecting the familiar production of knowledgeably grounded programmes of action. The metaphor of the therapeutic exchange is centrally important.[30]

Now much could be said about the schemes of Habermas: the idea of critique, the reworking of Marx, the borrowings from orthodox social science and the extent to which he is arguably properly to be regarded as a neo-Weberian rather than a neo-marxist; but these matters I shall once again set aside in favour of borrowing the one crucial motif. The nub of the issue, in respect of my present concerns, is the confusion that can occur between practical and technical matters. The ideal of (radical democratic) politics is discursive will-formation, whereas the ideal in respect of technical matters is efficient manipulative control. The planning mode of social-theoretic engagement exemplified by Gellner, Galbraith and Myrdal, and which fatally confuses these two patterns of enquiry, is in conception manipulatively interventionist and in intent corporatist. The schemes of social change they propose are, at best, restrictedly democratic and, given the particular mix of conception and intent affirmed, at worst straightforwardly non-democratic – a variety of authoritarian corporatist systems could be defended on the basis of their schemes. I find this a curious position for three such outstanding, and manifestly decent, theorists to come to adopt.[31]

4 The impact of the 'received model' of natural science upon social theorizing

1.0 Thus far in these essays I have been concerned, among other things, to advance a view of social theorizing which acknowledges the diversity of possible modes of theorizing. This view, which pays particular attention to the notion of ideology, runs counter to what has, arguably, been the orthodoxy of social science during the post-war period. That orthodoxy, like the orthodoxy of development studies, is now in decline. However, there are residual elements of thought which, it seems to me, remain very powerful. There is one crucial element of the declining orthodoxy (of social science and development studies) which I want to take note of, both for its continuing influence and for the contribution, a negative one, it has made to my views about the nature of social theorizing conceived as a diverse set of practices.

It is my view that the common sense image of natural scientific explanation, the 'received model', affirmed as the model of a useful and true explanation, occasions, quite routinely, a great deal of confusion within social theorizing. In this essay I want to draw attention to a series of examples, drawn from the ambit of development studies, which seem to me to lend support to my general contention.

The image of natural scientific explanation and the presumption of the cognitive superiority of that mode of thought can be found both in 'lay' thought, or common sense ordinarily understood, and in the common sense of social science. Consequently to cast social theorizing in terms of 'discovering how things are in fact' is to run with the cultural grain in both a general and a particular way. I think that this coincidence of disciplinary and 'lay' common sense (in respect of this particular matter) makes it all too easy for social-theoretic enquiry to become intellectually deformed.

But, it might be objected, these claims are familiar, and indeed they are: I want to advance two particular and related claims. First, that because of this 'double cultural grain' the error is routinely made. Second, that theorists adopting otherwise sharply divergent positions have this error in common.

I have made reference above to the 'received model' of science. This is usefully discussed by Giddens[1] within the context of orthodox social scientific concerns. The orthodox position is seen as having been concerned with a theory of industrial society and as having presented a series of views which now seem 'almost archaic'.[2] The orthodox cast their enquiry in functionalist and naturalistic guise and these elements retain, if I've understood Giddens's point, a residual and unremarked influence within social science. It is this area that concerns him and he advances five related claims, and of these it is the fifth which is most general and directly useful for my purposes. It is argued that the orthodox are: (a) wrong about the origins of social science *vis-à-vis* natural science and about the status of 'laws' in social science; (b) wrong about the nature of language; (c) wrong to see social science as 'revelatory'; (d) incapable of grasping the notions of agency and structure; and, finally, (e) wrong about their affirmation of the 'received model' (positivistic) of natural science.

When I speak of the 'received model', it designates a particular conception of natural scientific enquiry round which a series of other views cluster as that model is deployed in the context of social scientific concerns. In its narrow sense it is a view about natural science, in its wider sense it becomes an approach to social science.

Thus far I have made reference to the work of Giddens in an uncritical fashion. Now I want to indicate how my thinking, and this essay, diverges from his concerns.

To the above-noted characterization of the orthodox view of explanatory strategy is appended the declaration that the notion of 'explanation' must come to the fore in discussions of natural and social science and their relationship. If I have followed him, by this he means that the variety of explanations sought by diversely located social scientific actors are not to be forced into a ranking order (the best and the rest?) round the explanatory strategies of natural science as understood in the 'received model'. On the other hand, neither does Giddens want to retain any suggestion (as in Dilthey or even, residually, Habermas) of there being distinct – natural and social – sciences. Thus he goes on to assert: 'We cannot treat the natural and social sciences *as two independently constituted forms of intellectual endeavour*.'[3] Clearly, given the general and philosophically sophisticated level at which Giddens is working, and given also what seems to be his major concern, that is the *systematic reconstruction* of social science, this may very well be true. However, it seems to me that there remains the *present* 'double cultural grain' and its *present* impact upon social theorizing to deal with. To discuss the nature of social scientific explanation in the context of rethinking the philosophy of science and models of social action tends, arguably, to delay the immediate practical task of extirpating the influence of the orthodox notion of explanatory propriety – the 'received model'. This latter task might, possibly, be more readily accomplished if the precise nature of the reformulations necessary to prevalent conceptions of social science are clearly understood to be 'disciplinary matters arising'. The nature of social-theoretic engagement (and explanation) can be displayed, albeit in rough preliminary outline, by a simple, and (conceptually) self-conscious examination of a judiciously selected instance. I have argued elsewhere[4] that the post-war history of theories of development provides just such a revealing and multi-faceted instance.

The gist of my claims in respect of the nature of what is ordinarily labelled 'social science' centre on the view that social-theoretic engagement is about making problem-specific and circumstance-sensitive sense of particular, problematical, situations. The notion of social theorizing is thus generic, and the range of possible modes I map *via* a scheme which makes reference both to designated exemplars and to a schematic frame of roles. In the former case the prime example of social-theoretic engagement is the production of delimited-formal ideologies using the explanatory strategy of political economy. I think this is the main substantive tradition which social scientists inherit, though I do not deny that social scientists actually do lots of other things. A second exemplar, an extension of the first, so to say, is the mode of critique. The prime case of social theorizing, the main tradition of social science, and the particular narrow area of my interest in the self-conscious or deliberate making of sense, come together in the following summary claim: social theorizing presents itself as the business of the construction and thereafter the criticism and comparative ranking of ideologies. Now in the later case, using a schematic frame of roles, a broader sense of social theorizing which encompasses practical action in the world in addition to the production of texts thus far noted can be introduced. The range of social-theoretic engagements is wide: we can speak of (at least) the 'gross roles' of 'theorists', 'practitioners' and 'commentators' ('interpreters' and 'spokesmen') simply by considering in a naive fashion the chronological relation of thought and action – before, during or after.

Now this view of the nature of social theorizing entails among other things a specific role for scholarship. It seems to be interpretive commentary oriented to the display of the truth. Now once again this may seem utterly familiar and even banal, but the point is

69

that the business, thus conceived, is *not* reducible to the collection and description of facts. Scholarship is a particular process. It has its own particular embedding within the generality of processes in the social world. The formulations of scholarly social science have (if they are good or lucky) their own impacts upon the business of structuration. It seems to me (and here I am short-circuiting a complex of arguments both supposed and examined in these papers) that scholarship needs must adopt a Habermas-informed style, so to say. We argue on behalf of 'human kind' in pursuit of a 'reconstructed public'.

At which point a familiar and awkward question can be raised: Just who are the critical theorists addressing? I think at present that *any* answer rather seems both restricted to the circumstances of liberal democracy, on the face of it, and arguably rather bathetically nebulous in the light of the regular celebration of the importance of the unity of theory and practice within the tradition.

There is a related query. How do the set of schematically identified 'roles' relate to the designated exemplars in the circumstances of *decisions* in respect of engagement? Are all scholars everywhere enjoined to adopt the mode of interpretive commentary and adopt the style of critique? Conversely, just who uses political economy, and where and when? At present I rather suspect that all that is available is a schematic and general answer. Thus we say that circumstances and problems will dictate modes of engagement. Thereafter we can distinguish validation/authentication and say that, in the end, decisions in respect of engagements will be borne out to the extent that social-theoretic efforts are taken up (or not), and 'used' as anticipated (or not), in successful (or not) emancipatory (or otherwise) action in the world.

This dis-integrated and relativistic notion of social theorizing can be summarized, in a sloganistic fashion, in the following way. Different social beings in different places and times produce different sorts of knowledge designed to do different sorts of jobs. The crucial questions are, having rejected the assumption of the orthodoxy that all explanation revolves around the 'received model': How can we map this field? and, of most immediate importance: What sort of sense ought to be being produced by scholars in the social sciences?

To return now to the point of departure of these remarks, I think that it is clear that if the above ideas of explanation and role are affirmed, then the common sense idea of scientific explanation, the 'received model', presents itself as a source of deformation of social-theoretic engagements. Put simply, in the realm of what is called social science, the particular mode of social-theoretic engagement that concerns me in this essay, the familiar image of the natural sciences, serves only to sow confusion.

2.0 Having announced an intention to offer a series of examples of the deforming impact upon social science of the familiar image of the natural sciences, it would seem to be appropriate to offer some declarations as to the origins and extent of my thinking about the 'received model'. I take this sort of procedure to be appropriately reflexive.[5] However, in this section, I proceed anecdotally rather than formally, as the task of reviewing debates in respect of the nature of social scientific enquiry lies beyond the scope of this essay.

There are three principal foci for my interest in debates about 'science': the work that revolves round the Frankfurt School; a disposition to operate piecemeal which, following Hawthorn,[6] I take to represent my presentation of the 'British tradition' in social science; and finally a sympathy with the straightforwardness of certain marxian efforts in contrast to the strained 'scientificness' of much orthodox social science. And, if this seems a somewhat eclectic brew, then what I take to be its general thrust, and the basis for rejecting the 'received model', can be summed up in Bernard Crick's useful injunction: 'Theorists should grapple with practical problems in plain English.'[7]

The importance of the Frankfurt School within the marxian tradition is that it represents arguably the most interesting and widely influential general revision of Marx presented thus far. On the Frankfurt School view, the marxian tradition had, by the late 1920s, undergone a multiple decay. In place of the dialectical study of society in history there was, predominantly, an economistic and scientistic body of doctrine – the 'scientific socialism' of official Marxism-Leninism. The scientistic character of this area of marxian work was analogous to a more generally influential creed: that of logical empiricism (most emphatic in logical positivism). One of the familiarly characteristic elements of the Frankfurt School's reworking of marxism is their thoroughgoing denial of the justice of the elevation to epistemic priority of the positivist model of the natural sciences.

The Frankfurt School theorists represented a distinction, drawn from Hegelian philosophy, between understanding and reason. The former seeks an accurate descriptive accommodation to the facts as given, whereas the latter posits the creative intellectual display of the inherent dynamic of the particular complex situation in question. This is, of course, the now utterly familiar distinction between the pursuit of general descriptions on the one hand and critical enquiry on the other.[8] And in the context of marxian scholarship this stance entails affirming the critical aspect of Marx's thought. Put *very* simply, it is the early obviously Hegelian-inspired work as against the later English political-economy-informed work (subsequently (further) misdeveloped by Engels, the SPD, the Second International, and the Soviets into an economistic scientism, it is claimed) that is stressed.

This rejection of the positivistic or 'received model' of natural science as constituting the proper model for social scientific enquiry is, it seems to me, correct. It is this element that I am presently acknowledging having adopted. And while there is much to be said in favour of their idea of critique, I am not taking on board the entire set of positions – in respect of ideology, science, culture, aesthetics, philosophy, etc. – that are now associated with the school.[9]

Hawthorn,[10] in looking at the history of social science, has argued that the growth and character of social scientific work has been fashioned, in part, by the institutional locations of the various 'communities of scholars'. In particular it has been their relation to government that has been crucial. In the UK, on his account, the intelligentsia has been overwhelmingly 'liberal-reformist', and consequently social science has been, to simplify his tale, similarly reform-minded: piecemeal studies oriented to routinized, slow, bureaucratically ordered social change. If Hawthorn's thesis is correct then this is the tradition that social theorists in the UK currently inherit. A disposition to favour the careful display of 'bits of argument' might just have something to do with the particular unremarked common sense of the English tradition of social enquiry. However, even if this is one area where I am, perhaps, running with the 'cultural grain', the thesis in respect of social theorizing – that the business is about making sense and in the area of social science crucially a matter of *crafting arguments* – stands on its own merits. It is one of the notions that underlies all these essays.

A third proximate source for rejection of the 'received model' and the social scientific orthodoxy associated with it lies in my reading of Marx. A text which usefully summarized the fruitfulness of this line was Vic Allen's *Social Analysis*.[11] Allen argued for the importance and practicality of theory: 'It is present in all analyses . . . whether it is recognised and admitted or not.'[12] 'A social theory is a means for understanding social reality.'[13] Now what is impressive about Allen's text in the present context is his repeated urging of the *practicality* of social theorizing in the sense of its being, quite properly, *direct*.

These three, presented here in descending order of importance, represent the occasion and basis of my rejection of the 'received model'. However, before going on to consider examples of the deforming impact of the popular image of the natural sciences upon social theorizing, there is one argument brought against the 'humanist marxian' (includes Frankfurt School especially) critique of the positivist orthodoxy that must be noted.

It has been suggested that the humanists' notion of positivism is wrong and that this weakens, maybe fatally, much of their argument: the error resides, it is said, in the humanists' taking the positivists at their own valuation, in respect of natural science, and then denying that this stance can be extended to social science. I note this argument with Benton,[14] who, discussing the nature of enquiry, divides what he takes as the present disputants into two camps as noted. The positivists are taken to have argued for the extension of the 'received model' into the realm of the social, whereas the humanists have countered by arguing that persons and groups are not objects *qua* natural science objects and that, consequently, another method is required. Benton remarks that it is a central contention of his text that this dispute operates in a 'logical straitjacket which prevents the posing of important questions necessary to the development of this field.'[15] It is advocated that the positivist conception be challenged – at least more 'thoroughly'[16] than the humanists have managed to do. Benton argues:[17]

> If, however, the positivist conception of science is inadequate even as an account of the natural sciences then nothing whatsoever about the fundamental unity or division between the social and natural sciences will follow from a humanist demonstration that the social studies 'cannot' become sciences in the sense of the positivist model of the natural sciences. Because the 'humanist' criticism of positivism is primarily criticism of it as a source of social-science methodology, and not as a philosophical theory of science in general, such criticism is marred by the confusion between objections to positivist epistemology as such and objections to its extension in characterizing and informing a particular research field.

Benton thinks this misleads humanists into thinking that a method for social science can be established apart from discussions of natural science.

I want to make two sets of comments on this argument.

(A) In respect of social theorizing I want to distinguish between deployment and grounding. *Now* (1), I am interested in the deployment of arguments and claim this as the proper starting-point for scholarly, social scientific, reflection and consideration. The matter of (philosophical, epistemic) grounding is a 'matter arising': Benton would have us rebuild philosophically before we return to the world. *But* (2), as I remarked in the company of Giddens above, in the meantime the pervasive image of the natural sciences (which I assert is both positivistic and to be found in 'lay' and disciplinary common sense) will continue to sow confusion. *Thus* (3), in the

73

interests of the rapid amelioration of present problems (deformation) and, arguably, in the interests of clarity of formulation of the general problem of explanation (by moving away from discussion of natural science to establish a new intellectual area from which eventually to return to discuss natural science) I assert the *usefulness* of discussing modes of social-theoretic engagement.

(B) I want to suggest that we can reconstruct our idea of 'explanation' (to borrow Giddens's formulation) *directly*, so to say, by considering the area typical of social science. *Thus I assert* (1), that it is a prejudice to suppose that discussions of the nature of explanation *per se* must flow from discussion centred upon questions of the character of natural science. *Consequently* (2), I would urge that it is perfectly possible to contrive an adequate preliminary understanding of the nature of method in the social sciences *without* necessary recourse to discussions about natural science. (And that consequently much of what the humanists have said is correct.) *In particular* (3), the notion of ideology, which calls attention to the structured and continually recreated/restructured web of meanings inhabited by social actors, can be used as the basis of a preliminary, 'first approximation', of a method for social science. *In this vein* (4), the career of development studies offers an illuminating series of efforts of ideology construction which display both the varieties of social-theoretic engagements (broadly conceived) and also the craftsman-like nature of the business of making sense (narrow conception).

3.0 I have said that it is my view that the 'received model' sows confusion in the realm of social science. I have also indicated how this claim is engendered by my (developing) ideas about modes of social-theoretic engagement. Further, I have commented, briefly, on the original sources of my scepticism in regard to the 'received model', and, having entered a cursory defence of the humanist critique of positivism, have (again) suggested the usefulness of studying the post-war career of development studies. Now I want to make use of that career and treat the issue of the alleged deforming impact of the received model upon social enquiry. The career of development studies can provide us with a stock of examples. It seems to me that all these examples lend support to my general contentions and reveal how scientistic deformation is both routine and widespread. I shall now present five examples drawn from development studies: the sequence, though it is not important, is, roughly, both chronological and a matter of theoretical subtlety of error.

3.1 The first example presents what we can call the metaphorical use of the notion of a model in order to 'secure' claims to scientific status.

The earliest work in development studies, in the post-war period, was dominated by orthodox economics (initially a 'partial' Keynesianism, for the radical implications were muted, and then a reconstructed neo-classicism). Economics was conceived as a positive science and the problem of theorizing (as I would phrase it) development was taken to be essentially a technical matter. The established, proved intellectual tools of economic science could, in principle, be applied to any economic problem area. Theorizing development was the province of the expert, and a key explanatory strategy was the modelling of economies. The explicit, clear, preferably quantified, display of the strategic elements of the economic system was the basis of authoritative interventions in that system oriented to securing predetermined preferred states of affairs. Economics was, in Brian Fay's phrase, 'policy scientific'.[18]

Now this notion of modelling, which is, so far as I understand it, centrally important to orthodox economics, is thoroughly problematical. I made reference to Hindess and his critique of the 'epistemology of models' in chapter 1. To recapitulate, briefly, it is Hindess's contention that it is possible to trace a path of decay in terms of the notion of model such that the familiarly social scientific notion, where this includes economics, is best regarded as the deployment of persuasive metaphor. I think it is fairly easy to grant that this is so in the less 'hard' social sciences, where the use of models in pursuit of the status of scientificity is familiar. The use of formal models in economics, usually taken as the 'hardest' of the social sciences, can be seen as similarly misconceived.

Hindess traces a sequence whereby the rigour that the idea of a model has within mathematics (relating one area of formal discourse to another) declines *via* positivist philosophies of science which use, in effect, analogy (relating theoretical machineries to the extra-theoretic 'real world') and reaches its nadir in social science, where formalized description is just called modelling (the model is now a persuasive metaphor). It is this matter of formalized description that I first want to look at. In orthodox economics we find a curious admixture of syntactical apriorism (elaboration of frameworks) and semantical empiricism (the frameworks grasp the 'real world'). A second, minor, point I shall consider is how models might (a) be buttressed by the use of real definitions, while (b) being used within an explicitly argued political economic case.[19]

(1) In considering the post-war career of development studies it is Harrod's re-working of Keynes's short-run macro statics into a long run macro dynamics that establishes the analytical heart of growth theory.[20] Harrod presents an abstract model of the stable growth path of an economy using the familiar Keynesian lexicon in a typically formal manner. He makes a series of abstract assumptions,

75

expresses them in a formal manipulable fashion, and from them derives policy proposals.[21] This is the essence of the procedure of modelling, and it is this that Hindess objects to: this strategy, he argues, represents the mystifying elaboration of common sense notions such that the rigour of scientific enquiry is set aside in favour of mere plausibility.[22]

The dubious character of this procedure is revealed, *prima facie*, in the episode of the re-presentation of a neo-classical model of growth. The economist Solow confronts the inherent pessimism of Harrod using the simple procedure of reworking the equation's assumptions. Where Harrod's scheme offers a growth path that is difficult to find and difficult to keep to, Solow offers a scheme whereby the business of economic growth, once initiated, is virtually ensured and automatic.

We can consider this matter further *via* the work of Arthur Lewis, whom I take to have codified growth theory in his 1955 text.[23] Lewis declares that he is taking up the general study of economic growth that was last tackled by J. S. Mill, and that he is concerned to elucidate the matter of the 'growth of output per head of population'.[24] The explanatory level of proximate cause is fastened upon, and three such causes are specified. First, the 'effort to economize';[25] second, there is the growth of scientific knowledge; third, there is capital formation. Lewis then asks why these proximate causes operate in some societies more strongly than in others. The search is for the specification of 'social environments' conducive to growth and the detailing of the ways such 'social environments' change through time.

Lewis exemplifies the orthodox scientism of social science. In his economic analysis he begins with high-level 'formal' generalizations about economic behaviour *per se*. To these are added empirical generalizations detailing the typical behaviours of social groups and the general characters of social forms. The nature of economic growth can then be presented as a general model. This model is then put to work, in expert analysis of particular economies, by the judicious removal of simplifying assumptions so that the model is 'fitted' to the particular circumstances under consideration. But it is clear that this sort of approach has a great deal of intrinsic 'slack' built into it. The procedure is so inherently flexible as to permit the production of a favoured 'sort' of answer for the theoretician's client. And at this point the question – why not just argue an explicit case (where this would include centrally political and social commitments/evaluations)? – becomes a rather obvious one. And Lewis, it might be noted, is better than most.

(2) Hindess is highly critical of certain attempts to secure model-building as an explanatory mode by invoking either 'regularities in

nature' or (pre-)determined patterns of thought. Although I cannot treat these issues in the philosophically sophisticated manner of Hindess, I am obliged, it seems, to present a note on the use of *real definitions* to underpin sound theories. I have, in respect of the nature of political economic enquiry, supposed that the business if legitimately grounded must have a philosophical base that includes, *inter alia*, a set of real definitions that define essentially the scope of the theory. It seems as if I am condemned therefore on Hindess's view; though the determinism in respect of thought I would affirm, and my notion of theorizing, would *not* be the same as the empiricist modes noted by Hindess.

There are, in fact, two issues here, though I cannot tackle either of them in this essay. First, the matter of the nature of a marxian political economic analysis of some set of circumstances or other. Second, the business of the Althusserian critique of 'humanist' marxism.

These remarks have all centred upon the use of the notion of a model. In growth theory the notion is used to underpin policy scientific enquiry and as the basis, more generally, of claims to scientific status. I have pointed out why I think they fail. Clearly there remain a multiplicity of uses for the idea of models which I have not looked at, but any use after the fashion I have indicated would be illegitimate.

3.2 I want now to consider the persuasive use of the idea of a paradigm. Again we find claims to scientific status – in this instance to an emergent scientificity. Within the career of development studies there is a particularly complex and confused area of debate centring (to simplify) upon Latin American dependency work. It has been suggested that the shift from the structuralist economics of ECLA to the dependency of Furtado and from there to neo-marxism can be grasped by using the idea of paradigm shift. In this section I want to look at the idea of paradigms. I shall argue that recourse to the language of paradigms represents one more example of the deforming impact on social-theoretic discourse of the 'received model' of natural science.

The notion of a paradigm-shift has been used as the basis for a claim to theoretical progress. The notion of a paradigm-shift claims to encompass and render intelligible an *intra-disciplinary process whereby a failing orthodoxy is superseded and replaced*; given the scientific common sense of social science this is, inevitably, read as taking thinking closer to *how things in fact are*, notwithstanding the seeming relativistic elements in Kuhn. The notion of a paradigm is used persuasively to argue for an emerging scientific status.

Kuhn's work endeavours to capture science as a social activity and as a set of procedures for apprehending the nature of their given objects. Thus the Kuhnian notion of a paradigm has two related senses. In the first, it denotes that set of very general shared assumptions whereby the scientific community constitute their activities; and second, it denotes a particular practical exemplification of their practices. Kuhn later revises his terminology such that the former sense is presented as 'disciplinary matrix' and the latter as 'exemplar'. However, these revisions of terminology are unsatisfactory, given that Kuhn's objective is, as Bernstein points out, 'to help us understand what is distinctive about science'.[26] The problem is that what Kuhn has to say about science applies also to *other* disciplines: 'such as philosophy – which Kuhn distinguishes from science'.[27]

Now if there is nothing distinctive about the notion of a paradigm when it is used in reference to the natural sciences, then, clearly, to invoke that notion to illuminate events in the social sciences accomplishes little. The proposed conceptual link-up with the natural sciences turns out to be non-existent. There is no route here – *via* talk about pre-paradigm states – to scientific respectability as the orthodox social sciences would conceive it. Recourse to the notion of 'paradigm' (etc.) entails using an essentially unstable metaphor.

The use of the notion of 'paradigm', by social scientists, is seen by Bernstein to be so very vague as to suggest that a fundamental question is being begged. He observes:[28]

> What is at issue is not only whether political science is or is not a 'pre-paradigmatic' or 'paradigmatic phase', but whether this very way of speaking is appropriate and illuminating. . . If one thinks that political science is in a pre-paradigmatic stage, this suggests that surely a scientific paradigmatic stage must arise if we are patient and work towards it. But there is absolutely no warrant for such an inference on Kuhn's grounds or any others.

In other words, to argue thus is to beg the question of the precise nature of social science. In all these debates reference to paradigms entails the obfuscation of crucial issues. This claim can be illuminated further by considering the matter of debates (in general) within social sciences. These debates can be regarded as either *inevitable* or *transient*. Such a view entails a particular conception of social science *per se*.

Kuhn opts for transience – on, it can be suggested, the analogy of the established natural sciences – and then reworks the history of the natural sciences on the model of the social sciences. Thus he has 'pre-paradigm' debate (from the social sciences) culminating in eventual 'paradigm' agreement (from the natural sciences). There is one story, a sort of 'unified theory' for the natural and the social sciences. Reconstructing the argument strategy, we obtain the fol-

lowing picture. Working one way: the empiricist's model of incre-
mental science is denied in favour of suggestions drawn from the
image of the social sciences; thus natural science is seen as a social
activity. Working the other way: debate within the social sciences is
not taken to be endemic, neither is social science taken to be
hopelessly polluted by bias and ideology. The core of the natural
science effort, the agreed apprehension of a unitary truth of an
external world, is made available to social science. All the social
sciences have to do is sort out their agreed paradigm and thereafter
get on with it.

With regard to the research for an agreed paradigm, it is observed
that parties to debate (a) sketch out incompatible positions, and
that this is routine in social science; but (b) bother to do this only in
the natural sciences where there is doubt about how to proceed, and
that this is extremely rare in natural science. The Kuhnian 'unified
theory' then presents us with the notion of pre-paradigm debate
occasioning the critical identification of hitherto taken-for-granted
paradigms. These exercises in the critical identification of the presently assumed served to permit, or enable, the construction of the
new and superseding paradigm.

Looking at the whole business from our alternative starting-
point, that debate within social science is inevitable, we obtain a
different view. Having both affirmed that debate is inevitable, and
denied that this is evidence of futility of the whole enterprise, it
seems to me that we are forced towards a view of nature of social
science that centres upon *argument*. I have noted above (and argued
elsewhere[29]) that it is proper to regard the business of social science
as a variety of social theorizing. The history of social science is the
history of a series of *exchanges* between societal problems presented to it and the intellectual resource of the discipline. 'New
theory' is developed out of a debate with existing theory according
to the particular demands of the present problem. Thus established
theory is revised and reworked in the light of the demands of the
particular problem. There is no room in this conception of the
business of social science for the notion of theoretical progressivity
that is associated with the 'received model' of the natural sciences.
Crucially, there is no room for the idea of a *unitary* task.

It is my view that recourse to Kuhnian terminology does not
advance our understanding of how 'schools' emerge and how they
are constituted (except, maybe, in an *essentially descriptive*
fashion). Indeed it obscures investigation of the more plausible
view that revision of a set of concepts, within the realm of social
science, flows not from an improved apprehension of an independent reality, called forth by the 'anomalous behaviour' of that
reality, but rather from the advancing of the claims of a *novel*

79

ideology by a particular group in response to, or in the light of expectations of, changes in their social world. The matter of the various relationships involved in the switch from structuralist economics to dependency and thence to neo-marxism is better tackled with reference to the idea of the *construction of ideologies*.

3.3 The use, by social scientists, of the idea of a paradigm is relatively familiar. There is an analogous argument which draws on the 'received model', and which is found within development studies, that is not so familiar, yet which, it seems to me, is worth taking note of in this essay. It is an argument from the putative identification of a sequence of concepts or, rather more generally, positions, to the claim to general theoretical progress. The argument seems to crop up (quite often) in favourable commentaries upon dependency, but I would suppose that it is not unknown in social science 'review articles' generally.

Typically the reviewer identifies a number of positions (within a particular problem area) where each is taken as a conceptual advance from, and advance over, its predecessor. The claim is implicitly made that the mere existence of this sequence testifies to the truth of the final product. We have, then, two elements to consider: first, the sequence; and, second, the claims made for it or in the light of it. I will consider these points in the company of Ehrensaft,[30] as what I take to be the typical and erroneous fusion of these two issues is accessibly presented here.

Ehrensaft begins by observing: 'During the last decade a diverse stream of analyses emerged which taken together do much to update and correct our perceptions of the Third World',[31] and he goes on to declare that 'my intention in this essay is to give an initial synthesis of some of this new thinking'.[32] The typical and erroneous fusion of the matters of sequence and truth status is unequivocally displayed when he declares:[33]

> The central proposition of this essay argues [that the Third World bourgeoisie have been 'bought off']. . . This proposition emerges in five steps from the new writings on Third World political economies. Each successive step brings closer approximation to actual societal relationships . . . I will review these steps one by one, showing how each successive analysis builds intellectually on the ones which preceded.

What Ehrensaft is doing is attempting to assimilate to development studies the recent dependency work. The history (intellectual) of the post-war period is then reviewed in the light of this orientation. This procedure is familiar, legitimate, and entirely his own affair. But to my mind, in making his presentation, he commits a familiar error when he elects to relate the business of the establishment of his preferred view in the mould of the supposed progressiveness of conceptualization of the natural sciences. We are presented with a scheme of increasingly accurate approximations to a reality independent of the theorist's engagement.

We can look at his argument in a little more detail at this point. Ehrensaft claims to be able to identify a sequence of refinements of argument such that an unsatisfactory starting-point is replaced by his dependency-derived idea – this is his strategy of assimilation. I think there are three elements in this putative sequence. First, a simple chronological sequence – thus work gets better through time. Second, a logical sequence – thus concepts become more subtly expressed as we move through the sequence. Third, there is a sequence of improving descriptive accuracy – thus theories become better at grasping reality as we proceed. Now I find this trio of sequences buried in the one sequence both confusing and unpersuasive. Evidently element number one is simply an irrelevant aping of the 'received model'. Elements two and three are closely intertwined, and again the received model is in evidence, otherwise element two might be acceptable as retrospective intellectual history of ideas. In sum, Ehrensaft's identification of his sequence is problematical: it derives what force it has from one, mishandled, element only (element two). Turning to the claims made upon the basis of this 'sequence', matters become yet more problematic.

Now while it may be argued that natural science conceptualizations are progressive to the extent that they approximate more closely to an independent reality than their predecessors (and presumably Ehrensaft would affirm this), it should be noted that this formulation is, in the light of present debate within philosophy of science, both common sense and naive. Ehrensaft is, it seems to me, making two unwarranted assumptions: (1) that the history of the formulations of the natural sciences is one of increasingly subtle approximations to an independent reality; and, further (2) that the history of the formulations of the social sciences can be regarded as analogous to those of the natural sciences. These assumptions lie at the heart of Ehrensaft's project of assimilation: the sequence testifies to the truth of the product. The force of his argument is drawn from these claims. If these assumptions are called into question – and number (1) is at the *very least* open to serious questions and number (2) is widely denied – then so is the entire Ehrensaftian project. It seems to me that Ehrensaft's argument can be reduced to the status of a covert appeal to common sense to support his schema.

In contradistinction to what is seemingly assumed by Ehrensaft I would wish to argue, setting aside matters of the nature of the natural science effort, that with the social sciences there is no reason to expect, or look for, this progressive tendency. In respect of the history of dependency theory, or any other distinguishable school within the social sciences, there is no need to cast expositions in this natural-science-echoing style.

Recalling my preferred schema of social theorizing, it can be seen that the dynamic of theory is but one aspect of the production of social theory; the other is the dynamic of society. It is within the ambit of this second element that we can locate those societal conflicts and changes that issue in the demands made of theorists to produce useful explanations. Quite what the practical significance of autonomous developments in theory might be is, for the present, an open question. Clearly some role must be granted to such intra-disciplinary developments if we are to give the theorist a role broader than that of an apologist. However, it seems to be clear that, whatever the solution to this question, the idea of the double dynamic of social theory and social concern presents a sharply divergent picture of the nature of social theorizing from that of Ehrensaft's natural-science-deferring common sense. More particularly, if social theorizing involves, crucially, some measure of 'social practicality', then it is impossible to conceive of any progressivity of conceptualization on the model of that supposed to be present in the natural sciences The notion of 'progressivity' is at least *plausible* in respect of the natural sciences but seems wholly improbable in the realm of the social sciences. We can grant the facts of revision *within* a framework but this, of course, is a different idea of progressivity.

In sum I would say that: (1) Ehrensaft's pursuit of a progressive evolution of concepts towards a realistic economic sociology is, so far as I can determine, a misconceived project; (2) there is no reason to suppose that such a progressive sequence exists; (3) consequently the sequential presentation of the notion of dependency does not, in itself, say anything about the truth or usefulness of that scheme.

It is not enough to point to a (putative) sequence of concept development and claim thereby that the present end-point of the sequence is true and useful: the sequence establishes nothing about the position's validity; to argue, like Ehrensaft, that it does, is to draw wrongly upon a particular model of the natural sciences. The presentation of the claims of a novel ideology demands its own procedure. This is a point we can pursue with my next example.

3.4 Here I consider the confusion engendered by presenting ideologically novel departures as species of natural scientific progress. I focus upon the debate of Girvan and Cumper[34] in respect of the putative independence and superiority of dependency with regard to the conventional wisdom of economics. This debate is occasioned by the project of propounding an 'oppositional meaning system' using the syntax of orthodox social science. That is, Girvan does not present his exposition as the why and wherefore of a novel ideological departure. Rather, he claims to be revealing the manner in which the orthodox notions of a discipline came to be rendered liable to supersession.

Girvan argues that the school of dependency economics established not only an economics that was adequate to Latin America, but also an economics that could be taken as generally adequate.[35] This was in contrast to the hitherto unchallenged economics of the developed world – an approach that was now taken to be generally inadequate.

In the literature there seems to be a continual ambiguity in treatments of dependency; in particular with respect to what might be called the business of its proper disciplinary location. Are we treating an economic scheme, or some effort derived from the wider set of the social sciences? Girvan would seem to be firmly locating dependency within that sub-tradition of social thought called economics, and this opens up the possibility of debating the issue of dependency *versus* conventional wisdom on a *technical* level. This is a singularly unhelpful level of debate; yet it is the terrain chosen by Girvan and Cumper. Technical debates within an agreed ideological framework make sense; technical debates across the boundaries of ideological frames readily produce nonsense.

A further contribution to confusion flows from Girvan's intellectual expansionism. Having misread or misreported his ideological departure as (natural) scientific advance, Girvan, in the light of the notion of generality of formulation as being properly scientific, goes on to claim for his effort an area of broad application – that is, replacing the orthodoxy. Such a manoeuvre would be seen to be nonsensical if he had properly grasped the nature of his own effort as ideology. Further, it is obvious that such claims invite the proponents of the orthodoxy to reply in orthodox terms. Thus the fundamental points at issue, namely the disputes of the two ideologies, are missed or may be ignored.

Girvan adds a final element of confusion in that he presents his views with reference to an established debate within economics. That is, he takes the dependency line as resolving the issue of whether or not there is one general economics or two: one for the rich and one for the poor. (This debate derives from the dualism of Boeke.)

In respect of the debate (between Girvan and Cumper), my point of departure is the observation that the central axis of confusion is that between the received model – and its extension to social science – on the one hand, and ideology construction – or social theorizing as I understand it – on the other.

If we now move on to consider Cumper's reply to Girvan, we find that Girvan's synthesizing generality is confronted with detailed criticism. There are two interesting attacks. First, the matter of the rejected orthodoxy is pursued by Cumper. He presents a list of orthodox analytical techniques and asks, rhetorically, do the dependency theorists reject this, or this, etc.? As an argument strategy it is unconvincing. Even within the misleading syntax adopted by Girvan the proposed supersession of the orthodoxy cannot be taken to entail the wholesale rejection of particular technical constructs. In addition, if we note that Cumper goes on to lodge a sociology of knowledge critique of Girvan, it must be open to speculation that Cumper knows full well that what Girvan wants to do is reject the orthodoxy *qua* ideology. This line of attack from Cumper seems to me to be disingenuous. Second, Cumper launches a critique of Girvan which is informed by the notion of ideology; where this is taken in the fairly narrow sense of the presentation of a self-serving schema. It is suggested that dependency is the ideology of an intellectual in a post-independence state wishing to secure his position as an 'organic intellectual' at the expense of other intellectuals and groups generally. The general points about the status of the intelligentsia in newly independent states may be true, but Cumper undermines any force the attack might otherwise have by making ideology the *same* as bias. Claiming that Girvan *et al.* are unprincipled careerists is an argument that leads nowhere. Cumper grants this when he acknowledges a distinction beween origin and validity such that the former does not imply anything by way of the truth or falsity for the latter. Cumper retreats at this point into claiming that he is simply interested in sensitizing readers to 'ideological distortion'.

The equation of ideology with bias crops up again when Cumper grants that *his* stance could be called ideological. He answers that to go beyond this ideology-spotting routine requires a pragmatic test of what is or is not objective truth. Cumper proposes a crude notion of consensus; thus the more who accept an idea, the greater its likelihood of being objective. He further proposes 'track record': the more an analysis has been used operationally, the more we can take it to be objective. Evidently these both beg the question: orthodox views will be preferred and used by people whose views are orthodox. That a view is orthodox says nothing, *on Cumper's own terms* (origin/validity), about the truth of that view. Additionally we may observe that invoking notions of consensus and track record when treating a line which explicitly opposes the orthodox seems singularly inappropriate. (It is also an ambiguous position for Cumper to take up: consensus is usually, in the orthodox line, taken as an unsatisfactory criterion of truth in contrast to correspondence – it seems that Cumper is drifting towards being sensible despite himself!) The observations which Cumper makes in the light of the notion of ideology seem to run into the sand. The attack finally has no point and no force.

In sum we can see that the essential tentativeness of the project in respect of which Girvan makes his explicatory report (that is, in my view, the construction of a novel ideology), and the particular unfortunate syntax chosen (that is, a quasi-natural science revision of a discipline's concepts the better to grasp the given world) combine to present Cumper with a ready opportunity for 'missing the point' and launching a thinly disguised counterattack on behalf of the conventional wisdom. Girvan's presentation of the matter permits criticism to be couched in orthodox vein; it does not *require* the orthodox to confront the fundamental, ideological, issues at stake. The upshot is that Cumper feels able to dismiss dependency as a novel orientation and to condemn Girvan's paper on, and espousal of, dependency as slipshod, untenable and self-serving.

I would argue that the relationship of dependency theory and the conventional wisdom of economics is best understood as a matter of competing ideologies. In presenting any commentary the task is to compare and contrast the form and intent of two quite distinct approaches. Their comparative ranking is a difficult task. What is clear is that to cast the business in narrowly empiricist terms, and to pursue an argument in respect of the supposed supersession of a technical scientific discipline's notions by a new set of concepts, is positively to invite confusion.

3.5 I want now to look at examples of the influence of the 'received model' in neo-marxian work. I suggest that this unexpected influence occasions a variety of 'slides to the general' whereby specificity of engagement is either forgotten or presented in a simplistic fashion. Now at this point we must note an additional complication in the examples which I have in mind. Within the context of neo-marxism, as I treat it here, there are two 'received models' in operation. Thus far I have been concerned with epistemic 'received models'; now we meet political 'received models'. Where the orthodox defer to a model of proper explanation (which, of course, secretes a political stance) the neo-marxists defer to both a model of explanation and a model of political action. This additional aspect is, as might be expected, fairly close to the surface of the examples treated, so the parallel between 'bourgeois' and 'marxist' examples cannot be pushed too far.

In the work of the neo-marxists it seems to me that deference is paid to some model of 'properly marxian behaviour' where this tends to confine all radical activity within the one mould of 'marxian revolution-making'. This, clearly, has the effect of tending to suppress reflexivity of theorizing. Such reflexivity, which I take here as an injunction for the theorist to locate himself in the social processes of which he speaks and argue accordingly, would seem to entail that there can properly be a diversity of contributions to the pursuit of (radical) democracy. The mould of the 'one revolutionary mode' seems to be most emphatically presented in the work of those marxists influenced by the Althusserian tradition: a scientistic reading of Marx is conjoined to the left equivalent of the role of the expert. Thus, as I noted in chapter 2, where all these issues were touched upon in greater detail albeit in a slightly different context, we find absurdities such as Taylor's nascent 'left policy science'. A scientistic marxism is linked to a rather wooden understanding of what I have called the 'gross role' of the 'theorist'.

The 'slide to the general' is not, however, to be identified only with Althusserian-inspired material. In the case of A.G.Frank, whose early work, I think, can fruitfully be regarded as political pamphleteering, there is a similar disposition to pursue general formulations. Here I think Frank's method is, essentially, orthodox.

In sum; the burden of these cursory remarks upon neo-marxian work is that even within the ambit of an intellectual line that stresses reflexivity (a concern for theory and praxis) the impact of the 'received model', here a dual one, continues to sow confusion.

3.6 I have presented the foregoing as a series of (random) examples of the deformation of social enquiry consequent upon the affirmation of the received model. If we focus directly upon development studies, then one last point can be made. This point relates directly to development studies and is therefore somewhat outside the mainstream of this essay. However, at the outset I claimed that the errors in argument which flowed from affirming the received model became more subtle as we moved through the career of development studies. Here I attend to that claim.

Thus the earliest efforts at grasping the nature of the exchange of rich and poor nations (growth theory) revolve around the Harrod–Domar model. Growth theory was a narrowly conceived effort in that its aprioristic model-building, together with its use of the syntax of natural science, issues in policy science. Modelling – the pursuit of some (manipulative knowledge-generating) analogue of reality, corresponding to how things 'really are' – I take to be a fallacious procedure because descriptions of the world are theory-informed; that is, 'facts' are 'brute-relative'. Consequently a general description, or model, if you will, properly conceived, can be regarded only as the sum of the commitments entered into by the theorist in so far as he affirms some frame or other of analysis. If his work is to be plausible, then this would encompass the world of common sense (that is, those observations that the model-builders begin and end with), but would not be bound by it. With the orthodox model-builders the 'received model' acts to dissipate any residual sensitivity on the part of the thinker as to what is actually involved in social-theoretic work. The theorist comes to take his efforts as straightforwardly analogous with those of the natural scientist, and the role of the 'expert' thus emerges.

To my mind this is all low-grade ideology. This is very clear in the case of modernization theory, where a model of the modern is affirmed which is transparently a general characterization of the USA (*circa* mid-1960s) according to the orthodox view. This model of the modern is contrasted with a model of traditional society, called forth by negating the former, and this fundamental dichotomy is elucidated by reference to a further set of dichotomies: rural/urban, agrarian/industrial, etc. The process of modernizing entails losing one set of attributes and gaining the other.

More sophisticated in comparison are the efforts of the neo-institutionalists. Again we find that modelling is the basic approach, but here there are additional stresses on problem-specificity, realism in modelling and reflexivity in engagement. Neo-institutionalism is what can be called a sociologized economics and it is, arguably, the most plausible general effort from within the orthodox interventionist camp. However, their reflexivity does not extend to reading social theorizing as a matter of, in the first instance, ideology-making, but rather it is a partial effort: reflexivity appears as an additional technique which serves to permit better modelling.

When it comes to marxian-informed exercises, the issue of whether or not a correct strategy of explanation is being used becomes rather more cloudy. With Celso Furtado, who makes play in his late work with a 'rehabilitated' Marx, the tensions beween problem-specificity and generality of formulation colour his entire approach. In the end, what began as a search for an economics relevant to Latin America is taken to emerge in the construction of a new, generally appliable, economics.

The effects of the 'received model' are detectable in avowedly marxian efforts. Frank, for example, is taken by Palma to be pursuing 'mechanico-formal models', and Frank's habitual use of the syntax of natural science certainly does permit this reading. An analogous 'slide to the general' can be found, it would seem, in some academic marxian scholarship. In respect of marxian work we have to note, in addition to the 'received model' of *explanation,* a (different) 'received model' of *political engagement.* I have not, in the above notes, separated these two elements in any very precise way. However we can note, I think, that there is, in the work cited, a retrogressive collapse into the orthodox descriptive-general which results in schemes that ignore the matter of the necessary specificity of the theorists' engagement. General models of 'the one revolutionary path' are of little interest or use. It seems to me that the demands of specificity of social-theoretic engagement must result in an acknowledgment of these being *multiple modes of engagement*. The marxian 'reconstruction of the real' can proceed in various guises.

With regard to the post-war career of development studies, I think that we can identify an increasing subtlety of argument as attempts to constitute an 'autonomous discipline' fail. This failure leaves us to operate somewhere within the schema of modes of social-theoretic engagement that these essays are trying to elucidate and with the analytical machineries presently discussed under the heading of neo-marxism. But this is to anticipate my concluding remarks.

4.0 (1) I have argued throughout these essays for the key idea of specificity of engagement in social theorizing. It seems to me that this is the principal aid in translating down from the level of regarding social theorizing as generically concerned with making sense to the concrete level of treating specific constructs. (2) The modes of social-theoretic engagement which can be identified/ anticipated in the world are diverse, and the way in which they are embedded in the social processes they engage with are similarly diverse: most immediately we must note that their *intentions* and *explanatory modes* differ. (3) Within the career of development studies we can see a clear progression in terms of richness of practical intent (ethico-political stance affirmed) and subtlety of conception of appropriate theoretical machineries. (4) The implication for social science – the mode of engagement that is my particular concern in this paper – is that a coherent position in respect of theoretical machineries must entail specifying a particular intent. Following Habermas, in an untutored sort of way, I specify the intent of offering interpretive critical commentary. The notion of *critique* as developed by the Frankfurt School tradition seems, on the face of it, singularly appropriate to the social location of the scholar. (5) One immediate consequence of this line of argument is – recalling Giddens on 'explanation' – that the notion of science needs to be reclaimed from the positivistic orthodoxy. *There is no one model of scientificity in explanation.* The affirmation of the 'received model' only confuses matters. The notion of science will have to be understood as (something like) 'disciplined problem-solving': a loose array of modes of enquiry rather than a clear set of extensions of procedures drawn from (essentially) reflection upon experimental method. (6) I am not at present able to pursue these issues into the realm of the philosophy of natural science but – again recalling my earlier remarks upon the *present* impact of the 'double cultural grain' – within the ambit of the *social* sciences it seems to me to be clear that the notion of ideology (construction, critique and comparative ranking) must come to the fore. (7) Social theorizing – of which the institutionalized discourses of the various (and variously conceived) social sciences represent but one stream – is about 'making sense'; and this conception allows for multiple interests and strategies. The insistence of the orthodox line within social science of celebrating a scientistic self-understanding only serves to inhibit appreciation of the complexity of the business. As Bernstein puts it: 'the obsession with transforming social studies into natural sciences obscures, distorts, and suppresses the legitimacy of issues vital for theorizing about political and social life.'[36]

5 Comparative ranking: some approaches to the task of rationally adjudicating[1] between competing ideologies

1.0 This collection can be seen as presenting a series of explorations of elements of a particular view of the nature of social science: that the business is, at base, about *constructing arguments*.[2] And the matter of the comparative ranking of competing ideological schemas I take to be the most general problem of that line of thinking about social science.

The claim that the field of social science can be divided up on the basis of particular views about the 'fundamental character' of the endeavour is not new: indeed it is utterly familiar. The particular division I am resting upon in this paper – and in this set of essays – is dichotomous. Thus, on the one hand, there is the 'school' which thinks that social science is, or ought to be, like natural science (where this is usually conceived in an empiricist fashion); and, on the other hand, there is the 'school' which thinks that the business is best understood as a variety of social philosophy (where this is usually conceived in a rationalist fashion). These two views of the nature of social science involve their proponents in quite typical, and distinct, sets of problems in respect of *explanations*.

The familiar orthodox position, labelled 'empiricist' or 'positivist', would have us build a social science around a particular set of claims in respect of what is to count as knowledge. These claims are presented in terms that derive, in various ways, from philosophical traditions brought to a distinct peak in the inter-war period: natural science was the paradigm of knowledge production and logical empiricism was its philosophical elucidation. Consequently, any social science, if it is to lodge claims to the *status* of a science, must order its procedures in line with this model of knowledge production.

This line of thinking, which is now, it seems, less of an explicitly argued for position and more of an unspoken disciplinary common sense, would affirm a model of scientific explanation that was both informed by the empiricist tradition, and which was also – significantly for its plausibility – close to the ordinary common sense of our society. Thus we have the strategy of the collection of the facts, the preparation of descriptive generalizations and, finally, the presentation of summary theoretical statements. And the problems which thereafter concern this view – and I do not think my presentation is that much of a caricature – are those of data collection, data analysis (quantification and statistical manipulation) and, concomitantly, the extirpation of the influence of value positions. A 'summary anxiety' is that of the seeming immaturity of social science in relation to natural science, and the effecting of the appropriate methodological, procedural and conceptual refinements necessary to alleviate, and perhaps eliminate, this condition.

For the orthodox, the production of knowledge is essentially a matter of *reporting how things are*, and problems cluster around the *accuracy of reports*. The notions of science and ideology are resolutely divorced and ideology is seen as the repository for all the errors (indeed, *sins*, as some theorists actually embrace this sort of error!) to which social science is prey if ever value positions are affirmed.

The contrary view to this orthodoxy takes the production of social scientific knowledge to be less a matter of mimicking the (supposed) procedures of natural science and much more a matter of the construction of arguments. The philosophical traditions, in respect of the character of knowledge from which this position can be taken to derive are, of course, rationalist. However, it seems there is no recent and familiar presentation of the claims of the rationalist tradition that is equivalent to logical empiricism in terms of the pervasiveness of that theory's impact upon intellectual life. (Unless, that is, it is the humanist anti-positivist line of marxism running from Lukács down through the Frankfurt School to the early critical theory associated with Habermas.)

If social science is taken to revolve around argument construction, then it is not possible to regard the history of social science as involving the production of ever-improving techniques for the description of an external, given, reality. It is, on the contrary, a history of particularly located efforts of argument construction. Any progressivity in theorizing will be revealed in the *ways in which arguments*, appropriate to their circumstances, *are constructed*. The social *scientific* (and thus general) measure of progressivity centres upon the skill with which arguments are crafted so as to uncover the truth.[3] The multiplicity of pragmatic concerns which variously located social actors might have are measured internally, and thereafter to the measure central to social science.[4]

91

The concerns, in respect of propriety of explanation, which are typical of this line of thought centre upon the matters of appropriate premises, theoretical frameworks, the role of ideology and the rational judgment of competing claims: upon, that is, the business of *constructing, criticizing, and comparatively ranking,* ideological schemes.

This 'tradition' sees much debate about the merits/demerits of competing 'theoretical frameworks': Which set of premises, ordered how? Questions of value positions affirmed, crucial axes of explanation, relevant facts even, are all caught up in the over-riding concern for 'theoretical frameworks'. Additionally, if for the orthodox the notion of 'ideology' could be taken as the symbol of all the errors to which social science was prey, then for this 'rationalist' counter-tradition ideology, or better ideology construction (understood here, centrally, as the explicit, rational and prospective theorizing of society), represents the paradigm case of social theorizing. The culmination of this view is a concern for the comparative ranking, or rational adjudication, of competing schemes.

Constructing ideologies is thus constructing arguments: criticizing ideologies is thus criticizing arguments, and construction/critique are but two sides of the one coin. If we build a scheme of ideology construction/critique around a pure case which supposes that the proponents of particular arguments both *know their own minds* and are *concerned to utter the truth,* we have a reference point which can be used to designate the point at which social *science*, or social-theoretic commentary, fixes onto the world, and which can be used subsequently to order enquiry as we shift from 'pure cases' to 'real life'.

The above represent the most general occasion of my concern for judging between competing efforts to make sense of the social world. A more particular source for my interest was Bernstein.[5] In this text Bernstein devotes his first sections to a review of the empiricist orthodoxy and its critics. This exchange can be taken to be roughly analogous to the simple distinction I have drawn above. Bernstein comments:[6]

> Once the limiting perspective of mainstream social science has been challenged and the biases in its foundation exposed, new questions and problems emerge. These cluster around the interpretation and understanding of political and social reality. . . Looming in the background is the central question of how one can rationally adjudicate among competing and conflicting interpretations.

Bernstein will go on to review phenomenological and critical theory work and end, roughly speaking, by presenting a notion of *critique –*

exemplified by Marx and developed by Habermas – as central to social scientific enquiry. The social world must be deciphered in a theoretical discourse that is self-conscious and emancipatorily engaged (in dialogue with particular social groups).

In this essay I will look at a series of strategies for evaluating (comparatively ranking) ideologies. The particular schemes presented here will be developed from my earlier work on the history of development studies:[7] this material was reviewed briefly in chapter 1. It seems to me that this approach, of deriving criteria for the evaluation of ideologies from a study of ideologies, is a fruitful one in that it recalls attention to the fact that ideologies are concerned to *make practical sense* of, usually difficult, real situations. This I take to be a useful corrective to the, perhaps inevitable, tendency of scholarly reflection to drift towards the abstract and general. Similarly my focus counteracts the tendency of (directly political) engaged work to move toward the polemical.

Bernstein remarks that ideological schemas are interpretive and claim to display the truth:[8] thus we may critically and rationally inspect them. This is the locus of my present interests. Just how do we critically and rationally inspect ideological schemas? However, given the extensive discussion of the notion of ideology in the literature of social theory, I shall first have to pay some attention to familiar debates. Here I shall indicate, first, how my characterization of the notion of ideology relates to those usually present in the literature; and then, secondarily, how my present interests relate to the usual gamut of concerns displayed by social scientists (this is, of course, anticipated in general by the remarks immediately above).

2.0 I have said earlier, in chapter 2, that I take social theorizing to be concerned with the construction, and thereafter the criticism and comparative ranking, of ideologies. So far as I am concerned, this lodges my general intellectual commitments within the ambit of the 'humanist marxian' tradition. In this note on the notion of 'ideology' as it appears in the social scientific literature I present, within this declared frame, a very brief sketch of my own usage of the term. The literature of social science is replete with discussion of the notion of 'ideology', and while I have to take some cognisance of it I have no particular wish to contribute to it in any systematic way. The present essay is informed by my particular concerns: and these are kept very much to the fore when I come to look at ranking schemes. What follows here, then, is a *context-setting note* on the notion of 'ideology'.

2.1 As regards the question of how my characterization of ideology relates to those usually present in the literature, I would say that the following are the most crucial points. Thus against the common sense of social science I affirm the *centrality of debate*

93

where the orthodox would, in my view, affirm the centrality of the pursuit of *accurate descriptive enquiry*. To establish this point clearly in view I resurrect the positive sense of ideology: 'world views'. Social theorizing, generically, is about making sense of the social world: the prime case is prospective general theorizing – the production of argued cases, or delimited-formal ideologies.

If delimited-formal ideologies are seen as efforts to *make sense*, we can speak of some ideologies being better than others according to how well they are crafted (where this includes ethical inputs). In this way the familiar negative sense of ideology (partial and erroneous, non-scientific) is taken into my scheme. An ideology (pejoratively and familiarly understood) is in my terms to be regarded as a low-grade ideology because it makes errors of some sort; that is, it is badly crafted. It is from this intra-disciplinary point that we can shift to political critique proper; extra-disciplinary argument or engagement.

The related extension of this critical usage is accomplished *via* the notion of pervasive-informal ideology: the unreflective, casual, adoption of a position in common sense – for example, racism or sexism.

The business of social science is the elucidation of arguments – commentary pre-eminently: the display of the various efforts to make sense of the social world made by differently located social actors/groups. (In this I follow the 'classic' tradition in sociology – it is the same position as that adopted by Gellner[9] who makes sociology the heir to classical political philosophy, although I would make the business broader by using a notion of 'world capitalism' in place of his 'industrial society' as the fundamental concern of enquiry.)

With respect to the concern for the intellectual status of social science displayed in the literature, I reject notions of 'immaturity'. On the contrary, I regard debate within social science as both *inevitable and proper*. Both terms are important here. If I affirmed only 'inevitability', I could be taken as granting the logical possibility of a view of 'permanent immaturity', and if a discipline were 'permanently immature' then it would hardly be worth trying to distinguish maturity and immaturity. This is not my view: debate is proper because it is of the essential nature of the enterprise. The scientific status of social science is secured by its being a discipline of learning.

One issue which I have not tackled is the question of what I am to say about natural science. Briefly, I regard it as another discipline of learning: it has its objects and methods appropriate thereto. The term 'science' I use generically: thus scientific endeavour presents itself in several varieties and – and this I take to be an important corollary – if debate is to be intelligible and coherent, the particular variety at issue, or varieties being compared, must be specified.

In relation to the matter of the general political-cultural status and impact of the natural sciences, as they are ordinarily conceived, I follow the Frankfurt School tradition and regard it as ideological in the pejorative sense. Or in my own terms, as underpinning a low-grade politico-cultural ideology because it is the claimed basis of an attempt to reduce politics to technique in the interests of a retrogressive ethic. (Similarly I regard the common sense view of natural science as having a deforming impact upon social science: explicit notions of empiricism coincide with common sense and make it all too easy for social scientific enquiry to be fatally miscast in terms of methods and expectations.)

Against the positivist orthodoxy in social science I reject their claims about the unassailably pre-eminent status of empiricist positivist explanatory (knowledge-getting) strategies. I deny their positiv*ism* and their empiric*ism*. In contrast I affirm the role of prospective general thinking in knowledge production. That is, I affirm – in some fairly unspecific way thus far – a rationalist view in respect of knowledge. And, finally, I reject the orthodox distinction between science and ideology.

2.2 I shall now offer a brief note on how my present concerns relate to the usual gamut of concerns displayed by social scientists. These are, so far as I can see, lodged in the general tradition of the Frankfurt School: I have cited Bernstein above to indicate how.

My own interests stress the mundane connotations of the notion of *practicality* which I have used and which appears in the work of Habermas.

I am concerned here with comparative ranking. This is a narrow focus – the evaluation of texts. In the context of my set of roles ('general systematic framework for ordering modes of social-theoretic engagement') I am pursuing an element (technical) of the commentator's role. I am drawing a distinction between technical criticism (the business of the social scientist) and critique, as understood in the humanist marxian tradition. Clearly this is a fairly difficult distinction to draw in practice – the demolition of opposing interpretations is usually an aspect of the presentation of one's own interpretations – and it is also difficult to draw in principle. I could as easily speak of the 'moment of technical criticism' and the 'moment of critique'.

The strategies of comparative ranking I present below are heuristic: they are general, preliminary strategies which, usefully, recall the attention of commentary to the practical character of social theorizing. I look directly at the notion of critique in section 3.4.

3.0 In this section I shall present a series of ranking strategies. There are two points which should be borne in mind about these strategies. First, as I have already noted, these schemes are *heuristic*. They are fairly rough and ready procedures for ordering enquiry. They do not pretend to be the basis for any *mechanical routine* that could be substituted for the difficult and lengthy process of intra-disciplinary, social scientific, commentary. The use to which these schemes could be put (or the use to which I would envisage their unspelt-out cousins are already put in the minds of social scientists) is simply one of orientating enquiry in a fashion that makes central the practicality of social theorizing.

My second point is that all these strategies focus on the paradigm case of social theorizing: the production of delimited-formal ideological schemes. This involves another radical simplification: in practice, presenting an ideology (in my sense) is not likely to be a task that devolves upon one theorist; on the contrary the production process will be complex. The corollary of this is that the delimited-formal ideology is likely to be presented in, or *via*, many formulations, all slightly different, as the *process* of theorizing runs through time (for example, think of the business of theorizing 'socialism' in the nineteenth century). My ranking schemes posit a neat, tidy, packaged product: the fruit of the work of a single theorist who knows his mind and is concerned to utter the truth.

3.1 Analysing the extant products of particular theorists, or groups of theorists whose work has run together and who are thus a 'school', can be accomplished *via* a relatively simple sociology of knowledge approach. It is this simple, naive – in the sense of (i) taking the business of sociology of knowledge to be unproblematic, and (ii) taking sociology of knowledge analysis as being as straightforwardly practical as the products it treats – approach which I present here.

In an illuminating essay on the matter of ideology in the history of economic thought, Maurice Dobb[10] remarks that it is quite clear that theorizing is conditioned by history. Asking how this is so, he answers in terms of a dialectic between current practice and presently acceped theory, both having their own dynamics. Current social practice throws up 'problems' which are investigated by the theorist in terms of the intellectual, disciplinary, resources available to him. This exchange is complex.

It is pointed out that the social context which shapes 'problems' itself is a complex mixture and interaction of accepted ideas and systems of thought[11] – 'problems' emerge (slowly). Further, 'thought' is not to be taken as the passive recipient of problems simply presented to it; thus it is suggested that 'current problems are something created as much by thought inspired human action upon an existing situation as by the given objective (but changing) situation itself.'[12] The medium of enquiry, theoretical language, is itself reworked in the process of theorizing, and 'new ideas are necessarily shaped in part by the antithetical relation in which they stand to the old'.[13] Theoretical machineries are context-specific; thus when re-deployed they will be changed. A final point – and a crucial one given the orthodox desire to be 'objective' – is that theorizing needs to specify an agent of theory-execution: theories are built round the posited actions of a specified actor. As Dobb remarks: 'Social or economic action . . . can only be conceived with some subject in mind; and for problems to have an operational interpretation . . . they must have some implied reference of this kind.'[14]

Of these 'theoretical machineries' Dobb points out that it is at this 'level' that decisions are made as to the ways in which 'problems are framed and to the methods and instruments devised for yielding answers'.[15] Theorizing inevitably involves, in my terms, a conception of fruitful analysis and an intention in regard to the purpose of analysis. And while the *effective mixture* of these elements in any one specified effort of theorizing will be a matter of empirical enquiry, the *range* of possible mixtures can be described generally in terms of the roles available in social theorizing.

This notion of theorizing as comprising a conception and related intention can be used as the basis of a relatively simple strategy of interpretive exegesis of extant works. Thus we have the familiar sequence of interpretive analytical stages: milieu, the most general set of descriptions available to the theorist; demands, the particular problem relevant expectations made of the theorist; resources, the intellectual raw materials available to the theorist; and finally the product, the completed statement.

This strategy of interpretive exegesis accomplishes two things. First it displays the circumstance-sensitivity and problem-specificity of the effort of theorizing in question; and it can be recalled that I have claimed that circumstances and problems call forth engagements, and that particular engagements have corresponding forms of enquiry (see chapter 2). Second, the exegesis displays the argument-form of the effort: a necessary preliminary to any questions of comparative ranking.

I remarked in chapter 1 that I think the proper locus of any enquiry into the lessons to be taken from the post-war exchange between social theory and development studies lies in the field of 'humanist marxism'. Any concern to elucidate the notion of social theorizing *per se* must at least begin in that general area: this is the reason, of course, for my interest in ideology, and my affirmation of the specificity and practicality of theorizing.

Against that backdrop and more particularly with reference to

97

the above notes on Dobb, a *simple* schema for ranking ideologies can be presented. This schema centres upon the methodological subtlety with which a given product is crafted.

The abstract schema of conception and intent is taken and used to produce a scale which can be used to measure competing efforts. At the limits of the scale we have, respectively, *crude* and *subtle* efforts. These are distinguished according to the extent to which the effort in question displays a reflexive sensitivity to its own character and status. That is, the extent to which any effort acknowledges the implications of notion, centrally affirmed here, of the social construction of social theories. A 'crude' effort of social theorizing would be one that was un-reflective in both conception and intent. The sociology of knowledge derived terms, conception and intent, can be taken into a 'model of the crude' relevant, that is, to analyses of development, as the notions of europomorphism and europocentrism. (If the model is to be used in other contexts, then the two elements will have to be varied accordingly: for example, much work in 'industrial sociology' has been management-centred and concerned with efficiency of production of consumer goods – surely un-reflective and unsatisfactory if sociology is taken as scientific and thus, in some fashion, aspiring to the dispassionate display of the truth in its formulations.) The first can be understood as the affirmation of the priority of typically European categories of thought,[16] and the second as the affirmation of the priority of the material interests of the 'West'. A 'crude' effort of theorizing would thus be both europomorphic and europocentric. (In my discussion of the idea of development in chapter 6 I have used this 'model of the crude' as part of a ranking of the various post-war theoretical treatments of development.)

Now quite clearly such an analytical ranking scheme is of very limited use: it is hardly a sensitive analytical tool. In chapter 6, the ranking of competing schemes in this fashion is no more than a secondary motif in a discussion premised in quite another way. None the less, I have noted this procedure as it seems to me to be the simplest strategy of ranking which can be derived from the analytical strategy of the sociology of knowledge. I develop this strategy a little further in section 3.2 below.

However, there is an area of established thinking which is not unlike the position sketched here. I am referring to the work of Lucien Goldmann. (Dobb also, in the text mentioned, can be seen to be gesturing in the same sort of direction.) Goldmann's sociology is explicitly historically concrete: that is, theorizing appears as a sequence of historically-located attempts to make sense of the world. The scientistic pursuit of an abstract and general sociology is a waste of time, the goal is illusory, a 'concrete science of human reality . . . can only be a *historical sociology* or a *sociological history*.'[17] Problems of method are elucidated, by Goldmann, in contrast to those of the 'physio-chemical sciences' and with reference to the marxian tradition.

Goldmann presents two central issues of 'objectivity' and 'totality'; there is also the matter of 'potential consciousness', which is an element of the 'totality'. These issues flow from the 'two fundamental principles of method in the human sciences':[18] first, 'the *partial identity of the subject and object of knowledge*';[19] second, that 'the investigator must always strive to recover the total and concrete reality'.[20]

In his discussion of objectivity, Goldmann, having discussed and dismissed (in an uneasy fashion which begins by accepting the split fact/value and ends up by saying that valuation is inevitable so best be reflexive) orthodox treatments, asks if relativism is entailed: 'Are all ideologies of equal value . . . as far as the search for truth is concerned; and is the choice of one over another only a matter of individual preference?'[21] His answer is couched in terms of explanatory power. Thus he says:[22]

> Viewed in terms of their effect on scientific thought, *different perspectives and ideologies do not exist on the same plane.* Some value-judgments permit a better understanding of reality than others. When it is a question of determining which of two conflicting sociologies has the greater scientific value, the first step is to ask which of them *permits the understanding of the other as a social and human phenomenon, reveals its infrastructure, and clarifies, by means of an immanent critical principle, its inconsistencies and its limitations.*

He illustrates his notion by arguing that marxism encompasses Saint-Simon's work, and that marxian sociology encompasses orthodox material. Interestingly, given my earlier remarks upon the notion of the commentator, Goldmann goes on to argue that some individual scientists can move beyond the 'potential consciousness' of their class: the difficulties and procedures are also set out.[23] Now if social theorizing is a matter of, in an important sense, *crafting arguments,* then *practice* at this task is going to help. Thus does Goldmann secure his own position and the role of the commentator.

All these remarks are presented by Goldmann in the context of a discussion of 'objectivity', the problem occasioned by the 'partial fusion of subject and object' in the human sciences. From this point we turn to the notion of the 'totality', and here Goldmann presents a case for 'dialectical thinking' in contrast to the mode found in the 'physio-chemical' sciences and the orthodox descriptive social sciences. This I will not pursue, except to add a note on the idea of 'potential consciousness'. Of this notion Goldmann remarks that it seems to him 'to be the principal instrument of scientific thinking *in the human sciences*'.[24] Where the orthodox do not treat the ideologies of groups *as they might be* if all the distorting forces were removed, Goldmann, using the idea of 'potential consciousness', designates dialectical analysis as 'totalistic' because, as well as grasping the complex present, it includes this (ethical) element of future possibilities (of a class). The orthodox rest content with descriptions of how groups presently are. In this fashion the matter of the value engagements of theories in social science is acknowledged and brought into Goldmann's ranking scheme. Following a Lukácsian line, some value positions are progressive, because they are conceived of as eventually universal, while other positions are reactionary, being partial and attempting to fix change in place. Ethically Goldmann takes up his stance with the 'world-view' of the ascending proletarian class and against the partial ideology of the now reactionary bourgeoisie. In the matter of comparative ranking, explanatory scope thus involves ethical intent.

This question of how the value position present in a text can be used to rank the text in contrast to others is very problematical. It is made all the more difficult to grasp by the scientistic common sense of social science, and the common sense of our Western culture. However, I have made an attempt to rank theories of development on ethical grounds (in chapter 6), and the crucial issues here seem to be: first, how values are *inserted* into theorizing: and second, just what *value schedules* are used.

The claims to the ethical priority of the 'views' of one class taken as the potentially universal class are to be found in the humanist marxian line which includes Lukács, Gramsci, Goldmann and Habermas. Generally there is, it seems, a shift from lodging ethical priority in the class-consciousness of the proletariat towards lodging it in free discourse – language itself used in free communication. The whole tradition runs together, in various but relatedly characteristic ways, matters of (what I have called) conception and intent when they tackle issues of weighing claims: so ranking competing ideologies involves considering *both* elements.

Goldmann, in sum, attempts to offer a method of human science which lodges the social science commentator in history armed with conceptual machineries adequate to the task of comprehending and ranking conflicting patterns of meaning affirmed by groups in society. In the narrow area of what I have called delimited-formal ideologies, Goldmann presents a view which lets us see *some ideologies as being better than others*. Recalling my simple ranking strategy: ideologies get better to the extent that theorists acknowledge that social theorizing is socially accomplished, and craft their products accordingly.[25] This is developed below in section 3.2: however, before I look at that, I can usefully add, at this point, a brief note on the evaluative procedures hinted at in the essay by Dobb which I considered above.

Dobb is an interesting figure for my present concerns in that he offers a set of reflections upon ranking which echo, in a distant fashion, those of Goldmann, and he also anticipates my later notes on political economy. The evaluative criteria hinted at in the essay by Dobb flow from reflections upon the place of ideology in political economy: the text is allusive and not at all systematic as was Goldmann's. Dobb is concerned to re-present economics, and political economy, as comprising historically located efforts to make sense of the world. This claim is advanced as against the positivistic orthodoxy of economics and social science: but, like Goldmann, the rejection Dobb presents of the positivistic orthodoxy is apparently equivocal. Thus ideology is, sometimes, equated with bias, and at other times value-laden theoretical frames are made the prerequisite of theorizing. Again, the model of explanatory propriety advanced by the orthodox is granted at least in so far as Dobb tacitly grants their claims to the effect that natural science (conceived in empiricist fashion) constitutes the paradigm of knowledge production.

Given these provisos, it can be noted that Dobb reports that theorizing will be based upon *general ideas* about how the world actually *is*: these theoretical frames can be judged according to their being 'realistic'.[26] As theories claim to 'be about the world', so they can, roughly, be inspected according to the *gross facts,* as these are ordinarily understood. This I read as an echo of Bernstein's position: the claim which ideological efforts make to the effect that they 'are about the world' is the point at which the wedge of rational adjudication can be inserted, and the means to a general denial of any relativistic claims to insulation from criticism. It is also a point of criticism which the proponents of the orthodoxy are obliged, by their own views, to accept. Again Dobb notes, *contra* Popper and falsifiability of propositions, that '*generality* of statement'[27] is a relevant part of a social theoretical frame. But, and here is one example of what seems to me to be a slight malformation of enquiry, this generality allows 'the intrusion of ideological influence'.[28] Later he remarks that given these 'intrusions', debate between competing schemes is a long-drawn-out business and that the better effort could be decided 'in the very long term . . . by counting the number of prescriptions of the rival schools that seem to have "worked" in practice.'[29]

A very general ranking criteria lies between theories which

101

abstract and those which acknowledge the historicity of theories and theorizing. Dobb avers that 'historical assessment of theory and its unfolding is essential to any full appreciation of the theory itself'.[30]

Dobb follows Goldmann, as we might expect, in stressing the requirement that theorizing must acknowledge the process of its construction. This reflexivity is one criteria of ranking: thereafter Dobb hints at explanatory scope ordered to some context-defined problem area. Choosing between one or another of them will be *slow*: this is the useful corrective to Goldmann's more schematic presentation. Progress in social theorizing is *elusive in principle and non-obvious in practice*.

3.2 I want to return now to the consideration of material drawn from my studies in the history of theories of development and to the business of presenting 'heuristic strategies' for ranking ideologies. In this section I offer an extended ranking scheme derived from reflections upon social theorizing taken as ideology *construction*.

If the production of delimited-formal ideologies is taken as the prime case of social theorizing, it is clear that there is much that could be said about the *production* process. Elsewhere[31] I have argued that any exercise in ideology construction can be regarded as involving the deployment of a morally informed categorial frame: which procedure properly moves from the rationalist conceived 'general' to some set of empirically relevant 'particulars'. The resultant product can then be analysed in terms of conception and intent. So I have two complementary approaches to reflection upon the character of delimited-formal schemes. The former line is how I have argued that ideologies are constructed, and the latter line is how I have said that completed, extant, schemes can be analysed.

I want now simply to juxtapose these two approaches and try to extend the strategy used for analysing completed products. Thus as regards 'conception' I ask how this notion can be extended in light of the slogan presented in respect of construction – deployment of a morally informed categorial frame. Similarly I can ask how the notion of intent might be extended. In addition to these two lines of analytical commentary it should also be noted that as ideologies are here taken to be exercises in argument construction, then the usual rules of intellectual discourse hold. The upshot of this attempt to refine the analytical power of an approach derived from a simple sociology of knowledge can be presented, in line with my remarks about the scheme's heuristic status, as a check list.

This check list involves three main elements: the matter of conception, the matter of intention and the business of the exchange between the two. These we can now review.

(1) *As regards conception* it can be asked whether or not the

product in question displays 'reflexive consistency' in the crafting of argument. Briefly, is the scheme being considered actually acknowledged by its authors to be an ideology? There seem to be three readily identifiable sorts of 'reflexive consistency'. In addition there is the business of consistency ordinarily understood.

(a) Reflexive consistency I (Internal). Here we can ask: Does the product in question acknowledge its own value engagement? Is there, in the text, a routine demonstration of an awareness of social theorizing as issuing in value-suffused products? It can be noted both that claims to the status of 'objectivity', taken as displayed by the natural sciences, are simply fatuous and similarly that pro-forma declarations are unsatisfactory. I have already said, following Bernstein, that Mannheimian-style claims to the relativity of value-informed schemas are unacceptable.

(b) Reflexive consistency II (External). Here we ask: Does the stance in question specify an agent of theory execution whereby the effort can latch onto the world? This agent of theory execution is understood to be integral to any stance (that is reflexively consistent in the present sense). Consequently any agent that appears simply as an addendum, to abstract and general reflections, designed merely to satisfy the requirements of the logic of theorizing will not do. Put crudely, the effort has to be genuinely engaged. The plausibility of the schema, which will rest in part on the agent chosen and its supposed role, is another question.

(c) Reflexive consistency III (General). This seems, loosely, to be a matter of the particular commitments undertaken in affirming any particular stance. So we ask: Does the product in question explain itself? To put this another way, is the effort itself compatible with the claims lodged in the effort? For example, according to the principle of verification proposed as the criteria of scientific meaningfulness by the positivist philosophers, the propositions of logical positivism themselves could not be verified and thus could not be regarded as meaningful. Conversely, the claims of Marx are consistent: he locates his theorizing in history as a historical process. Again, for example, Giddens reports in respect of Habermas's treatment of the notion of ideology that 'the concept of ideology, Habermas argued, did not just come into being with the rise of bourgeois society; it is actually only relevant to the conditions of public debate forged by that society.'[32] Thus Habermas inserts his concern for ideology into a historical schema which explains the general occasion for his interest.

(d) Formal consistency. Of any text it can be asked whether or not that text is *formally consistent*. As this is the basic and wholly routine demand of all intellectual work, I do not think that we need to pursue it.

(2) *As regards the exchange* between conception and intention, it can be asked whether the product in question is based on a set of premises explanatorily rich enough to be able to display the nature of whatever problematic situation is addressed *adequately* (to the facts ordinarily understood) and *usefully* (given the anxieties underlying the problem addressed).

So analysis entails enquiring whether the effort in question has recourse to a categorial frame whose explanatory scope is commensurate with the demands for explanations flowing from the declared intent. That is: Is the set of premises used adequate to the task of grasping – rendering relevantly intelligible – the world as it is ordinarily understood? This 'ordinarily understood world' will be the practical starting-point of the product's engagement. Relatedly, the set of premises must grasp the world usefully: that is, in a fashion that displays the possibilities for the future lodged in the present.

Girvan, for example, seemingly invokes these related points when, reviewing the construction of 'dependency economics', he remarks: 'The development in thought, generally, took the forms of (i) adding a historical perspective and analysis to the structural and institutional method, (ii) giving the historical/structural/institutional method the kind of theoretical and empirical content needed to construct a general theory of dependence.'[33]

A second example, again from economics, can be offered. This is an example of *failure*. In respect of the Great Depression it is argued that the conceptual apparatus of orthodox neo-classicism was incapable of treating the events. It was not a matter of the appropriate sub-areas of the discipline being un-developed; rather, the economic orthodoxy *denied* that such a depression could happen. Clearly it was inadequate, conceptually, to its task of interpreting the economic world in such a manner as to inform rational action in respect of that world.

(3) *As regards intent* the matter concerns the value-positions, and objectives, underpinning and guiding the product in question. Generally it seems as if we confront an issue of *practicality*. Here I would identify two relevant cases of practicality.

(a) Intent I (External). Here it may be asked: Is the posited intent tenable? The notion of delimited-formal ideology, so far as it is presented here, is understood to be practical. Ideology, as I understand it, is not to be assimilated to expressive exchanges with the world – it is not, for example, religion, neither is it art. In this light, if an ideology is intended to secure for its adherents/agents, say, 'eternal cosmic wisdom', then I would wish to rank it lower than an effort intended to secure, say, some piecemeal change in the distribution of economic power in society.

(b) Intent II (Internal). Here it may be asked: Is the stated intent ethically sustainable? In my remarks on the idea of development in chapter 6, I argue that there is a general determinism in respect of the ethical schedules any 'Western' commentator, or theorist, could plausibly and defensibly affirm. An ideology affirming a notion of 'progress-as-the-maximization-of-democracy' would have to be ranked higher than one either denying it or declining to affirm it.

So much for the check list. In sum it can be seen that a schedule of necessary elements of any analysis of an extant scheme can be derived from the affirmation of the notion of conception and intent as characterizing centrally the crucial elements of any delimited-formal ideology. This schedule, it should be noted, is predicated on the 'pure case' of a theorist who both 'knows his own mind' and is 'concerned to utter the truth'. It is a reference point around which investigations into the effective ideologies of the 'real world' might be ordered.

3.3 The foregoing elements of this part of the essay were derived, respectively, from reflections on the sociology of knowledge, on the one hand, and, on the other, reflections on the sociology of knowledge coupled with a simple notion taken from a consideration of the nature of the work of Marx. In this element (**3.3**) it is from this last-noted area that my central interest is taken. The ranking scheme proposed here derives from discussions in respect of the explanatory strategy of political economy. It can be noted that here we tackle a contentious aspect of the material presented above: that is, the business of conceptual richness/usefulness. More particularly, having made the matter of conceptual richness/usefulness fairly central to ranking strategies, just how do we judge this? It is hoped that the discussion of the nature of political economy will reveal some sort of an answer.

3.31 Political economy is, I have argued, to be regarded as the prime case of social theorizing: it is the basis of delimited-formal ideology construction. However, before looking at political economy directly, it can be noted that the issues I have pointed to – of conceptual scope and usefulness – have been addressed by more than a few theorists.

The orthodoxy, given their claimed pursuit of neutral factual description, would measure the justifiability of their own theoretical frameworks (presented after the fact-gathering were done in the simplist formulations) in terms of summary elegance: Occam's razor as intellectual polish for accurate description. The more the orthodoxy refined their formulations in respect of explanation-strategy the greater would be the stress on the investigatory aspect of theory-construction: accuracy of reportage might be expected to come to the fore with notions of *realism* in modelling. I have elsewhere followed Hindess[34] in seeing 'modelling' as central to empiricist explanation. Conceptual scope and usefulness are judged according to the policy scientific relevance of realistic models. A final version, Popperian, might elect to dispense with anxieties about premises and focus upon the business of successful predictions and error elimination: the goal remains the same in terms of the use to which it is thought that theorizing can properly be put.

A related strategy which, in various ways, reads the business of authoritative judgment more politically – that is, self-consciously and with reference to the social process of securing political judgments – can be found in the work of the 'intelligent orthodox': the 'reformist' line of thought on the matter of not only development but also the future of industrialism (their term).

Gellner, Myrdal and Galbraith can be taken as a representative group of the 'intelligent orthodox'.[35] Their work has, notwithstanding its several roots and areas of concern, a general similarity in approach. Myrdal follows the orthodoxy, albeit in a heavily revised fashion, in the pursuit of realistic models. They are the key to ordering politically a resolution of the morally demanding crisis of underdevelopment. What is useful is, in outline, *obvious* (because there is a *crisis*) and the explanatory scope of theories is read as realistic modelling to that moral end.[36] Similarly Gellner,[37] arguing from the recent attention paid to industrialization, advances the notion of industrialism (taken as sociology's central concern) as uniquely useful in any legitimating theorem of modern society. Explanatory scope and usefulness derive from the scientific (where this is a seventeenth-century notion of *method*) elucidation of the nature of the 'transition' (where this is a reworking of the idea of progress) to industrialism so as to permit the experts to order this process. For the presently industrializing, Gellner favours the 'rule of the Graduate Student Kings' and for the industrialized the effective rule of the expert.

Galbraith, in the final work of what he designates a trilogy, *Economics and the Public Purpose*,[38] offers no directly 'methodological' discussion. However, from scattered remarks and the style and manner of his work, we can conclude that he does indeed take social theorizing to be about the construction and criticism of arguments. His treatments of economics and society proceed in this fashion. So Galbraith reports: 'The ultimate test of a set of economic ideas – a system, is whether it illuminates the anxieties of the time. Does it explain the problems that people find urgent?'[39]

These two strategies of deciding upon the scope and usefulness of conceptual machineries can be taken, roughly, to represent conservative and reformist thinking. With political economy, taken as the prime case of social theorizing, and as best exemplified by Marx, we can introduce the third element of the usual trio of political positions. It is here that I shall try to sharpen the criteria whereby matters of scope and usefulness can be gauged. These, to recall, are but elements of broader-based strategies of ranking competing ideologies.

3.32 Political economy, as a particular mode of producing social-theoretic explanation, can be characterized simply, and in contrast to orthodox description-biased disciplines, in a threefold fashion. First, there is the catholicity of intellectual interest displayed in political economy: the reduction of enquiry into matters political-economic to given disciplinary frameworks is eschewed. To say that political economy is multi-disciplinary would be anachronistic: the breadth of scope characteristic of this strategy of explanation is crucial and relates to the second way of typifying political economy. Thus, second, there is a thoroughgoing practicality of intent. There is little attention paid to that pursuit of 'general statement' displayed by the scientistic orthodox of today. This relates, in part, to the idea of science affirmed: centring on disciplined enquiry rather than experimentation. Third, there is what can be called the 'shape' of enquiry: the business of social theorizing involved the 'intellectual reconstruction of the real'. A movement from (rationalist conceived) general statements to (empirically relevant) particulars.

As a scheme of enquiry/explanation, political economy is clearly sharply distinct from any empiricist orthodoxy. Enquiry does not proceed by abstraction from the given, generalization and model-building. Nor is explanation linked with, or made analogous to, causal predictiveness. Rather, enquiry proceeds by the technically explicit 'reconstruction of the real'. The notion of scientific explanation used here, and by Marx, 'was essentially active, investigative, critical and practical. . . one which solved conceptual mysteries and presented the human world accurately, intelligibly and politically.'[40]

3.33 The criteria of adequacy implied by my note on the nature of political economic argument can be taken as relevant to the questions of problem appropriateness, or usefulness, and conceptual richness of categorial framework, or adequacy.

The first criterion to be drawn from the above notes is that of *breadth of scope*. In political economy we find, typically, the pursuit of a 'comprehensive social science': the approach is general both in the sense of its 'level' of treatment (it is prospective ideology-making, so it would be 'general') and in respect of the intellectual resource-base used.

The second criterion derives from the requirement that political economic enquiry must be practical in intent. The attempt to construct abstract and neutral theorems – the bases of applied social technologies – is taken to be misconceived; there is no such neutral theory to be found. Again, the reformist 'social engineering' familiar in certain theories of development would be regarded as the politics of the planner: ideologically self-denying and concerned with effecting piecemeal change to the slowly moving *status quo*.

The third criterion derives from the note on argument 'shape'. The intellectual reconstruction of the real is taken as appropriate and scientific. Orthodox schemes of modelling are taken as misconceived.

To these three, which focus on argument strategy, two more points may be added. These refer to some wider commitments in respect of the nature of the world and the relation of thought to it. Thus the fourth criterion recalls that, following Marx's materialist thesis, concepts are occasioned by specific economic forms and that whilst their application is – inevitably – going to be general, their fullest expression is going to be specific to some historical economic form. Theorizing is thus inevitably and thoroughgoingly circumstance-specific. It is so in a related sense: the fifth criterion derives from the argument that the economic form 'bourgeois capitalism' is complex enough to occasion a set of economic categories adequate to the comprehension of all other, existing and preceding, economic forms. Political economy needs must revolve round the notion of capitalism.

3.34 I want now to turn to the consideration of my illustrative material taken from the career of development studies. This will enable me to offer some specimens of the criticism and comparative ranking of ideologies. The above criteria are, for ease of enquiry, re-presented thus: (a) (3.341) practicality of intent/engagement (elements 1 and 2); (b) (3.342) strategy of explanation (elements 3 and 4); (c) (3.343) substantive categories used (element 5).

3.341 I shall begin this illustrative critical and comparative review of theories of development with the criterion of practicality of intent/engagement. I have argued that any social-theoretic effort of ideology construction has to specify an agent of theory execution if the departure is to engage with the world. The absence of a specified agent entails the decline of theorizing into ideology, pejoratively understood. In the post-war career of development studies, a variety of engagements can be identified.

In the ambit of the orthodox *interventionist* schemes, this is typically a matter of affirming the role of the 'expert'. In the case of growth theory, informed by the Harrod-Domar model,[41] the expert is presented as a technician. Development is equated with economic growth, which is to be identified by the movement of technical statistical indices, and is to be secured by the implementation of policies determined in accordance with the results of the positive science of economics. This determination of policy proposals tends to become a simple, if hugely elaborated, technical matter of professional problem-solving. These elaborations are nowhere more grandiose than in modernization theory. Here engagement is conceived as technical but the role of the expert is represented as 'master scientist'. Development is still taken as evidenced primarily by economic growth but this is now related to a host of 'non-economic factors', and the theorem itself – modernization theory – claims to treat the wider issue of social change.

I would argue that the role of the 'expert' is, in actuality, an evasion of the problems attendant upon taking up a value position. Writers using this stratagem neither pretend to complete neutrality, for that would be immediately implausible (practically, and theoretically untenable I would add), nor do they explicitly argue a case. The role of the 'expert', as a claim to a particular status in the political process, is grasped as the social science analogue of the role of the natural scientist. This serves to provide a legitimating scheme which allows the 'expert' to adopt, or aspire to, the position of an extra-systemic cause. This attempt to render just their behaviour non-determined is a functional requisite of state power in (mature) capitalist society: that is, authoritatively interventionist. In this mode of enquiry/action social *theory* becomes a technical manipulative summary of the results of modelling the world.

With the political reformism of neo-institutional social theory we find a third variety of the role of the 'expert'; but this time there is also an argued case. The neo-institutionalists take the 'expert' to be the planner and lodge this figure within a view of the world which argues that in periods of acute social crisis the resolution of questions about value positions becomes obvious: indeed, politics reduces to planning. This scheme might, at first glance, appear to be quite untenable, yet it is, so far as I can see, by far the most plausible of all these early schemes. It is plausible, but at the same time flawed, yet it is a position which is of continuing interest and relevance because it is probably the nearest (single statement) to the disciplinary 'common sense' of development studies. The solution to the problem of values proposed, that is, the appeal to a crisis-occasioned obviousness, is simply sophistry. And the engagement of the scheme, *via* the reasonable actions of the reasonable men in charge of the state planning machinery, is implausible. This implausibility is announced in the notion of the 'soft state' which specifies the reasons why the agent cannot accomplish the tasks the theory sets for it.

In the case of the Latin American dependency theorists, this issue of engagement is slightly more involved. In the case of Celso Furtado,[42] whom I take here as exemplar, there is an initial affirmation of the pursuit of relevance (in economic theorizing), but this

109

is cast within the framework of an orthodox empiricism. His early work is dominated by the idea of a *typology of models* of structures of dependent economies. The later work broadens this conception: Marx is invoked, in a distant fashion, and the 'historical/structural/ institutional method' is affirmed. At this point the familiar dependency line emerges. Furtado seemingly conceives his efforts as interpretive and interventionist: the engagement resembles that of the 'expert'. Yet there are problems of interpretation here, for the engagement of the 'expert' is joined by a general political nationalism. More difficulties arise when it is noted that this dependency scheme is taken by Furtado to be the basis not only of an economics relevant to Latin America, but also of an economics relevant to the situation of the developed – a new *general* economics. The tension in Furtado's work between problem specificity on the one hand, and the urge to generality, taken it seems from the orthodox notions of scientific explanation, on the other, recurs throughout his work and through the work of the dependency 'school'. It rather seems to me that, in contrast to the neo-institutionalists, the 'reasonable men' to whom Furtado would naturally appeal are *not*, typically, in charge of the state machineries and that *this* is the basis of the drift to the general that can be seen.

In the case of marxian-derived attempts to theorize development, the matter of engagement is very problematic: a long period of comparative neglect marked only by the seminal work of Paul Baran[43] has recently given way to a veritable flood of material. Neo-marxian work – that which derives from Baran – has taken itself as marxian political economy but has been variously and vigorously challenged. I shall offer two remarks here, as I cannot adequately reduce this marxian material to a length suitable to the present context; one concerning A. G. Frank and the other the analogy 'agents/allies'.

Frank[44] has presented versions of Baran's political economy as the theory of the development of underdevelopment. Among the criticisms this work has attracted, Palma[45] has argued that it is merely a 'mechanico-formal' inversion of the (neo-classical) economic orthodoxy. I think this point has some force, yet contrariwise I would argue that Frank's work is *coherently engaged*. It is so in the mode of the pamphleteer (commentator-spokesman): that is, Frank's agent of theory execution is the political activist and is omnipresent in Frank's work precisely because he casts himself in that role.

The business of 'agents/allies' involves taking the exchange between Third World bourgeoisies and multi-national corporations and asking if there is a radical political equivalent. The exchange between multi-national corporations and their local agents is cemented in routine commercial/industrial/financial practice. But what of the exchange between theorists based in the developed world and those based in the Third World? The role of *ally* is necessary if it is to be said that Third World theorists and their allies need to use political economic analyses. But how plausible is this role? It seems as though the declaration is of political solidarity rather than, except on a very general level, shared practical circumstance. I have insisted, above, that politics is specific: that being so, the business of theorizing the political economy of peripheral capitalisms rather seems to be a matter for Third World theorists. Baran, and anyone similarly located, can reasonably offer commentary only if another version of the slide of the general is not to be presented.[46]

3.342 In any treatment of the matter of strategies of explanation in theories of development since the end of World War II, a major concern must be the shifting impact upon formulations of the orthodox image of the procedures of natural science. This impact is, to my mind, a deforming one. I will review my illustrative material in terms of the *increasing subtlety of impact* of the image of the natural sciences.

The earliest attempts to grasp the nature of development revolve round those models of capital-generated growth associated with Harrod and Domar. I have called these formulations 'growth theory' and I would argue that, of the material presented in the post-war period, these are the most narrowly conceived. Growth theory typically mixes an empiricist concern for descriptive adequacy with an aprioristic strategy of model-building. I would follow Hindess[47] in regard to the misuse of the idea of model within social science. Modelling, in this sense, entails the pursuit of some analogue of reality which might then, in turn, be manipulated to generate new knowledge about the world. It is a procedure which is misconceived; and when this is taken along with the routine adoption of the syntax of natural science, then a variety of policy science[48] is the ready upshot. The theorists come to regard their efforts as analogous to those of the natural scientist, and the (intellectually deadening) role of the 'expert' thus emerges.

So far as I am concerned this is all very low-grade ideology: this is perhaps nowhere clearer than in the case of modernization theory. Here a model of the modern is affirmed which is transparently a general characterization of the USA according to the conventional view. This model of the modern is contrasted with a model of traditional society – called forth by negating the former – and this fundamental dichotomy is elucidated by reference to a further set of dichotomies: rural/urban, agricultural/industrial, folk culture/literary culture, and so on. The business of 'modernizing' involves losing one set of attributes and gaining the other, thereby effecting the shift from 'traditional' to 'modern'. Its basic crudity is quite evident, even in its elaborated versions. Indeed, one is reminded of Martin Shaw's sharply polemical comment upon Parsonian sociology: the real question is not how was this material assembled and what are its strengths and weaknesses, but rather how are 'such intellectual monstrosities possible'.[49]

Considerably more sophisticated in comparison are the proposals of the neo-institutionalists. Again it is modelling that is adopted as the basic technique. Here, though, there are additional stresses on problem specificity, realism in modelling and reflexivity in engagement. Neo-institutionalism represents what has been called a 'sociologized economics', and it is the particular use made of the resources of the social sciences that provides a key to considering the strategy of argument in detail. Briefly, I would argue that, epistemologically, fine-grained social science data are necessary for the construction and checking of concepts. Methodologically, social science data establish the possibility of realistic models and social science concepts their general structure. Finally, procedurally, the habit of reflexive scepticism is used to generate criticisms of proffered formulations. This reflexivity does not extend to reading social theorizing as a matter of ideology-making; it is, rather, a partial effort. That is to say, reflexivity appears as an additional technique which serves to permit better modelling.

When it comes to marxian-informed exercises, the issue of whether or not a tenable strategy of explanation is being used becomes rather more cloudy. It is clear that the impact of the 'epistemology of models'[50] is evidenced in some marxian work. A. G. Frank, for example, is taken to be pursuing a 'mechanico-formal model' by Palma.[51] Frank's use of simple explanatory framework, derived from Baran, and the syntax of the natural science mimicking orthodoxy does permit this critical reading. An analogous, and, so far as I am concerned pernicious, slide to the general can be detected in some academic marxian scholarship. Deference is paid, so it seems, to some model of 'properly marxian behaviour' which attempts to concentrate all radical activity into the pursuit of 'the one model of revolutionary change'.[52] Any sensitivity to the *multiplicity of circumstances of theorizing/action* is denied and this does seem to me to be a gross error.

Turning to the matter of the 'reconstruction of the real', the procedure of logical synthesis, in contrast to modelling, then with 'neo-marxism' there is a furious debate in progress. The originator of the approach, Baran, begins with a notion of surplus which is both an economic and an ethico-political term. Baran uses this term to elucidate the present circumstances and future possibilities of peripheral capitalism. Now on the face of it this does look like logical synthesis. However, Baran's work has been called 'left-Keynesian', and neo-marxism has been subjected to detailed (and often plausible) criticisms. I have noted above my doubts in respect of Baran's location and role. Yet it is also true that many of the criticisms levelled against Baran *et al.* tend to focus on showing how the analytical machineries used diverge from those deployed by Marx. Strictly this would seem to be irrelevant, unless we are to suppose that the world has stood still over the last century or so. The more appropriate question – suggested by Palma – is not whether or not this or that approach closes with or diverges from the detailed analytical substance of Marx's work, but rather whether the effort is good or bad political economy. It would be difficult to deny that Baran's work is political economy, but, for myself, the issue of the precise quality of his product remains open.

3.343 In respect of the substantive categories deployed, I shall offer here only a summary note. At a most general level we can note a shift from narrowly conceived technical schemes of economics through elaborated 'sociologized economics', to fully developed (marxian-informed) efforts of political economy. This sequence of 'orthodox', 'radical' and 'political economic (marxian)', I think, can be regarded as a sequence of increasing richness of categorial frame. The ideological schemes presented become subtler as attempts to constitute an autonomous, technical social scientific, discipline of 'development studies' fail.

3.35 It is no simple matter to summarize the disparate, yet some-what overlapping, ranking strategies noted above. There is clearly a movement from relative simplicity to a more elaborated concern for details of argument construction. My simple sociology-of-knowledge-derived model of 'the crude' requires little more of any product than that it display a minimal appreciation of the problems attendant upon granting that social theorizing was indeed a social process. Theorists must argue cases, I would argue, and not anxiously concern themselves with borrowing from the procedures of the natural sciences. Enquiry may be structured and ordered by invoking the entirely serviceable notion of a discipline of learning.

The business of disciplined enquiry was the focus of my second ranking scheme. This approach was contrived by running together ideas about constructing ideologies and ideas. about criticizing extant schemes. Both sets of ideas derive from the common root, noted above, of an idea about the social nature of the manufacture of social theory: constructing and criticizing are but different deployments of the one simple idea. The resultant 'check list' drew attention to the breadth of intellectual scope of the business of social theorizing and the inevitably problematical nature of its production (use). The image of theorizing presented here can be seen to be in stark contrast to the hunch-shouldered anality of the empiricist orthodoxy.

Finally I attempted to derive criteria of ranking from the explanatory strategy of political economy. Here the problems of complexity met with in 'ranking strategy two' were found to be compounded. Given that political economy can be characterized by, among other things, a thoroughgoing practicality of intent, that the derivation of formal criteria was difficult should be no surprise. It seems that with the criteria of practicality of intent, strategy of explanation and categorial notions used we have reached a point at which any simple (preliminary) ranking procedure has to give way to the intra-disciplinary procedure of scholarly criticism. None the less I think the trio of criteria I presented – and exemplified with reference to my 'stock of examples' – do allow a preliminary analysis of delimited-formal ideological schemes which allows due attention to be paid not just to the detail of their construction, but also to their 'status' as elaborated attempts to render intelligible real situations.

All three strategies of comparative ranking indicate, so far as I am concerned, that the post-war career of development studies can be regarded, speaking most generally, as displaying an increasing subtlety of argument construction and deployment as the empiricist orthodoxy is variously revised and superseded. An initial determination to constitute a specialist social science of development disintegrates as the full complexities of social theorizing are discovered to be inevitably germane to the business of comprehending 'development'.

3.4 I have remarked above that I take social theorizing (narrowly construed) to be concerned with the construction, and, thereafter, the criticism and comparative ranking of ideologies. Thus far, in this essay, I have been concerned with the business of the comparative ranking of ideologies and to that end have presented critical schemes which derive, variously, from reflections upon the business of constructing ideologies. However, I have also said that theorizing grows out of circumstances and problems and that as modes of engagement differ, so too do explanation strategies. The paradigm case of prospective social theorizing I took to be the production of delimited-formal ideologies *via* the explanatory strategy of political economy. Clearly, though, this does not exhaust the business of theorizing: it is with Habermas that I would mark down a second mode of engagement that is of major importance. It is here that my simple notion of criticism can be developed into the idea of *critique*. In the context of this essay the relationship presents itself, most simply, as between technical enquiry and politically engaged enquiry. However, as the criticism of political economic theorizing (and to a lesser extent the schemes using reflexivity and invoking ethics) also involved commentary upon substantive theoretical engagements, this simple distinction is not to be pressed too far. Similarly, working in the reverse direction, so to say, the Habermasian scheme of critique can be used for (technical) ranking. There is also the related matter of using critique in development issues. It seems, to put the matter in a banal way, to be matter of stress and emphasis. There are roughly three points, then, in this introduction to the extended notion of critique. First, the matter of a more overtly politically engaged scholarship. Second, the possibility of another, yet more subtle, scheme of technical ranking. Third, the question of whether, and how, this scheme can be used in Third World matters of development.

3.41 Ideology critique, as it is presented in the work of the Frankfurt School,[53] can be taken as a circumstance-sensitive and problem-specific extension of the marxian tradition. This 'humanist' tradition includes the figures of Lukács, Gramsci, Horkheimer and Adorno. Marcuse and Goldmann are related figures, and recently the concerns of this tradition have been extensively developed by Habermas.

Habermas's project involves re-presenting the undeveloped and neglected elements of critique within Marx's work. This is to be accomplished *via* a Freudianized historical materialism. Thus 'distorted communication', ideology, is regarded both as a block to rational behaviour and as supportive of the irrational (capitalist) *status quo*. The critique of ideology aims to fracture common sense and thus contribute to satisfying a necessary condition of change in society. Moreover, the ideal of an autonomous self-hood and free social exchange is anticipated in the structure of language itself. So communication anticipates and implies free communication which, in turn, implies the practical requirements of such free communication; that is, a free polity. In sum, the pursuit of open debate, a 'reconstructed public', is compatible with scholarship,[54] appropriate to modern scientific civilization and tends to the realization of democracy.

In respect of the notion of ideology as 'distorted communication' Giddens notes: 'There are two strands in Habermas' writing relevant to the characterization of ideology – and its critique. The first is part of Habermas' discussion of the development of modern society and politics, the second locates ideology on the level of methodological analysis.'[55] The former is the critique of technocratic consciousness, the reduction of politics to technical expertise

– the pursuit of policy science and the affirmation of the role of the expert. The second presents ideology critique as the central mode of enquiry for social science. Thus the social scientist (critical theorist) analyses the process of the creation and maintainance of structures of meaning and their extension in the social world. The results of such enquiry are presented in therapeutic exchange with specified audiences. In this exchange, critical theory is authenticated to the extent that it becomes a significant cultural object, that is, is taken up by those to whom it was addressed. This therapeutic exchange is governed by the regulative ideal of an ideal speech situation, intrinsic to language, which supposes free debate and an open society.

The emancipatory role of the intellectual, including the social scientist, is grounded, it seems, upon the truth inherent in language. Habermas's value-position is built into his critical theory, just as Lukács and Goldmann invoked the proletariat. Habermas differs, in one presently relevant particular, in the ease with which a slide to the (philosophical) general can, from this point, be accomplished.

3.42 This emancipatory role is secured *via* the technical business of critique. Thus we have a distinction between speech and discourse. Where communication becomes problematical, where consensus breaks down, we have resort to discourse. In discourse, competing ideologies confront each other in pursuit of rational adjudication *via* explicit argumentation: the deployment and counterdeployment of arguments. Quite how intradisciplinary consideration is fitted in with extradisciplinary emancipatory critique I am not clear. Bauman[56] has proposed a distinction between validation (intra-disciplinary) and authentication (extra-disciplinary). Here again the question of quite who is supposed to be being addressed by critical theory reappears. None the less the theorists of this school claim that critical theory, in contradistinction to the orthodoxy, is a coherent social science and the correct radical democratic social-theoretic mode in advanced capitalism.

There is a schedule for this discourse, and this would be a ranking strategy of sorts: ranking is actually just a matter of rational argument. Bernstein presents an exposition of this in terms of consensus, positing four irreducible claims (which derive in Habermas's work from philosophical enquiry into the nature of language). The claims, entailed in consensus, 'include the *comprehensibility* of the utterance; the *truth* of its propositional content (when assertions are made); the *legitimacy* of rightness of its performative content; and the *veracity* of the speaker'.[57] When consensus breaks down we have recourse to discourse – in the appropriate area – to re-establish *rational consensus*. So ranking competing ideological schemes is, at base, a matter of arguing it out.

There are no fixed criteria and no mechanical procedures.

3.43 I have not had occasion to use an extended notion of critique, one resting on what I have called a pervasive-informal notion of ideology, in the context of discussions of theorizing the development of the Third World. In the Frankfurt School line the critique of ideology is a prerequisite of social change where the culture is repressive (or repressively tolerant) and the economic form advanced. In this set of circumstances, mature metropolitan capitalism, the emancipatory critique of the dominant hegemonic meaning system does indeed seem plausible as a proposal for action. However, in the Third World, where the economic form of capitalism is of a different – dependent – type and the polity rarely equivalent to the bourgeois liberal-democracy of the capitalist metropoles, the critique of ideology in a more classically marxian guise seems more appropriate.

In terms of ranking competing schemes treating the development of the Third World, then, it seems to me that the subtle schemes of ideology critique that are presented in Habermas's work are overly elaborate. In my opinion, if we would grasp the issue of development, then the simpler notions of criticism will be more fruitful. I do not want to claim that the pervasive-informal notion of ideology cannot be used in the context of the societies of the Third World: to do so would seem to involve making claims to the relative simplicity of Third World forms of life which, at a guess, would be wholly untenable. What I do say is that if theorizing would be practical then maybe the delimited-formal notion will be found to be more immediately useful in determining, among competing schemes, what best will secure 'development'.

4.0 In conclusion it can be recalled that Bernstein has made it clear that if the orthodox – descriptive – model of social scientific enquiry is rejected in favour of a model which centres, in some fashion, upon the business of the production of argument, then inevitably the proponents of such a replacement scheme have to confront the task of indicating just how they propose to tackle the inevitable and central problem of rationally adjudicating between competing schemes.

I have tried to offer an answer to this question which centres, in line with my claims about the importance of recent theorizing of the Third World for ideas about social theorizing *per se* (that the material is informative and reveals the business to be essentially practical), and in the light of the established theoretical 'school' I have made the locus of these enquiries (that is, humanist marxian), on the practical nature of social theorizing. I have considered, in particular, the business of the production of delimited-formal ideological schemes. I take this to be the prime case of social theorizing, and in thus presenting the issue of ranking I hope that I have usefully recalled attention to the proper centre of social scientific commentary. An excessive concern for either, on the one hand, theoretical (epistemic) 'grounding' or, on the other (polemically), effective 'deployment' will serve only to skew social scientific enquiry. Commentary must centre upon the quality of crafting of ideological schemas which are concerned to make sense of the world.

The particular ranking schemes I have presented are, as I have said, heuristic. That is, they are general strategies which might usefully serve to order enquiry. There is, so far as I can see, no substitute to be found in this material, or elsewhere, for the lengthy, and continuing, process of intra-disciplinary debate in respect of the particular nature and quality of any ideological product.

I have no doubt that the remarks in this essay will not be the last on the matter – hardly! – nor are they likely to be to the intellectual taste of many (little better than nonsense to the orthodox, and rather philosophically crude for Habermas and Marx scholars), but what I hope I have achieved is an approximation to a practical and plausible answer to a question that is central to the humanist marxian line. This, it should be clear, is a fairly modest claim.

6 The ethico-political notion of development: a memorandum on commitments

1.0 In this chapter I want to consider the nature of the idea of 'development'.[1] In the literature of development studies the term seems to be taken – and here I pick out the two 'pure' cases – as either *technical* or *obvious*. In the former case, development is conceived as a matter of building appropriate physical, social and economic structures – largely a matter of accumulating a set of characteristics familiar in the experience of the developed nations. In the latter case, development is taken to be the fundamentally uncontentious business of organizing decent lives for the presently disadvantaged Third World peoples. It is my view that these two uses of the term development can be located in particular periods of the post-war career of development studies, and that both are wrongheaded. In contrast to these two familiar uses I would argue that the term development is essentially ethico-political. It is a complex notion and one whose deployment in matters of the Third World is by no means unproblematical.

1.1 The original impetus for these enquiries was the intuition[2] that Winch[3] had come close to displaying how philosophical work could help the business of social theorizing. In particular he seemed to show how the richness of philosophical discourse might be joined, productively, to the relevance of social scientific researches. Such an exchange has now been accomplished by more than one subsequent writer – I am thinking of, say, Lukes, Giddens, MacIntyre and Bernstein[4] for example (and I dare say it would be possible to identify anticipators in the history of social theorizing too), and this essay follows their general lead. My actual point of departure was the juxtaposition of Winch and Hawthorn.[5] On the one hand Winch had argued that sociology might be seen as 'misbegotten epistemology'[6] and had been criticized (by, say, Giddens[7]) for, among other things, leaving off the investigation of 'forms of life' just where a sociologist would want to begin. That is with issues relating to genesis and change within the 'form of life' in question. On the other hand I took from Hawthorn the remark that the easiest way to grasp the work of any theorist of society was to ask after that thinker's moral vision.

The general theoretical underpinnings affirmed by Hawthorn in his study – his 'voluntaristic idealism' – are, to me, unconvincing. Rewriting Hawthorn's suggestion, after the style of Marx ('men make their own social theories but not as they choose') and in the light of Winch's remark, occasioned the question of whether social theorizing could be taken as being, in some significant measure, misbegotten moral philosophy (where this is taken as a broader task than talk about the logic of moral statements). If such a view is given credence then one set of questions in respect of treatments of Third World issues immediately presents itself. Given that moral valuation will be integral to a 'form of life', just what scope has any (Western) theorist in adopting a stance in regard to what is to count as development in the Third World? Is the work of any (Western) thinker inevitably more or less euromorphic and eurocentric? Is there, contrariwise, any set of 'ethical simples' that could be invoked? In sum, what stance can we adopt and how (if it is possible) do we legitimate it?

I shall begin this chapter (continuing this section 1) by offering reasons why it is both proper and helpful to regard 'development' as an ethico-political term. And I shall note that a focus upon this ethical intention is a rapid way to come to grips with given theoretical efforts. I shall then consider the origins and scope of the idea (section 2) and, having made a brief (secondary) note about subtlety of argument forms being a matter of acknowledged reflexivity, shall treat its various presentations in the post-war career of development studies (section 3). Finally, I shall note what seem to me to be the obvious practical implications for theorizing (section 4). My remarks, and the lessons I draw from them, will not be novel intellectual departures. Indeed, the reverse is the case: so this paper is a memorandum on commitments; it recalls attention to neglected, and not unimportant, aspects of the business of theorizing the development of the Third World.

1.2 It seems to me that it is both proper and helpful to treat the notion of 'development' as an ethico-political term. It is helpful in that it allows debate on matters of development to be reflexively sensitive: that is, it permits better argument. This is in contrast to the orthodox 'technical' or 'obvious' stances. The paper as a whole aims to show how it is helpful, and I return directly to this aspect in section 4.

Gellner's work[8] will let me establish, in a preliminary way, the propriety of regarding 'development' as an ethico-political term. My argument strategy here involves invoking an authority, rather than presenting complex arguments from first principles. If there are any such 'arguments from first principles', which I touch on, then they are buried/scattered throughout these essays. And, in any case, as my style of theorizing is essentially one of identifying commitments I make (reflexivity), as and when it becomes clear that I have to, then constructing 'arguments from first principles' is really the business of the moral philosopher.

Gellner begins constructing his general scheme, an outline of a now-needed politics of transition, of indeed, 'modernization',[9] by observing: 'Men generally have a view of the nature of their society. They also have views concerning what validates the society's arrangements. The two things, image and validation, never are, and cannot be wholly distinct.'[10] The idea of progress is taken as central to European schemes, and three general positions are identified: the 'episodic', the 'evolutionist' and the 'neo-episodic'. It is the last variety that Gellner looks to, and he argues that at present a social order is valid if it is nationalist and industrialized or industrializing. This is the core of the 'substantive' position advanced. Gellner looks for a politics of 'the transition'; where this is an episode whose general end point is known ('modern world') and whose typical mode of thought, science, is historically novel in that it is reflexive, thus ensuring its successfulness on Gellner's scheme. These two: destination, and means to achievement (both *given* so far as Gellner is concerned), are the keys to ordering the 'transition'.

This 'transition' is seen as a pervasive phenomenon and Gellner urges that it is self-deluding to deny the attendant absence of settled views of the world and of our place in it. Gellner, in his remarks on the appropriate intellectual (here ethical) response to this pervasive phenomenon, argues two related cases. On the one hand that the absence of surety should be acknowledged, and second that this absence can be embraced in the guise of an ironical doubt (a general analogue of scientific thought). Of the lack of surety Gellner argues that it means the loss of a settled identity:[11]

> and 'identity' of course embraces picture-of-world, values, crucial concepts, priorities, tools, connections – all those things which, if only they were retained, could help one to jerk oneself back into a fixed self. This situation constitutes the very paradigm of a moral problem. Interesting moral crises are not those in which the question is simply whether individual or group will or will not succeed in maintaining or attaining some given or assumed standard – a kind of moral weight lifting – but those in

121

which the aims or criteria, the identity of the solution are
themselves in serious doubt.

Gellner does not look for any simple *technical* solutions.

Now this over-all argument of Gellner has the intriguing result
that if he is right about the centrality of the 'transition', then 'the
heir of "classical" political theory is now sociology. It is sociology
which is concerned with the understanding of that process, which is
now central to validating or even conceptualizing society.'[12] (It
might be noted that by 'sociology' Gellner means the efforts of the
'classical sociologists'[13] of the eighteenth and nineteenth centuries
to grasp the massive changes attendant upon the rise of what is now
called the 'modern world'. He does not mean the 'jejune official
textbook definitions'.[14]) Notwithstanding that I do not agree with
Gellner's treatments of the issues that he raises, so far as I am able
to comment at all, his general line I follow. The business of making
sense of the modern world is a central task of social theorizing; and
one that is essentially problematical in character, practical in intent
and catholic in its interests. The eighteenth- and nineteenth-century
'classical sociologists' (plus for my part the nineteenth-century
political economists), as their lines of enquiry culminate in the work
of Marx, are appropriate exemplars for present social theorizing.

This (very brief) discussion of Gellner's complex arguments
serves the purpose of indicating how social theorizing can be seen to
be centrally concerned with the business of making sense of novel
situations – where this is paradigmatically a moral problem and
typically sociology's concern. Gellner focuses upon the issues of
industrialization and takes the countries of the Third World to be
repeating the process experienced last century by the presently
developed. Here Gellner, notwithstanding the Popperian liberalism and modernization-theory infusions in his work, recalls Hilal[15]
on the importance of 'development': central issues of social theorizing are *re-presented* for our fresh consideration. The notion of
'development' – on Gellner's argument – is central to an enquiry,
into the 'transition', itself central to society's conceptualization and
validation, whose character recalls 'classical' political philosophy.

1.3   Gellner has been cited as a means to the rapid preliminary
establishment of our claim to the effect that 'development' is an
ethico-political term and that so to regard it is, among other things,
to affirm a particular view of social theorizing. Now these remarks
can be extended in another, more immediately useful, fashion.
From argument presented in order to establish the view of theorizing advanced, I turn to a writer who would grant it (albeit in an
idiosyncratic and, to my mind, eventually unhelpful fashion) in
order to deploy it as a means to the analysis of extant schools.

Hawthorn, in his history of sociological thought, argues to the effect that all eighteenth- and nineteenth-century theorists had a moral model of man as a key part of their efforts. A reference point round which data, explanations, arguments, illustrations, and so on, might be organized. Confronted with a given theorist, he advises, as I noted above, that we look to what was taken as a 'defensible social, political and moral order'.[16] This injunction is interesting for two general reasons. First, following on from the points made in the company of Gellner, it lets us link in an intuitively persuasive way theorist and theory. It 'solves' the 'problem of value freedom' by denying that it is at base a coherent notion. An element of the theorist's self-image is included as the basic organizing element of the theorist's product.[17] Second, to advance matters into the realm of method, it can be noted that Hawthorn takes social theories as 'actions. . . in part actually constituted by the intentions within them'.[18] It seems as though Hawthorn might grant my notion of 'engagement';[19] but in trying to avoid the (false) dilemma of theory as ideas *versus* theory as epiphenomenal responses, he rather slides off into an idealist stance. The pursuit of intentions is, for Hawthorn, the proper route into history writing. I will borrow this entry route, but with two provisos. First that my notion of intent is more robust than Hawthorn seems to want to make his. Whereas, in the end, Hawthorn refuses to acknowledge the sociologist's (deterministic) view of man and instead affirms his rationality,[20] I place less stress upon individual rationality. Indeed, my notion of intent is not constructed in the light of philosophical disputes about free will/determinism or causes/reasons. Men live in the mundane world – their use of their reason is both circumscribed and practical, and unless this is granted then there is a danger of drifting towards idealism.[21] My second proviso is that my notion of social-theoretic engagement embraces both intent and conception. As Hollis has noted, 'Every social theory needs a metaphysic. . . in which a model of man and a method of science complement each other.'[22] We need to consider method even if we are interested, as in this paper, in the ethical side of things.

Hawthorn's affirmation of the centrality of ethical/political intent is a restricted, though convenient, entry point into the analysis of extant social theories and I subsume it under the broader, prospective, schemes hinted at above with Gellner: 'classical political philosophy' and its 'heir'. The helpfulness of regarding 'development' as an ethico-political term will become clear, I hope, as I construct a history of post-war development studies as a series of morally informed efforts of analysis.

The stress on 'rational action' made by Hawthorn would have us write a history of efforts of analysis in an essentially piecemeal fashion: where attaching the theorist to this world was a tentative, empirically piecemeal, business to be attempted only when explanations in terms of reasons/intentions ran out. However it seems to me that the traditions of enquiry we inherit are just as solid, structuring, as the forms of society given us. The sociology of knowledge I would affirm is more straightforwardly marxian: granted that social theorizing is complex, and presents itself in diverse guises, it seems to me that some very general patterns can be seen. I want, in this paper, to uncover the structure of ideas, historically occasioned, within which theorists of development, in the post-war period, have acted. I want to look for a root metaphor around which the efforts of theorists of development can be ordered: this metaphor is the idea of progress.

1.4 The idea of progress is made central by Gellner: 'it seems obvious that European thought since the eighteenth century has come to assume the idea of progress; and indeed, that the idea has come to permeate ordinary thought and be built into its assumptions and language'.[23] I would agree with this claim, and I assume it would command general consent; the question that now arises is: What is the character of this familiar idea? An approach to an answer to this question will be made by looking at two related areas: first, the history of the notion, and second, its analytical spread. Having sketched the character of the idea of progress, I shall go on to look at the various presentations of the idea in the post-war career of development studies.

2.0 I shall begin with the 'historical' approach and trace the debate in the modern world about the development of man and society. Here I shall use the work of, in the main, two writers. The general ideas will be presented by using Passmore's[24] philosophical history of ideas, and the particular contexts will be reviewed using Pollard's[25] naive[26] sociology of knowledge treatment. Passmore presents the career of the notion as a history of ideas – mostly – tracing the shifts in argument, and the various problems thrown up, faced, evaded or simply not seen, as theorists sought to formulate a coherent schema of progress. Pollard traces the notion of progress against the backdrop of European history from the eighteenth century to the present.

Following the 'historical' side, I shall present the 'analytical' side, and offer a sketch of the ethical substance of the notion. This discussion will rest largely upon the work of C. B. Macpherson[27] and will centre upon the notion of man's essentially human powers and their realization – which, incidentally, I take to be the core of Marx's ethic.

2.1 It can be said that the idea of progress is modern. That is, it belongs to the post-Renaissance period of European thought. But if it is a modern notion then it can also be seen as one recent manoeuvre in an even longer argument – that which Passmore identifies as treating the idea of the achievement of perfection.

These notions of perfection are based in Greek philosophy, where contemplation of the notion of perfection, and the manner of its achievement by man in society, achieves its most thorough presentation in Plato. The Greek legacy involves, centrally, the idea of perfection as 'harmonious being' (and this can be unpacked metaphysically, aesthetically, teleologically or morally[28]) and the idea that such perfection can be achieved by man though this involves some sort of 'withdrawal' from the world. These ideas are taken up by Christian theologians. What is of note in this Christian thinking is that, as a rule, the possibility of perfection here on earth has been denied. What we have instead is the business of preparing for perfection in some after-life. This is argued for by Augustine. Yet in the fifth century the contrary view is put by Pelagius (the 'heresy of Pelagius'). Denying the notion of 'original sin' and affirming a duty to strive for perfection in earthly life, he argues that perfection can indeed be achieved in the here and now. These two can be taken to set the terms for the Christian debate. It is in the fourteenth century that we find the crucial change. The Renaissance humanists present a notion drawn from a re-interpreted Aristotle: that of civic perfection. This is the first step in a radical change which establishes a third route to perfection, social action.

The impact of Renaissance humanism, its ethic, its science and its success results in a shift in the centre of gravity of discussions of perfection which Passmore sums up under three points. First, perfection comes to be defined in natural rather than metaphysical terms and slowly comes to mean 'improvement' and 'doing the maximum of good'. Second, it is now seen that perfection has to be gained with the help of one's fellows rather than God's grace or individual effort. Third, the stress on motives is reduced and perfection is taken to be less a matter of (un-realizable) purity of motive and rather more to do with pursuing the maximum of good. This shift in the terms of theorizing the model of perfection sees a concomitant move in respect of achieving such perfection. The new position involves the view that the contemplative life is now, paradigmatically, that of the scholar/scientist and not that of the mystic. It is the rise of science that is taken by progressives of the time as the key to subsequent change.

2.11 The culmination of these movements, as they are present in the consciousness of our modern world, can be taken to be the idea of progress. The notion 'permeates' our thinking, as Gellner remarked. The idea of progress emerges in the eighteenth century, and this emergence can be read in two ways: as an idea, and as an element of wider social movement.

As an idea, it can be interpreted as an answer to the problem presented by the work of Locke in respect of the matter of education and its control. Thus it can be seen that in the course of the complex theoretical shift noted above the ideas of *perfection* and *perfectibility* are divorced. The general doctrine of perfection is reformulated, says Passmore, and it is represented in the claim that 'all men are capable of being perfected and to a degree that has no limit'.[29] If it is then asked *how*, then the most obvious candidate was education. It is Locke who lays the ground for subsequent (eighteenth- and nineteenth-century) discussions of education and social action as means to progressive change by showing that education can in fact achieve this. He does so by proposing a simple pleasure/pain psychology and by taking virtue to be the possession of 'good habits'. Passmore explains that 'the new moral psychology opened the way to the suggestion that men could be to an infinite degree improved by the use of appropriate social mechanisms – in the first place education.'[30]

However, the reliance upon education to secure improvement runs into the problem that the educator is already a member of a corrupt society: the educator needs educating. It is at this point that a familiar area of concern opens up – the relationship of changes in education and changes in the social system. The stress on education as the route to general improvement seems to open up this circle of non-movement. One important line of reply is that which Passmore calls 'governmentalism', by which he seems to mean the social reformist stance most readily associated at the present time with the Fabian tradition. Bentham, J. S. Mill and the Fabians are cited: in the post-war career of development studies one immediately thinks of Myrdal and the neo-institutionalist line which was described in chapter 1 as an ideology of 'co-operative (revised authoritative) interventionism'.

It seems that the most the Lockean can claim to have established is that man can be perfected. The gap between the possibility of being perfected and actually being perfected still has to be bridged. Secular perfectibilism lacked the metaphysical guarantor of a god, but the position was retrieved by two steps. In the first of these the educator is made subsidiary to a method, and in the second he is abolished altogether (and this second move I look at in section 2.12 below).

The educator was made subsidiary to a method in the course of formulating a doctrine whereby human history was taken to afford a guarantee that man would continue to improve his position. If man's history is conceived in such a way that improvement is guaranteed, then the occasional errors by educators (etc.) can be dismissed as relatively unimportant. It is here that we arrive at the idea of *progress*.

The idea of progress was argued for on two main grounds. On the one hand it was pointed out that, as a matter of fact, there had been progress in man's affairs. The optics of Newton for example were better than those of Descartes. However, the major discovery of the early modern thinkers was *scientific method*: it was, reports Passmore, the dominant theme of the seventeenth and eighteenth centuries. The early successes of natural science were immediately taken note of. Bauman observes: 'Hence the attitude of *techne*, of manipulation, inducing deliberate and planned change, first forged in the course of wrestling with Nature, could be, without much further reflection, stretched to embrace human relations.'[31]

This intellectual movement can be summarized in the following way:[32]

> There gradually developed then, in the 18th century, a chain of inference which ran thus: man had until that time been a mere child in respect of knowledge and, in consequence, of virtue; he was now at last in a position as a result of the development of science, to determine how human nature develops and what is the best thing for human beings to do; this new knowledge could be expressed in a form in which all men would find it intelligible; once they knew what is best to do men would act accordingly and so would constantly improve their moral, political and physical condition. Provided only then, that 'sinister interests' did not prevent the communication of knowledge, the development of science was bound to carry with it the constant improvement of the human condition, to a degree which would be, like the growth of science itself, unlimited.

As I noted above, this intellectual change can also be seen as an element of broader social movements. It is to the matter of the social location of the idea of progress that I now turn. The social historian Pollard presents a useful view of the modern period and uses the image of a pyramid to capture the degrees of radicalism of those who have affirmed the idea of progress. Thus he argues that few would deny that there has been technical and natural scientific progress. Fewer would expect it to continue and to include social progress. Fewer still would expect the character of men to improve and it is only a small minority who would expect actual biological change. Pollard agrees with Passmore in seeing the Renaissance as the point when the idea of human socially achieved advance was first presented. The preceding theistic schemes are embraced in the phrase 'the pre-history of the idea of progress'.[33] The key to the new optimism is again seen as the discovery of scientific method. However, it is rightly pointed out that these ideas were not generated, or taken up, in a vacuum. The advance of science was not the result of a new tolerance on the part of the Church, neither was it the result of the sudden evident superiority of scientific thinking. Rather, the advance of science was a result of a complex of social factors, not least the support of powerful groups. Pollard's summary is worth citing at length:[34]

> Thus it was the New Men of Europe, the merchants and traders and manufacturers, the owners of mines and mills and of banks, and their technicians and managers and doctors and clerks, whose experience tallied with the new philosophy, and whose needs called forth the new science. They had little regard for the privileges of birth or for divine rights, but required instead rewards for merit, freedom of contract, protection of property and defencelessness of labour, and in the end they won, for their economy was more efficient. In the two or three centuries before the 1680's or 1690's, their advance and the growing acceptance of their values were sufficiently marked to make a doctrine of progress seem plausible to them. When they made their bid for power against a well entrenched landed class system which used tradition as its ideology, they would find the slogan of Progress most useful. . . The idea of progress will be much misunderstood unless it is viewed as playing its role within the real, concrete history of the men who held it.

The first wave of optimism peaks in the eighteenth century, particularly in France; though it is the English anarchist and freethinker Godwin who most unequivocally reduces the mechanism of progress to the result of the free play of rational discourse (Godwin looks to the establishment of 'a free community of rational beings in which it is the opinions of those who are informed and objective that will carry weight'[35]). Passmore notes that the Enlighteners were confident that a science to improve man had been established *and* that it would be used. This confidence is taken to rest on the Enlighteners' self-perception: this involved their emergence as a new and distinct social group. They were, it seems, self-consciously a 'community' – thus Hume feels obliged to offer Rousseau a place to stay while the latter is in exile in England. Pollard calls the area of agreement in their doctrines 'astonishingly wide'[36] and unique until the rise of marxism in the nineteenth century. These thinkers took themselves to be the natural governors of society through an equally natural alliance with the rising bourgeoisie. As Passmore has it: 'Overt power to the middle class, actual power to the intellectuals.'[37] Progress is, then, evident in history, appropriate to the needs of the day, and underpinned by reason.

2.12 This optimism, in respect of progress, reaches a peak in the work of the *philosophes* and thereafter declines and becomes diffuse. The idea of progress is generally accepted throughout the nineteenth century, but it is presented by various groups in various countries. The intellectual and social history of the notion, so to say, is very complex. Greatly simplifying matters, I will sketch a twofold reading.

So if we first consider the history-of-ideas side, it can be noted that, as an idea, the notion of secular progress lacks the metaphysical guarantor that theistic schemes could invoke. The response to this, after the unsatisfactory nature of the focus upon method is seen, is to abolish the educator altogether and to invoke natural guarantors in the shape of history and biology. Thus we have theories of *progress as natural development*.

With Darwin we can associate a range of evolutionisms. Pollard remarks that 'Darwinism permeated every philosophy at least to the extent of postulating some process of evolution'.[38] Now while the precise intellectual status of Darwin's theory, and, more importantly, the extent and nature of his contribution to and borrowings from theories of *social* evolution, is disputed, it seems to me to be reasonable in this essay to let the simple association stand. It is so because I do not propose to discuss evolutionist schemes: they have been presented in theories of development of the Third World and have been sharply criticized.[39] That 'evolutionisms' display a marked tendency to shift from any initial precision of formulation towards the descriptive general characterization (celebration) of society (Western *status quo*) is surely true.

Turning to the schemes which make some reference to history, it is clear that theories positing immanent 'laws', and which present schemes of gradual unfolding (of inherent potentialities) animated by means of a social dialectic, offer mechanisms of progressive change and are better explanatory strategies. Passmore sums up the intellectual career of such approaches:[40]

> The roots of this theory of immanent laws lie in Aristotle or in Leibniz's version of Aristotelianism; they are laws of 'unfolding' by which man, or Spirit, or Idea, or God, gradually comes to a full realization of his nature, achieving a complete rationality and freedom – which are, so it is supposed, inherent in that nature – in a form of society in which rationality and freedom can fully express themselves. The disagreement amongst developmentalists turns about the nature of the immanent laws and the form of society in which they will finally issue.

The central nineteenth-century figure here is Marx: 'he sees capitalism itself as a highly developed stage in the unfolding of man's creative powers'.[41] The analysis of the class dialectic of capi-

129

talist society, through the critical revision of the political economic theorizing then current, served to inform progressivist pressure for political change – 'shortening the birth pangs'.

Turning to the complementary matter of the social location of these sets of ideas, the central point is that the victorious nineteenth-century bourgeoisie found, on the morrow of their victory, that the culmination of the tradition of thought and action of which they had been prime movers did not serve their interests unreservedly. The pattern of intellectual change reviewed above was blocked, and the extension of political economic enquiry into the area of socialist prognoses of the future of capitalism was left to Marx *et al*.

The alliance of commerce with science is seen as restrictedly progressive given the incompatibility of an open-ended method oriented to the closure implied in the establishment of the bourgeois state. One response is the search for a new motor of progress, and we have noted its best exponent above. But for the orthodox, and their theorists, the progressiveness of science is curbed and classical political economy collapses into social science. For Pollard, the decay of political economy into social science with economics mathematicized was 'a mark of triumph. . . of the new liberal capitalist order. . . by making economics a-historical the economists made social conservatism orthodox. To advocate further progress by basic social change, as had occurred in the past, was not only politically deplorable, but economically nonsensical.'[42]

I have now traced the origins and career of the ideas of progress from its inception in Greek philosophy to the forms presented in the writings of the nineteenth-century theorists of 'industrialism'. The range of debate, relevant to matters of theorizing society, I take to have been more of less fixed at this time. *On the one hand* we have progressivist schemes of natural development which we can associate with classical-marxian work centred on political economic enquiry. If I have understood Passmore rightly, then it is here that we have the intellectually coherent schemes of 'progress'. Equally it is true that, even if this is the intellectually coherent line of this general and familiar tradition, it is none the less a frequently submerged and ridiculed line. It does not lend itself to the policy-scientific elaboration of short-term detail which mature monopoly capitalism demands of its intellectual help-mates. *On the other hand* we have those schemes of orthodox social science that tend to the positivistic, scientistic, policy scientific.

These two, presented here summarily, are the *reference points* I shall use in considering the notion of progress presented in post-war treatments of development. I shall not treat the complex history of the idea of progress through the nineteenth and twentieth centuries as it is presented in various guises by various groupings – Hawthorn offers one history of this. Instead I move straight to my particular area of concern: the post-war career of development studies. Before that, however, I shall look at the *scope* of the idea of progress: this will provide a related set of reference points for organizing commentary upon the career of development studies.

2.2 I have now sketched the route whereby the idea of the individual pursuit of perfection was transformed into naturally guaranteed social progress. Additionally it was pointed out that as this key idea of the tradition of political thought we inhabit was in point of formation, it simultaneously assumed two forms. The one pursued the core of the idea, though it was now taken as the radical line, and looked to schemes of the 'dialectical unfolding' of societal tendencies. The other line, which became the orthodox view, aborted its intellectual development and endeavoured to fix change either in place – by invoking schemes of overweening generality, that is, evolutionisms – or in a mundane realm – by reducing progress to the efficient functioning of the free market and the individual consumption of proliferating consumer goods.

I now turn to the ethico-political substance of these two lines: it will allow us to consider the *scope* of the idea of progress. That there are two such distinguishable positions in political philosophy is a familiar claim. Berlin, for example, distinguishes 'positive' and 'negative' ideas of liberty, where only the latter is helpful. The former is taken as pernicious and is characterized thus: 'I wish, above all, to be conscious of myself as a thinking, willing, active being, bearing responsibility for my choices and able to explain them by reference to my own ideas and purposes. I feel free to the degree that I believe this to be true and enslaved to the degree that I am made to realize that it is not.'[43] This passage is quoted with approval – quite rightly in my view – by Macpherson,[44] whose work I shall largely rely upon here.

The over-all drift of Macpherson's work is that we can separate two traditions of politico-moral thought, and argue that the more familiar, orthodox, scheme is unsatisfactory and should be replaced by a new position which acknowledges the over-shadowed counter-tradition. I shall review the claim made by Macpherson that the doctrines of liberal capitalism are either irrelevant to the needs of modern society, or incoherent, or both.

The justificatory theorems of liberal capitalist market society centre upon the notion of individualism. It can be seen as a central element of the Enlightenment. Thus Goldmann argues: 'Between the age of traditional Christianity and the beginning of dialectical philosophy there grew up the great individualist traditions which have continued to develop to this day. . . these. . . dispensed with all trans-individual concepts.'[45] This individualism is, he argues, manifestly the ethic of the market-place. There is a stress on the formal, reflecting the needs of the market and the act of exchange, to the detriment of the substantive contents of moral codes. The insufficiency of liberal individualism is a central concern for Macpherson. In liberal democratic theory two incompatible lines are run together; thus Macpherson observes: 'The justifying theory of our Western democracies rests on two maximizing claims – a claim to maximize individual utilities and a claim to maximize individual powers.'[46] Resting upon his work we can, first, look at the claims of liberal democratic justificatory theory to the effect that liberal capitalism maximizes utilities. And then consider the related point that it maximizes 'powers'.

The claim that market capitalism maximizes utilities requires that economic science grant that individual utilities can be measured against a common scale – else the set of satisfactions satisfied by liberal capitalism cannot be held to be greater than those of some other system. The orthodox position in economics denies that satisfactions can be compared. Macpherson takes these claims at face value and points to the resultant logical difficulty – orthodox economics cannot claim that liberal democracies' set of utilities are maximal.[47]

The claim that the system maximizes utilities *equitably* runs into similar logical difficulties. The abstract formal calculus of economics can demonstrate equitable distribution only upon a given initial allocation of wealth, etc. The calculus says nothing about that original allocation. These two arguments I take to be fairly familiar, so I shall not pursue them at length. More interesting, for my purposes, are Macpherson's remarks upon 'powers'.

Here the way in which the justificatory theorem of liberal democracy runs together two incompatible traditions – exemplified in the work of J. S. Mill for Macpherson – is most clearly visible.

The familiar use of the notion of 'power' in social-theoretic work appears in the context of discussions of political and social conflict. Thus, for example, Marx remarks in the *Communist Manifesto* that political power is simply the means to the oppression of one class by another. However, we can note that the notion of 'powers' is not the same as the notion of 'power'. Lukes[48] analyses the idea of 'power' in the familiar way and distinguishes three characterizations, which he calls the one, two and three dimensional views. The shift is from voluntaristic decision-making towards an idea of structural determination that lets in notions of false consciousness and real interests. Lukes's focus is upon the idea of 'power' as 'power over'.

Macpherson considers the pair of notions: 'power over' and 'power to do'. Conventional discussions of power begin with matters of its source in the political realm and particular deployment thereafter. However, Macpherson invites us to consider the purpose of the exercise of power. It is claimed that treating matters of purpose reintroduces the classical political theorist's concern for developmental power – 'power *to do*' – human powers.

In the case of liberal democracy, Macpherson argues that the democratic elements included are extra-liberal and represent an attempt to co-opt pre-seventeenth-century notions of democracy. Here the notions of man affirmed made human actions intrinsically valuable – this is the Aristotelian-derived scheme of civic virtue and of the flowering of natural capacities. The liberal model of man, in contrast, affirms that man is a bundle of appetites in search of satisfaction, and this view, it is suggested, is to be found in Hobbes and Locke and occasioned by the needs of the incipient bourgeois revolution and the establishment of capitalism.

There are thus two notions of power: what Macpherson calls the *ethical* concept and the *descriptive* concept. The former he associates with the democratic tradition and the latter with the liberal tradition.

The ethical concept of powers centres upon a man's natural attributes and potentials and includes access to whatever external means (tools, say) are needed for their exercise. Any limitation of access to the means to the exercise of powers is therefore an effective diminution of those powers. This pattern of argument does not hold when we turn to the descriptive notion of power. The descriptive notion includes both natural endowment plus extra skills acquired at second hand *via* effective social control of other people's powers. A man's powers are just those which he controls. There is no place in this schema for the notion of diminution as it appears above.

Now one way of transferring powers is by denying free access to the means of exercising these powers. If a society systematically employs such restrictions then, on the ethical concept, there will be a continuous net transfer of powers. On the other hand, using the descriptive concept, there will be no transfer.

It is J. S. Mill, Macpherson argues, who introduces the ethical concept into the liberal capitalist scheme. The descriptive concept of powers is used in analysis and the ethical in justifications. The claim to maximize powers rests upon the use of the ethical notion. But the two are not compatible, and the powers which liberal democracy is claimed to maximize are not in fact those which it actually does maximize. The theorem is thus incoherent. It is also presently irrelevant.

The net transfer of powers can be seen to be necessary only upon a certain set of assumptions – relating to material scarcity and human desire – which, arguably, were historically necessary for the establishment of capitalism but which are not, arguably, necessary now.

The assumptions of infinite desirousness and scarcity are bound up with the justificatory theorems of liberal capitalism. Macpherson presents the argument in summary form as follows:[49]

> We may now summarize the logical chain that leads to the transfer of powers. The net transfer of powers in a free society is the result of the accumulation of the material means of labour in the hands of one set of people. This accumulation is the result of two factors: (a) the society's decision to set up a right of un-limited individual appropriation, and (b) the natural inequality of individual capacities. Of these two factors, I assume that (b) is inherent in any society short of a genetically managed one. Factor (a) I find to be the result of the society's double value judgment: (i) that individual freedom is preferable to authorita-tive allocation of work and reward, and (ii) that the chief purpose of man is an endless battle against scarcity in relation to infinite desire. Assumption (ii) can be restated as, or reduced to, the assumption that unlimited desire is natural and rational.
>
> Putting the logical chain in the reverse order and compressing it, we get: the acceptance, by the most active part of society, of the belief that unlimited desire is natural and rational *leads to* the establishment of the right of unlimited appropriation, which *leads to* the concentration of ownership of the material means of labour, which *leads to* the continual net transfer of powers.

The assumptions of infinite desirousness are taken to be no longer historically necessary. The development of the forces of material production has been so dramatically successful that there is no longer any need to 'maintain this perverse, artificial, and tem-porary concept of man'.[50] The circumstances of capitalist produc-tive skill, plus competition with both the 'Eastern Bloc' and Third World in respect of notions of social development, make the re-instatement of the ethical concept of powers appropriate and urgent.

The ethical concept of powers has been reviewed in the context of the claim that powers are maximized by liberal democracy. But what, it may be asked, do we take this ethical concept to entail? In Macpherson's work it is granted that various *lists* may be made, and he remarks that the familiar notions of liberal democracy probably cover the ground. The positive content is not made specific, as the assumption of 'essentially human powers' is both a very general empirical postulate *and* a necessary assumption for any democratic theory.

The notion can be read, more simply, as an evaluative standard against which particular social states of affairs can be judged. As regards liberal-democracy it has been argued that in presenting its defences/theorems of liberal market society a crucial distinction (between ethical and descriptive notions of powers) is blurred. This failing allows the (routine) neglect of systematic inequalities in access to the means of life. Liberal-democratic analysis is strong in the area of civil liberties, but hopelessly weak in respect of inequality of access to the means of labour and the general social inequality that results therefrom.

In regard to the scope of the idea of progress I would summarize this brief discussion of Macpherson as follows. The liberal democratic notion of progress – accumulation of material possessions – is incoherent and, now, irrelevant. It must be reworked in the light of the submerged 'radical democratic' idea of progress as maximization of essentially human powers. These two I take to set the presently effective limits to the scope of the idea of progress as it appears in present social theorizing about development.

2.3 I can summarize this section as follows: I have looked at the historical career of notions of perfectibility and at the scope of the ideas of social progress routinely presented in contemporary social-theoretic discourse. My treatment of these has been, inevitably, derivative and cursory, but my goal has not been the preparation of a satisfactory analytical history but rather the *establishment of reference points* against which the ethical substance of theories of development might be ordered.

The notion of progress can be traced back to the Renaissance humanist restructuring of the notion of perfectibility. The influence of a rediscovered Aristotle, read as concerned with civic rather than mystic virtue, is taken to prompt the view that the contemplative life is now that of the scholar/scientist. It is the rise of science that is taken by 'progressives' of the time as the key to subsequent change, and the notion of progress emerges in the eighteenth century. This emergence can be read in two ways. As an idea it is taken to be the response to the problem of control of the educator or law-giver. As a social phenomenon it reflects the expectations of the theorist in alliance with the commercial bourgeoisie – the idea is thus socially located.

This optimism reaches its climax in the *philosophes,* and then becomes diffuse. Again a twofold treatment was offered. As an idea the notion of secular perfectibilism lacks a guarantor and the response is to invoke natural guarantors in the guise of history and biology. Or, moving into a familiar and restricted area of theorizing, the market of the economists. As a social phenomenon we saw that the alliance of commerce and science is restrictedly progressive. It is limited by the incompatibility of an open-ended progressive method oriented to the closure that is implied in the establishment of the bourgeois state. The response of the theorists is, as with Marx, the identification of other class agents or system tendencies. Or, more narrowly, the construction of marginalist economics and subsequently positive social science.

On Passmore's account – if I have understood him – it is the nineteenth-century tradition of classical political economy that inherits the intellectually coherent notion of progressive development. This line of enquiry has been left, pre-eminently, to Marx and his subsequent followers. Orthodox social science represents the area of restricted enquiry compatible with the requirements of the bourgeois state – we have scientistic policy science.

Resting upon Macpherson's work, I considered the scope of these two lines of enquiry. The progressivist – democratic – tradition affirms notions of 'powers' which are integral to the humanist perfectibilism of the classically-inspired Renaissance. Against this the orthodox – liberal individualist – scheme has been presented as a, now dangerous, historical novelty whose roots lie in Hobbes and Locke and the needs of the Puritan revolution. I have rehearsed the view, advanced by Macpherson, that with Hobbes and Locke the perfectibilist ideal is not only brought down to earth but presented in a very narrow version. The model of man presented is unique in the history of moral and political philosophy in that it makes rational the limitless pursuit of utilities and political power as a means thereto. The philosophy of liberalism peaks in the eighteenth and early nineteenth centuries and, reworked as liberal democracy, is now the conventional wisdom of Western capitalism. The contrary view – evoking the older line of thought – is presented by Macpherson as the democratic tradition: a now half-submerged position in our political culture.

The intellectually coherent notion of progress (Passmore) can be associated with the radical democratic stance (Macpherson); and the restricted, and incoherent, notion of progress (Passmore) can be associated with the liberal democratic stance (Macpherson). These two dually characterized positions I shall use as the reference-points against which theories of development produced in the post-World War II period can be located.[51]

3.0 Earlier in this chapter I quoted Hollis to the effect that social theorizing must have a model of man and a complementary method of enquiry. Although I am interested in the ethical character of the various attempts to comprehend the problem of development, I shall acknowledge Hollis's claim by introducing, in this section, a secondary motif: that of method.

Whether it is possible to link, in a logically rigorous fashion, definite ethical and methodological positions in the way that Fay, in his *Social Theory and Political Practice*, links methodology and practice, I do not know. What is clear, as the following material shows, is that ethical stances certainly characteristically *associate* with particular methodological strategies. Thus the early 'positivist' work combines the pursuit of a descriptive general social science with an unexamined – descriptively derived – ethic of growth. Similarly, the later 'marxist' work combines dialectical analytical engagement with an explicit ethic (a philosophical anthropology).

It seems clear that conceptions of explanatory propriety entail definite stances on the matter of valuation generally. But it is not clear that substantive ethical commitments are similarly entailed.

Given this association, and given that the issue of necessary linkages is not an issue that I propose to pursue, what I shall present is a simple schema of varieties of explanation. Once again, as with the above discussions of progress, I am looking for reference-points which will allow discussion in respect of development to be ordered.

What I propose, then, is to examine the theories of development which I identified in chapter 1 and ask of each: (a) how does it stand with respect to the idea of progress; and (b) how does it stand in respect of my simple model of explanatory strategies?

This schema of explanatory strategies involves only one axis built around one idea, or claim. I have claimed that social theorizing is essentially practical and, for purposes of inspection, can be characterized as comprising a given *conception* (of how explanations ought to be constructed) and a related *intent* (in respect of how practice is to be effected). Most centrally social theorizing involves ideology construction and the key to the production of intellectually plausible work seems to me to be a routine reflexivity. This being so I can contrive a reference-point by presenting a 'model of the crude' (in explanations) simply by negating the above image of social theorizing.

The sociology-of-knowledge-informed terms – of conception and intent – present themselves in the required definitions of a 'crude' stance as the notions of europomorphism and europocentrism. The first can be understood as the affirmation of the priority of (what are taken to be) typically Western categories of thought relating to the areas of social and political enquiry. The second can be understood as the affirmation of the priority of the material and practical interests of the West.

With this simple model of the explanatory character of theories, and with the models of progress presented above, I can now go on to look at those theories of development produced in the post-war period which I identified in chapter 1. In respect of each departure I shall ask how does it stand in respect of the idea of progress and how close is it to my model of the 'crude'.

3.1 The first presentations of the idea of progress in the context of post-war development theories are to be found in that period which Ehrensaft[52] has dubbed the 'pre-Seers consensus'. There are two versions of essentially the same schema: an earlier UK/UN-flavoured effort and a latter distinctly US scheme. The former I have called an *authoritative interventionism* and the latter an *elaborated authoritative interventionism*.

If we look at this notion of authoritative intervention, which I take to be analogous to Fay's[53] 'policy science', and attempt to unpack it, then we come up with the following model of social theorizing. It is a scheme of analysis and engagement which takes the exchange between the theorist and the world (of objects) to be, in essence, the knowing manipulation of the latter by the former. Typically an empiricist epistemology, which takes 'theory' to be a complex summary statement of the correspondences of events and reports, is used. The analytical methodology of this approach is that of modelling. And although the theorists characteristically lodge disclaimers in respect of the status they would wish to accord these models, they are, given their formalism, empiricism and technical manipulative orientation, more or less scientistic. The theorist adopts the role of the expert, and the procedure for any practical enquiry involves the disaggregation of abstract models (produced by abstraction and generalization from many cases) to fit given circumstances.

With regard to the ideological function of this scheme it can be seen that the strategy of explanation serves to legitimate a relationship of super- and sub-ordination whereby the 'development' of the present UDC is ordered by the experts of the DC and their agents. 'Development' or progress is understood as a technical matter which is elicited by this authoritative intervention, and which presents itself in the various indices of economic growth. Progress is taken as evidenced by economic growth: progress *is* economic growth.

In the earlier versions of this over-all line, those I have categorized as producing an ideology of authoritative interventionism, there is an underlying pessimism in respect of the chances of contriving steady growth. This early scheme has a general Keynesian backdrop and two particular theorists. They were Colin Clark[54] and his ideas of growth as sectoral redistribution of productive effort, and Roy Harrod[55] with his Keynesian-derived model of the growth path. These schemes occasioned much concern for statistical indices – GNP, ICOR, etc. – and the more embracing social context of change tended to be discussed in terms of 'non-economic factors' helping or hindering what was seen as an essentially economic process. This view was not unimportant, as I note below, given the economists' (and others') own estimation of their worth. Yet, over-all, this early work was cautious in respect of its claims. Not so the later version.

The theorists of modernization produced what I have called an ideology of elaborated authoritative interventionism. The economics core of the scheme remained, but with one crucial altera-tion. The pessimism of Harrod's scheme was denied. Indeed it was replaced[56] by a new model which simply restated the problem minus the problematical elements of the old one. Economic growth was now largely automatic and guaranteed.

The theorists of modernization also effected the relative emanci-pation of the general family of the social sciences from the thrall of economics: the essentially economic-technical character of the theorem was largely lost from sight in the profusion of social scientific characterizations of the 'Grand Process of Moderniza-tion'.[57] W. W. Rostow presented the most influential general scheme.[58]

Looked at through the eyes of a sociologist of knowledge, or a historian, both these departures reveal the character of their respec-tive times and places. The earlier growth theory was contrived in the immediate aftermath of war, when the prospects for the develop-ment of what came to be called the Third World looked dim when set against the daunting tasks of reconstruction of extensive war damage, and when the extent to which economics admitted of the possibility of effective state intervention was limited. Keynesianism seems familiar today; then it was not. Growth theory is con-sequently rather cautious. Modernization, however, is a product of the period of the high tide of positivist social scientific conceit. Affluence, full employment attendant upon an unprecedented and unexpected economic boom, burgeoning social science research, and the demands of governments for effective policies when con-fronted with political pressures from new Third World states com-bined to call forth modernization. One theorist has remarked that it is now 'hard to see the former mood of assurance in perspective'.[59]

The idea of progress affirmed by these early positivistic efforts is, in the light of my treatments of the origin and scope of the idea, firmly lodged within the intellectually incoherent and ethically im-poverished line. The idea of progress appears in an entirely orthodox and narrowly materialistic guise: and it is to be secured by social scientific policy science.

In respect of method and the model of the 'crude' presented above it is clear that the theorists of the orthodoxy would reply to a question in respect of the propriety of their efforts with a dual affirmation. Their work is europomorphic because economics just are scientific, and therefore of general application. And their work is europocentric because the developed world shows the under-developed its future. Any route to that future which does not rest upon a continuation of the economic relationships already established is inconceivable. Inequalities between central and peripheral areas are contingent problems to be resolved – they are not the inevitable adjuncts to a fundamentally exploitative and unequal relationship.

I shall pursue this point about method in a general fashion (I think the claim made is true of both growth and modernization theory, though the sketch of a history following does not treat these lines separately as a more detailed treatment would).

As regards the europomorphism and 'centrism of this particular 'school' of thinking it is possible to identify a long history of pre-sumption. This routine assumption of the correctness of the Western 'stance' cuts across a spectrum of issues from questions of the participation in government to debates in respect of rationality itself: from regarding colonies as reservoirs of resources for the home economy to treating them as responsibilities to be discharged.

Perhaps the most uncompromising general statement appears in the late nineteenth-century jingoist themes of the complete superiority of Western man in contrast to the childish natives. These images, it can be suggested, are not called forth as a result of the exchange between people in Third World areas and Westerners, but by the politics of colonialism. Sachs[60] points out that the image of the 'native' shifts. From, say, Rousseau, in the period prior to the French Revolution, who used it as a model of mankind untainted by civilization's vices. Then towards the routine deprecatory view which reaches its rawest presentation in the late nineteenth century – the period in which formal empires were completed. Sachs notes: 'After the French revolution of 1789 the noble savage ceased to be indispensable to the development of European ideas, and further-more the race for the colonies resulted in a hardening of attitudes on the part of the Europeans.'[61] As an ideology it assumes that the Europeans have a 'civilising mission'; and if we wanted a practical elaborated paradigmatic specimen of a 'crude' approach, then this would seem to be the place to start gathering material.

Subsequently this jingoistic stance relaxes. Hetherington,[62] who is looking at the British in particular, reports that the period 1920–40 saw a clear shift in position. From the above-noted straight-forwardly exploitative stance there is a move toward an ethic of responsibility which is now taken as entailing some measure of preparation for eventual separation, and the colonial territories' eventual independence. Curiously enough, looking at this parti-cular episode (actors, time, place) it was the demands of the

German government for the return of 'their' colonies, taken after Versailles, which prodded the British into action. Hetherington notes: 'In the 1920s the colonies were still largely thought of as an extension of Great Britain. . . By the late 1930s the eventual separation of the African colonies . . . could be envisaged.'[63] Though the *pace* of any such *political* change was a matter for debate, it remains the case that few envisaged any profound *economic* change. Davidson sums up the shifts in attitude in the inter-war period in the following way:[64]

> Exactly when the British began thinking seriously of withdrawing their political control from a system whose structural substance could then be conserved by African successors has remained a matter of controversy: in no systematic way, probably, before the end of the 1940s. . . Onwards from the great slump, however, one's impression is that a situation began to shape itself in the minds of leading officials wherein they ought to begin to look for reliable African successors.

There is a further softening of the position in the case of the orthodoxy of the immediate post-war years. I think it would be quite clearly unreasonable to link in any very direct way the proponents of growth and modernization with those jingoistic sentiments noted above. However it seems clear that there is an underlying family resemblance. The modern version of this stance – whose character was noted above – would *deny* that its various theorems were anthropomorphic/anthropocentric, if by this it was understood that an error of some sort were being made. Both growth and modernization theorists argue, or assume, that the developed West is the model (and in saying that I declare that I do not take theories of 'industrialism' or 'convergence' seriously), and that conventional economics – with their Ricardian scheme of specialization and exchange in the international economy – are scientific, and consequently of general application.

It is at this point that critics of these orthodox lines become suspicious that what is in progress is a largely verbal shift – akin to replacing 'backward' with 'developing' – and that what we in fact have is a thoroughly sophisticated reformulation of the jingoistic scheme. Critics point out, quite correctly in my view, that orthodox economics is not scientific in the sense its practitioners would like to (and often do) claim. Neither is the history of the West a simple programme for subsequent nation states to follow. The idea of 'recapitulation' is a nonsense, and the suggestion, drawn from orthodox theories of international economics, that the interests of the West are inevitably helpful to the UDCs, is a proposition to be believed only by those with a strong interest in doing so.[65]

In summary, I take the view that the idea of progress affirmed by these positivist theorists is, of those we shall investigate, by far the most impoverished and implausible. Furthermore I take the mode of theoretical enquiry/engagement utilized by this school to be the least routinely self-critical – methodologically this work is (or aspires to be) policy scientific and comes closest to my model of a 'crude' approach.

3.2   The second presentation of the idea of progress in the post-war period occurs in the context of a revision of the intellectual machineries of the above-noted orthodoxy. There is also a parallel revision of the objectives sought. The idea of progress in this period, and in this distinct theoretical context, is presented in several guises; but it would be beyond the scope of this paper to run down all, or even most, of the variants on what I will present as a common core. I shall refer to two theorists: Myrdal and Furtado. Both of these 'radical' theorists begin with orthodox economics – though in each case the exchange of cited theorist and 'general economic orthodoxy' is quite specific – and reject them for what have been called 'sociologized economics'. Progress is no longer associated with economic growth, called forth by the application of the technical scientific expertise of the economists, but is conceived more broadly: it becomes equated with ordered social reform.[66]

The two schemes that I shall consider are Myrdal's 'world welfareism' and the Latin American school of dependency as it is presented by Furtado. Of these two it can be noted that both are interventionist schemes, seeing it as the business of the theorist to produce, among other things, knowledge of an instrumentally effective kind. However, they do differ. I have called the Myrdalian work the pursuit of an ideology of *co-operative (revised authoritative) interventionism*, and the dependency work of Furtado an ideology of *reactive (populist interpretive) interventionism*. These differences flow from their particular circumstances of production and their differing sets of intellectual resources. It is none the less the case that, while these theoretical departures are distinct, they both share common features and represent, to my mind, considerably richer efforts of social theorizing than those of the economics-dominated orthodoxy.

The notions of progress affirmed by these two theorists – taken as exemplars of their schools – can be elucidated by tracing the revisions to the orthodoxy made by these two thinkers. As restricted explanations of social change, dominated by an intellectually narrow economics, are adjusted, in the light of the contributions of the social sciences generally and the experience of the failure of the orthodoxy either to grasp the scale of the development task or provide any useful insights into it, then the notion of progress affirmed is revised in a parallel fashion. The idea of ordered social reform emerges slowly. This emergence can be traced via three crucial areas of revision to the orthodoxy made by the 'radicals'. These areas of revision are: (1) *problem specificity* – which is affirmed against the pursuit of the (natural scientific) general; (2) *valuation* – the inevitability of valuation in social theorizing is acknowledged, even if it is regarded as problematic; (3) *scientism* – this habit of thinking is less evident.

(1) Problem specificity: here the claims of the orthodox to the effect that they are applying a generally relevant economic science (to the circumstances of the Third World) are denied. The Myrdalian approach is piecemeal, sceptical and pragmatic. There is a resolute insistence upon the pursuit of realism in models. This in turn attaches to the key epistemological notion which is that concepts have ecologies. This to say that a particular concept will work only within certain circumstances and that, consequently, shifting concepts produced in the developed West to the different situation of the UDCs is fraught with difficulties. Indeed new concepts, locally contrived as it were, are needed. A rich knowledge of the problem situation is a prerequisite of the construction of appropriate concepts – any simple 'export' of ready-made 'Western' concepts is far from being the application of established scientific notions; it is rather a gross and fundamental error. The general explanatory strategy, for those in the Myrdalian line, is the pursuit of problem/situation specific formulations and not the search for general theories, or partial statements made in the light of a commitment to such an ideal.

The 'dependency' school of thought takes as one of its starting-points a rejection of the claims of orthodox economics in respect of the generally beneficial nature of 'free' international trade. The revisions made to orthodox economics then proceed through a series of stages until the formal, ahistorical, mathematicized manipulation of formulae is abandoned for the affirmation of a structural, institutional and historical method. This method is claimed – justifiably – to be more appropriate to the circumstances of the UDCs than ever orthodox economics could be. Dependency thus resembles the Myrdalian neo-institutional work in that it begins with the attempt to theorize the situation of particular economies – Latin American: there was a 'pursuit of relevance'. However, paradoxically, the dependency approach ends up with claims being lodged to the effect that dependency is now the first *generally adequate* economics, in contradistinction to the limited scope of the now superseded orthodoxy.

The impact of these revisions of conception upon notions of progress affirmed is fairly clear. The progressive broadening of the explanatory task – from the deployment of technical economic formulae to the interpretive social scientific display of underlying social forms – sees a concomitant enriching of the notion of progress. Progress is not now to be revealed in growth and other statistical indices but rather in the effective changes induced in deformed or moribund social forms.

(2) Valuation: here the claims made by the adherents of orthodox economics to the privileged status of 'experts', with the claimed value-neutrality attached thereto, are denied. These claims are, however, denied in slightly different ways.

Both the neo-institutionalist and dependency lines acknowledge their own engagement in the social processes of which they write. Neither would aspire to the (incoherent) view of the orthodox, that is the extra-social role of the expert. But the proposals made for accommodating to the inevitability of value involvement differ for the neo-institutionalists and the dependency theorists. These differences of treatment can be taken to flow from differences in circumstances of theorizing.

The neo-institutionalist approach can be seen to be lodged within the experience of 'decolonization' (taken here to be a particular 'solution' to the problem of nationalist developmentalism and as *the* model for subsequent aid programmes, and the like). The theorists' concern, typically, is to assist in the reworking of long-established colonial relationships. Power is to be handed over, there is a continuity of governmental procedure, and development is to be ordered authoritatively. The neo-institutionalists write for the reasonable men who are taken to be in charge of the developing states' planning machinery. In this, as in other respects, Myrdal is an appropriate exemplar. However, the scheme's implausibility is acknowledged, in Myrdal, by the presentation of the idea of the 'soft state' – where this is the summation of the reasons why the state cannot play the role accorded to it in the theory. Ehrensaft[67] rightly calls the whole approach Fabian. The position adopted on problems of valuation is an appeal to 'obviousness'. Myrdal speaks of 'crisis politics' where the urgency of the requirements of practical action swamps any doubts about the moral commitments of the theorist. This is Myrdal's way of 'wearing his values on his sleeve' – they are declared, declared to be obvious and unproblematic, and the theorist simply thereafter gets on with the job. Any further problems with 'values' are simply those of avoiding bias, of avoiding smuggling in unannounced values, of avoiding any intellectually polluting 'value seepage'.

With dependency the position is rather different. The injunction to the 'pursuit of relevance' which moved early dependency work admits of a range of development that is different from that which is permitted by the injunction to 'problem specificity' which informed neo-institutionalism. Dependency has a more visibly orthodox intellectual framework than neo-institutionalism. When this is coupled to the theorists' evidently blocked political circumstances – for in Latin America it is typically the right-wing military rather than the reasonable men who are in control of the state – the result is a drift towards generality in formulation of theoretical statements. Thus we have the claims to have replaced the orthodoxy of economics on a general level; and politically we find a general, non-class-specific reformist populism. Value positions affirmed, and the manner of their affirmation, flow out of these circumstances: the material hovers uneasily between an explicit engagement and a technical neutrality.

(3) Scientism: I have argued above that both dependency and neo-institutionalism remain close to the orthodox, 'positivist' view. They do so in that both are empiricst interventionist schemes – though their theorizing is suffused with an appreciation of the social character of that which they study and of their own study of it. Indeed much of what is theoretically characteristic of these efforts flows from the tension between the restrictions they place upon themselves by their respective acknowledgments of the dictates of the orthodox conceptions of science and its extension to the social, on the one hand, and their continuing and central impulse to practical engagement, on the other. This acknowledgment of the problems attendant upon granting the conception of the 'social construction of social theories', so to say (even if it is, as I would claim, a partial acknowledgment), has the effect of blunting the scientism of the orthodoxy which they otherwise do not quite manage to free themselves from. This blunting effect, though it flows largely from revisions to method, has the related consequence of replacing any simple identification of progress with technical economic criteria: the idea of progress broadens along with the theorists' conception of their role.

For the neo-institutionalist and dependency theorists the idea of progress is interpreted as meaning *ordered social reform*. If it is now asked: So where should they be located against the spread of the ideas of progress given above?, then the answer would seem to be that they remain within the line of the orthodoxy. This is the schema of progress which affirms a model of man as consumer and which takes progress to be secured by the (largely) automatic mechanisms of the market: I called it, following Macpherson and Passmore, ethically impoverished and intellectually incoherent.

However, that said, it is clear that while the theorists treated here do remain, in general, with the orthodox position, the particular conceptions of progress affirmed are richer (as are their methodo-

145

logical remarks). Indeed if it were desired to construct a plausible policy science in the area of development studies then these departures must be regarded as prime candidates. Both theoretical lines can be seen as subtle, plausible and humane, even if, in the end, unsatisfactory. And if this judgment seems ambiguous then it reveals, again, my view that social theorizing is always incomplete, partial and tentative, and that this is of the nature of the business – not a measure of its failing.

That the early post-war orthodoxy of development studies could be seen to be unreflexive – 'crude' – in construction was made plain by comparing a series of stages in its development. I noted three: jingoistic, inter-war revised, and present. With the work of the neo-institutionalist and dependency theorists the matter is a little more difficult. I have traced out above, looking at their ideas of progress, three areas in which the methodology of the positivistic orthodoxy was revised. I now look at the methods of the neo-institutionalist and dependency theorists under the headings of conception and intent.

In respect of intent both the neo-institutionalist and dependency theorists would deny any suggestion of favouring the interests of the metropolitan centres. Their work is thus not europocentric, and indeed it is explicitly claimed that their practical interests are in the establishment of new economies, not in the reinforcing or sustaining of the subordinate incorporation of the UDCs in the capitalist world economy. So far as I am presently aware in neither case has this declaration of intent been questioned. There is no suggestion, as there has been in respect of the orthodoxy noted above, that the efforts of the neo-institutionalist and dependency theorists might be taken as (possibly self-deluding) reformulations of an unreflective metropolitan-interest-serving orthodoxy. Both theoretical lines work within the injunction of 'nationalist developmentalism'.

When it comes to the question of conception – that is, notions of explanatory propriety – and my definition of a 'crude' approach, both theoretical lines would reject any claim that their approaches were 'crude'. The nature of the rejections would be different.

With the dependency line, as exemplified in Furtado, there is a progression in formulation from a scientist pursuit of a typology of models of economies and their sectors to the dynamic scheme of dependency with its structural, institutional, and historical method. Furtado, having begun, in a reaction against the orthodoxy of economics, with the 'pursuit of relevance', claims that the dependency scheme offers a *generally adequate economics* in contradistinction to the claims of the orthodox which are now seen as partial. Thus Furtado lodges himself within a realm of discourse which claims to transcend and encompass that orthodoxy which I have taken as the remote inheritors of the jingoistic view of the late nineteenth century. The denial of charges of europomorphism (and europocentrism) is emergent: *now* we have a generally adequate economics.

It is this claim to general adequacy that seems to me to be ambiguous: it is a formulation that is redolent of the scientistic, interventionist, conceptions of that orthodoxy which dependency rejects.

If we turn to Myrdal and his neo-institutionalist approach and look for evidence of sensitivity to the problems attendant upon acknowledging the notion of the social construction of social theories, then we can find it quite easily. This is because Myrdal takes the issue of valuation as one of the key points of departure in his theorizing. This is made quite clear by his exegetist, Streeten.[68] This evidence of reflexivity is at the same time the ground for a denial of europomorphism. Myrdal would claim that his efforts are free of any taint of the illicit importation of foreign concepts, of dispositions, as his epistemic starting-point was the idea of concepts having ecologies and his procedure was problem-specific. In terms of the dispositions the position taken would be one of the *obviousness* of welfarism in crisis politics.

Once again it seems that this is an ambiguous effort. The epistemology is an elaborately revised empiricism and is unpersuasive. So too is the idea that appealing to the obviousness of courses of action in times of crisis is a satisfactory resolution of the problems attendant upon deploying the politico-ethical term 'development'. Myrdal may claim to be free of the taint of unreflexiveness, but to the extent that his effort is justly called Fabian – as Ehrensaft jibes – then to that extent the work must be 'tainted' because Fabianism is evidently a circumstance specific policy science.

However, even after entering these caveats in respect of the precise status of neo-institutionalist and dependency theory, it still remains the case that both departures represent a marked distancing from the positivistic orthodoxy noted, and from what is implied by my model of the 'crude'.

In summary, I take the idea of progress affirmed by this group, in their different ways, to be the most readily acceptable of all those I shall review. That is to say I regard the idea of 'progress-as-social-reform' as representing the common sense of much of development studies. It is undoubtedly a much richer idea of progress than that which was presented by the earlier theorists reviewed above. Yet it still remains within that familiar liberal democratic line which, on my reading, Passmore and Macpherson between them would regard as incoherent and impoverished.

A similarly cautious judgment is repeated in the context of my review of their methods – with both groups we find theoretical approaches which are centrally concerned with government's role in the ordering of development. Once again it can be suggested that this bids fair to be understood as the common sense of development studies. However, that said, we should not let ourselves become blind to the defects of these approaches in order, as their proponents might well say, 'to get on with the job'.

3.3 I have argued above that the particular work of the classical political economists, and in particular Marx, constitutes the paradigm case of prospective and general social theorizing – of the construction of a delimited and formal ideology. I have also claimed that the marxian tradition continues the main thread of argument from the career of the idea of perfection/progress. It does so by presenting a notion of democracy as entailing 'the free development of all' and by treating the occasion/realization of democracy as having a natural guarantor in the historical dialectic of class conflict. The notion of progress affirmed is, in brief, both intellectually coherent and ethically rich.

I take the classical-marxian mode of enquiry to be, routinely, *engaged*. That is to say its value orientation suffuses it and requires effective deployment. The idea of the unity of theory and practice demands that moral commitment, so to say, be practically developed. With regard to this injunction to practicality, the theoretical mode adopted is that of categorial analysis of the social situation – thus the intellectual/ethical machineries called upon in enquiry are (again routinely) *displayed* and *reviewed*. It is thus apparent that the classical line is the antithesis of any 'crude' effort: that is, an explicitly revolutionary, or critical, theory and practice is affirmed.

It can be noted that while this mode of enquiry may be the antithesis of the 'crude', there is no basis for any claim to be lodged to the effect that the stance can be made free of the circumstances of its production. This style of theorizing requires a thoroughgoing reflexivity. Theorizing is located self-consciously in society and history. It is this reflexivity that, so far as I can see, is the basis of the claims that can be made for this approach in contrast to those approximating to my model of the 'crude': that last-mentioned position is, so to say, turned inside out.

The history of marxian analyses should, in the light of this conception of it, appear as a history of the circumstances of theorizing. Marxian theorizing I want to claim should always appear as a circumstance-specific and problem-centred deployment of fundamental explanatory categories. If it does not, then we may suspect that something has gone awry.

Palma[69] identifies three major efforts of marxian analysis of the exchange of 'rich' and 'poor'. First, the work of Marx and Engels themselves who treat 'capitalism as a historically progressive system. . . which will spread through the backward nations by a continual process of destruction and replacement of pre-capitalist structures.'[70] Second, the work of the original theorists of imperialism: schemes presented in the circumstances of attempts to grasp the situation of Russia as a 'backward' state. Capitalism is taken as progressive but altered in its effects by the dictates of monopoly. By the 1920s the emphasis in theorizing had switched to the idea that post-colonial change might be blocked by metropolitan monopoly capital in alliance with local bourgeoisie. Third, the neo-marxism of the post-war period. Now capitalism is no longer taken as progressive. In the metropolitan centres 'crisis management' seems to offer to guarantee an irrational longevity, and the peripheral areas are condemned to subordinate incorporation. The political implications for the 'poor' are that disengagement from the world capitalist system is the prerequisite of planned socialist development, which is now the only available route into the modern world.

In respect of what Palma has identified as the third major marxian attempt to theorize the Third World I am presenting the last group of theorists who make up my schematic history of post-war development studies. In looking at this group I will pick out the major line of enquiry, that is, the 'orthodoxy' of neo-marxism, as it were. Palma distinguishes three lines within neo-marxism: a Baran-inspired line; a revision of the ECLA position; and the work of Cardoso. It is the Baran-inspired work that I shall consider here.[71]

In respect of the idea of progress affirmed by the neo-marxists, it seems to me to be quite clear that this is, of those I have looked at, by far the richest – at least on the face of it. Not only is the idea of progress richest, but it is also made integral to their analyses. In the case of Baran, who is usually regarded as the 'father' of this approach, a notion of economic surplus is used as a measure of the over-all level of functioning of the economy. Social forms are then ranked according to how rational is the realization of their economic surplus and how humane its allocation through society. Monopoly capitalism with its militarism, imperialism and inegalitarian consumerism is deemed both irrational and inhumane.

The impact of monopoly capitalism in its peripheral areas is treated by noting its socially and economically deforming misuse of locally generated economic surplus. Subordinate incorporation is the fate of the peripheral areas and the possibility of an autonomous capitalism and thereafter some higher social form is blocked.

The whole line of enquiry adopted by Baran, and subsequent theorists in this line, is an argument for socialist planning as the only presently available route to economic and social rationality, for both central and peripheral areas: and with the latter this requires disengagement.

The extent to which neo-marxism actually is marxist has been a subject of intense debate. It is a debate that bears upon my present concerns. The critics on the left have tended to suggest that the schemes of Baran (and those who have followed his lead) are those of an 'idealist left Keynesian'. Aggregative economics is used in conjunction with the sentiments of a liberal reformer. In similar vein, Palma has argued that the work of A. G. Frank is essentially orthodox in that he (Frank) tries to build a general 'mechanico-formal' model[72] of the process of the underdevelopment of the periphery. Palma suggests that this is, in a relevant sense, tantamount to an inversion of the orthodox economics view. It is the extent to which the work of the neo-marxists actually manages to be problem-specific and reflexive that is being called into question. There is, it seems, a strong suspicion that what is happening with neo-marxism is that a radical (moral) disapproval is, when explicitly theorized, tending towards a retrogressive collapse to the descriptive general.

This all raises important questions in respect of the precise status of neo-marxism with reference to both the marxian tradition and the proper theorizing of the Third World. Yet for the present I would still affirm that *within the particular context of my enquiries here,* that is, broad comparative evaluation resting upon a schematic history, neo-marxism represents the richest idea of progress (a transformation of an irrational and degraded polity into a rational and humane one) and deploys the subtlest scheme of analysis (in that it treats the dynamic of the world historical development of the capitalist system). The issue of the extent to which Baran, and his followers, either have or have not got their analyses right (i.e. 'really' marxian) is not an issue that I wish to pursue here.[73] Although it does seem to me that, given the difficulties of the issues tackled, any quick decision to the effect that Baran is 'left Keynesian' and therefore to be dismissed is unhelpful.

4.0 I began this chapter by noting that the idea of development is, typically, taken for granted: the notion is seen as *technical* or *obvious* or both. I undertook to show that, on the contrary, it was an ethico-political term whose deployment, in matters of theorizing the Third World, entailed definite presumptions in respect of goals, procedures for attaining these, and explanatory strategies informing action.

It was from Gellner that I took the central claim that theories of progress are central to the 'legitimating myths' of modern societies. Current ideas of progress have been sedimented in discourse by long chains of philosophical and socially practical activity. This history I reviewed and distilled to a doubly characterized pair of ideas which I asserted could be seen to set the limits of subsequent debate in the late nineteenth and twentieth centuries. These were: (a) the orthodox liberal democratic idea of progress which, I argued (following Passmore and Macpherson), was intellectually incoherent and ethically impoverished; and (b) the (radical) democratic idea of progress which I argued, in a similar fashion, was intellectually coherent and ethically rich. To this device for ordering my particular explorations of the material of the post-war career of development studies I added a similar one treating, albeit in an even simpler way, methods of explanation, arguing that the more systematically and routinely reflexive social theorizing is then the better it is.

The post-war career of development studies can be taken to comprise a series of intellectual departures: in my terms, efforts of ideology construction.

The theorists of the earliest period presented, in two principal versions, ideologies of authoritative intervention. Development was conceived as the social scientifically ordered establishment of market economy based liberal democracy. Progress is taken as (economic) growth and as evidenced by authoritatively engendered movements in social scientific indices. The ethics are impoverished and the explanatory strategy crude.

The theorists of the middle period of my history revise both methods and ethics. In doing so, they present what I think is probably the common sense of development studies. It is a humane and plausible scheme. The idea of progress affirmed is broadened. In place of growth we find ordered social reform. The methodological strategies are softened. In place of positivistic schemes we find 'sociologized economics'. The basic approach, which presents itself in distinct guises as I pointed out, is co-operative in spirit. The intellectual tools of the West are to be modified, perhaps radically, to fit the particular problem situations of the UDCs as they embark upon their own processes of industrialization.

In the final part of my historical schema I presented the neomarxian work inspired by Paul Baran. Taking note that this area of theoretical enquiry is riven by conflicting positions, I declared that, so far as could be seen, it was *this* school that presented the ethically richest idea of progress and the most intellectually coherent scheme. We have an idea of progress as the maximization of democracy and it is to be secured, or at least moved toward, by practical activity informed by a marxian political economy.

What are the general lessons to be taken from this memorandum on commitments? They centre, so far as I can see, upon the assertion of an undeniably *practical* core to social theorizing.

151

It seems to me that despite the scientist orthodoxy, which increasingly seems unspoken and left to the common sense of social science, *all* social theorizing is suffused with value judgment. Charles Taylor[74] has the useful phrase, 'value-sloped', to catch that characteristic of *any* theoretical frame whereby the frame secretes a disposition to approve/disapprove before ever a particular episode/event/case is considered directly. This now strikes me as being so well established – Taylor was writing in 1967 – as to have attained the status of a truism. If social theorists are to produce intellectually plausible work, then it would seem that this point had best be embraced. The scientist common sense of social science continually invites us to backslide. This temptation is made all the more attractive as it accords so well with habits of thought widespread in our culture. If we would produce defensible social scientific work then we had best resist this temptation to slide into the scientist neglect of crucial elements of our own arguments.

Following on from this general point and looking directly at the career of development studies, it seems that it is foolish to try to make development either technical or obvious. If we are talking about the efforts of one group (whoever they might be – academics, civil servants, managerial staffs of multi-nationals, or revolutionary guerrilla groups) to theorize the circumstances of a particular part of the Third World, then if we wish to present an intellectually adequate story then we needs must take note of the *interests informing those specimens of theorizing we treat.* Blandly assuming that the common sense judgments our own cultural background disposes us to make are unproblematic entails (at least the possibility of) doing violence to the views taken by others.

Similarly, and reflexively, academics, it would seem, need to consider the nature of their own valuations and the audiences they address. At the end of the day academic social theorizing is a socially located activity, and our return to the 'real world' must be consistent with general claims made about social theorizing *per se.* This seems to imply that the claims of academically based theorists must be *restricted*: if there are no 'general theories' (as the orthodoxy would in some way claim), we are forced back to the role of commentary: the examination of arguments.

I said in chapter 2 that social theorists, wherever they are located, must pay attention to what it *makes sense to say or do.* For academics, writing on development studies in a more or less detached fashion, in an unremarked atmosphere of scientist descriptive accommodation to the facts, it is all too easy to slide toward the production of general schemes.

It seems to me that neo-marxists should affirm these points *against* the familiar lexicon of Althusserian condemnation.

Further, it seems to me that what is *going to count* as development, if that term is ethico-political, in a practical and engaged sense will inevitably depend upon circumstance-sensitive and problem-specific analyses or actions. The idea of development represents, loosely, an orientating frame. I cannot see that any useful purpose can be served by trying to establish a *fixed set* of criteria of progress. If social theorizing is practical, then what is to count as development will have to be locally determined. We can step back and rank such efforts against the standards I have presented.

The above point can be represented in the following fashion. In the circumstances of the Third World, what is to count as development will be a negotiated meaning among those groups involved. It is not a term that can be given any fixed sense and thereafter just simply imposed. It is not technical, and it certainly is not obvious.

7   The common sense of development studies: elements of reconsideration

1.0   Work relating to the areas of concern which can be subsumed under the heading of 'development' has now been in progress, in its 'modern' guise, for nearly forty years.[1] The output of material has been vast. Inevitably the presentation of any retrospective and synthetic survey will involve a large measure of simplification. This seems acceptable: we appropriate 'the past' in order to make sense of the present and set tentative agendas for the future. And it seems to me that within the diversely theorized field of 'development' there is a discernible element of reconsideration taking place: an attempt to take stock. In this essay I want to explore some elements of this process.

   As a route into these matters I shall identify three ways of appropriating the past of studies on development. I shall speak of three – not mutually exclusive – motifs within that history. I shall begin with what seems to me to be a relatively minor motif: the attempt to constitute an autonomous discipline; move from there to a major theme: the construction of a series of ideologies; and, finally, I shall note that the career of development studies can be read as a progressive movement away from a technical 'ghetto' back into the 'mainstream' of the concerns of social science. All this, let us note, will be by way of an introduction to my main concern with the reworking of the 'basics' of studies of development now, arguably, in train.

1.1   I have argued elsewhere[2] that the post-World War II period has seen the attempt to constitute an autonomous discipline of development studies. Autonomous in the intra-social sense of being one distinct social science among others; and autonomous in the extra-social sense of the study having its own external object and methods of enquiry appropriate thereto. This, clearly, is a strategy of conceptualization which is informed by the 'received model' of natural scientific explanation, and there are direct links to practical engagement which can now be noted with the familiar term 'policy science'.

I further argued that this attempt to constitute an autonomous discipline was identifiable in orthodox work, growth theory and modernization theory, where matters of development were conceived (variously) as an extension of positive economic science. I then went on to claim that it was with neo-institutional work, and some dependency work (in particular, Furtado), that claims to autonomous status were most forcefully and persuasively made.

In neo-marxian work, and in the products of some of its 'left' critics, there is an analogous concern. I can introduce this 'analogous concern' by indicating the nature of the 'received model' that is at work within these marxian enquiries. Thus it can be noted that the received model of the orthodox, 'bourgeois', theorists is primarily (on the claims of the practitioners) epistemological; that is, positivistic, and the interventionist policies just flow from this. In contrast, in the case of the marxists, the received model at work is, so far as I can presently see, both political and epistemic (again on the claims of the practitioners). More specifically I find the celebration of the idea of 'the one revolutionary mode' and, further, a residually scientistic analytical approach.

Clearly, the general resemblances between 'bourgeois' and 'marxist' in respect of the 'pursuit of autonomy'/'presentation of a latent orthodox' have to be treated cautiously. The differences between the two approaches are profound, and likely to become ever more clearly appreciated as both delve into their intellectual and social histories.

When I speak of the attempt to constitute an autonomous discipline, it will be the bourgeois theorists that I have in view. The marxists I shall read as adopting an analogous position which flows from a failure of the reflexivity (of theory and practice) one would have expected them to display.

Returning to the business of the attempt to constitute an autonomous discipline of development studies, it is my view that the attempt failed. It failed for two general sets of reasons.

The first was the project's own inherent implausibility: the attempt (made by academic theorists, technical experts in government and international agencies, plus a host of miscellaneous commentators) to characterize authoritatively the major elements of the process of transition to the modern world and to lay claim to particular, technical manipulative, expertise in respect of these identified elements was doomed to failure, it seems to me, from the outset. The over-all problem area was both too complex and of interest to too many diversely located groups for it to be amenable

155

to the process of reduction of attention and focusing of enquiry which must be necessary to the constitution of a 'discipline'. Failure was built into the project design.

A second area of explanation for this failure is to be found in the success that repeated enquiry had in occasioning refinement of argument. From the narrowly economics-based work of the 'committee of experts'[3] in 1951 there was refinement of argument, in concert with extensive practical experience, along two axes. First we can identify a fairly obvious *spread* of enquiry. The work of a wide range of social sciences was called upon in the efforts to theorize development. Second there was a process of increasing *depth* of enquiry. By this I do not mean the refinement of technical detail; it was, rather, the increasing reflexivity of enquiry that was important.

And when we put together this dual process of refinement, then, it seems to me, the upshot is that 'development studies' is tending to move back into the main-stream of social theorizing. As regards the marxists, the analogous move is clear: in much recent marxian work there has been great concern to identify the core of a properly marxian analysis of development and underdevelopment. The matters which students of 'development' now typically address are those which exercised the 'founding fathers': widespread and pervasive social change and the extent to which it can be comprehended and its direction made subject to human will. The self-consciousness of students of development now coincides with that of other social scientists: it revolves round the continuing effort to clarify the nature of social theorizing. In slightly over three decades the project first enunciated by the 'committee of experts', as a technical matter, has reached a point of being poised to crumble back into social philosophy. The question thus arises: Where does all this leave the community of (academic) students of development and the problems they have typically addressed?

At the outset it can be said that it does *not* leave them with a crisis, and it is not my intention in this essay to offer any such declamatory announcement. There are two reasons for eschewing such a course of action, of which the first is stylistic. More important, I do not think that a notion of crisis fits into a plausible metatheory of social theorizing. The business of social theorizing presents itself in diverse guises. The generic notion of 'making sense' has to be unpacked in a variety of historical/social/economic/political locations and this view holds for development studies. The range of interests in matters of development is very broad – to speak of a general crisis would be absurd. To speak of a series of crises would be both theatrical and false. I do not think either that it is helpful or correct to speak of a particular crisis (in, say, the work of those who most enthusiastically affirmed the autonomous status of development studies). Rather I would speak of a diffuse pattern of reconsideration. Thus, out of the range of modes of engagement with matters of development, I think we can now pick out some impulses to reconsider, in the 'depth' noted above, the familiar assumptions of development studies. These impulses are evidenced in academic commentary, though the extent of reconsideration may, of course, be much broader.

1.2 The idea of reconsideration is helpful in attempting to grasp and contribute to present discussion of development. It is so because it is a non-apocalyptic term which allows for the acknowledgment of both the tentativeness of my claims and the multiple ways in which the process could be occurring.

Discussions of development can be characterized in several ways. One such is to distinguish 'bourgeois' and 'marxist' approaches. Resting, for the moment, upon this useful (if misleading) shorthand, we can see that it is possible to select texts, treating matters of development from these positions, which reveal that over the last few years confidence in respect of the adequacy of the various characterizations of development has been in decline. (It is possible here to distinguish between theoretical doubts and practical doubts: that is to say, the 'real world' process of development has routinely been scrutinized and 'found wanting' in this or that respect whereas fundamental theoretical constructions have not been similarly inspected.) The ready suppositions of the orthodox, bourgeois, theorists centred upon the view that the business of development was clearly 'obvious' and 'technical'. Empiricist social scientific enquiry was adequate to the task of preparing authoritative knowledge for the use of state planning agencies in pursuit of the uncontentious goal of adjusting the patterns of life of the presently disadvantaged in line with standards holding in the industrialized areas. Equally confident were the 'marxists': thus development was taken to be a quite clearly political matter. Critical enquiry identified the bifurcation of the world into exploitative metropolitan capitalist centres and exploited peripheral regions – the official communist bloc constituted an ambiguous and massive special case – with the practical political implication of the pursuit (variously conceived) of autonomy (again variously conceived).

We can identify a series of texts which indicate a diminution of confidence in such straightforward positions. Further, these texts do not merely offer exercises in either unfocused or narrowly practical reflection but, I think, clearly tend to look to central traditions (substantive and formal) of social theory.

It is not my intention in this paper to attempt to map the present extent, and depth, of reflection *via* a series of critical commentaries upon particular texts, but none the less a few such texts can usefully be mentioned in order to confirm/illustrate my general contentions. The following constitute an unsystematically generated group. There may well be anticipations and adumbrations[4] in earlier/other work.

Thus the earliest text I would cite is that of Ernest Gellner: in his *Thought and Change* (1964) he addresses the business of theorizing development directly in his attempts to provide an intelligent grounding for modernization/industrialism. It would seem that this sophisticated and sceptical work was too far ahead of its time, for it is now rarely referred to. It is certainly true that the sophisticated modernization theory which Gellner pointed to never was constructed. However, the one thoroughly thoughtful scheme which 'bourgeois' theorizing did produce – neo-institutionalism – also involved a routinized self-scrutiny. The reflexive scepticism of theorists such as Myrdal, Streeten and Seers, while usually oriented to producing a technically better mode of essentially orthodox theorizing, has also thrown up evidence of more general doubt. Seers wrote a classic paper on conceptualizing development as long ago as 1963,[5] and Streeten has run together philosophical material with development material in much of his work.[6]

Other evidence of a mood of reflection can be found in the strategy of enquiry into the discipline's history. Thus Brookfield,[7] or again, and with reference to political science issues, Kitching.[8]

Turning to avowedly marxian work, there is a plethora of texts that might be illustratively invoked. In the process of the general rediscovery of the marxian tradition during the 1970s, the work of Paul Baran in respect of development was extensively discussed. Often it has been the work of A.G. Frank, which drew upon Latin American work and used the frame of Baran, that has drawn most attention. Argument has centred upon the issue of what is to count as a properly marxian analysis of the circumstances of the Third World. Recent debates have resulted in the situation that any so-called 'marxian' enquiry would first have to settle a whole series of issues in respect of, roughly speaking, just how the legacy of Marx was to be appropriated. Frank himself, whose own corpus of work neatly illustrates my claims in respect of the diversity of social-theoretic modes, in a recent text (comprising earlier material) has evidenced the process of reconsideration most directly. Thus *Dependent Accumulation and Underdevelopment* (1978) seeks to rework the legacy of the classical political economists (including Marx). Doubtless other texts could be cited and better characterized. However, it is enough for the present that assent be given to the plausibility of my claims.

Reconsideration of the nature of the project of development studies is, as I have claimed above, one element of current work on development. Modes of engagement are diverse and I can speak only (here) of some trends in (academic) commentary. This reconsideration is also, itself, 'work in progress'. I have contributed one text addressed to this concern and I do not now wish to attempt to anticipate the outcomes of this reconsideration. What I am interested in investigating in this paper is the question of the nature of the *common sense* of what I see as a disintegrating development studies. This is both an area of enquiry the pursuit of which will contribute – indirectly – to the reconsideration in progress and an area of enquiry which follows on from my earlier work (just how, is elucidated below).

1.3 The post-war career of development studies can be read in several ways. Above I have made reference to the attempt to constitute an autonomous discipline: a project which failed and has resulted in a disposition to reconsideration. A similar disposition is visible in the work of those within the marxian tradition. This pursuit of an 'autonomous discipline'/'latent orthodoxy' is, as I noted at the outset, a subsidiary motif in the history of the career of development studies. I want now to introduce a major one. This will serve as a corrective to any reading of the post-war career of development studies which is inclined to draw upon the 'received model' and thus be encouraged to look for a spurious coherence.

Thus it seems to me that this career can much more plausibly be analysed in terms of the construction of a series of 'schools'. I have argued that it is both possible and useful to identify five such schools. The process of the construction of these schools I have discussed elsewhere.[9] However, what I have not treated is the subsequent pattern of decay of these various positions. My purpose here is to discover whether the decay of these particular schools has generated any legacy of widely accepted ideas – a *'residual common sense'* of development studies.

The attempt to institutionalize discourse in this substantive area upon the basis of affirming the 'received model'[10] may have failed, but none the less the set of problems addressed (now liable to reformulation) remains. Development studies is now to be seen as just that which students of development actually do study. In this period of diffuse reconsideration I want, in this paper, to focus on one aspect of the multiple patterns and complex process of the decay of schools. I do not intend even to sketch a history of these patterns and processes. Instead I shall seek to identify familiar notions within the ambit of development studies and attempt to relate those to particular schools. It can then be asked whether or not these identifiable elements are widely used or assumed. If we can identify such a stock of ideas, we have discovered, on the face of it, something of the residual common sense of development studies.

159

This indicates how this paper flows from my earlier work. The contribution to the claimed process of reconsideration can be indicated as follows. The fruitful legacy of development studies, or its fatal flaws, will be found in those ideas which have commanded widespread assent from theorists: either way, the process of reconsideration can only be aided by an attempt to elucidate that set of ideas.

The patterns of concerns which are to be revealed, and the nature of the debate which is generated when the hitherto assumed is problematized, presents us with a third synthetic motif. The career of development studies entails a progressive shift from a narrowly technical enquiry detached from the concerns of the main-stream of the social scientific tradition back into that main-stream. Indeed this motif recalls the claims I have associated elsewhere[11] with Gellner and Hilal: the issue of development recalls the work of the 'founding fathers' in terms of the breadth of scope, complexity of elements and demanding urgency of the problems addressed.

In sum, in this essay I want to see if we can identify a residual common sense in discussions about development and then go on to ask whether these common sense elements actually help or hinder the theorists' appreciation of the process of development and of the ways in which it may be engaged with.

2.0   Above I have identified a trio of motifs whereby the long and complex history of development theorizing might be grasped in a single synthesizing move. I remarked that this inevitably involved a large measure of simplification. This problem is repeated here. I do not wish to undertake a detailed survey of patterns of decay of schools and identify, piece by piece, their contribution to a residual common sense. That sort of approach would be, I suspect, disproportionate to the value of the product. Instead I will offer another, possibly rather more impressionistic, synthesizing motif and use it as a thread upon which to hang a variety of particular reflections.

The motif which I think runs through much of the work produced in the last forty years is that of the *assumption of responsibility*. This assumption of responsibility is made by academic theorists, agency officials and other commentators. It relates to the production of theories, presentation of policies, and – for First Worlders – the behaviour of their national states. Routinely we find a variegated pattern of intellectuals assuming these styles of responsibility. Familiarly this 'responsibility' is conjoined with the presentation of general programmes of development.

It is not very hard to fathom the reasons for this approach. A knowledge of circumstances, a supposition of requisite expertise and an appropriate ethic logically entail action. Streeten[12] has eloquently reviewed the early days of development studies: in the wake of World War II there was a realization of the extent of poverty and, it was thought, its amenability to ameliorative action. Coupled to the reformist ethic of First World social scientists, the pursuit, once initiated by political needs, of authoritative and interventionist strategies of development flowed automatically.

It rather seems to me that there has been a triple change of mind in this area: in respect of the claims to knowledge that would be made in the area of development, increasing sophistication makes for modesty of claims; in respect of claims to expertise – who would now even vaguely think of calling for *carte blanche* for the economic planners (or any group of planners) as did the committee of experts?; finally, a salutary doubt in respect of ethics has emerged – from naive orthodoxies of growth through arguably equally naive orthodoxies of socialist disengagement through to an awareness of the multiplicity and complexity of stances than can be taken up.[13] So, in sum, the hitherto accepted triune claim to knowledge, expertise and moral vision is now in respect of each element open to question.

2.1 The first area of concern that I wish to investigate revolves round the idea of intervention. That this idea should figure so crucially in studies of development is not surprising. The idea was available within the historically recent experience of the DCs. In the political-intellectual realm there had been the experience of the USSR – successful and influential argues Clairmonte[14] – and, pre-eminently, for the First World the work of Keynes. It is with the name of that great economist that in the First World the legitimacy of planning can be associated. Keynes made it respectable and safe. In the economic realm the requirement of planning was systemic. The nature of the capitalist system had, by the 1930s, clearly entered into a period of change and while the upshot has been variously labelled – monopoly capitalism, advanced capitalism, welfare capitalism – the key to these changes resides in the dual process of economic concentration (private and public sector monopolies dominating a residual, if extensive, market sector) and state direction.

So extensive has the role of the state become in monopoly capitalism, so pervasive its involvement in the lives of its citizens, so routinized the pressure to a technocratic politics, that the possibilities of a reconstruction of the public sphere – the key to a politics adequate for modern society – have become a principal concern for the inheritor of the mantle of the Frankfurt School, Jürgen Habermas. And here is the crucial, and for my purposes relevant, point: the perceptions of the role of the state as planning machine have become increasingly jaundiced. This realization of the essential ambiguity of the system-sustaining role of the monopoly capitalist state has not been restricted to Habermas or to the work of those for whom the line he inherits has been influential. However, it seems fair to report that it was with the New Left in Europe and the USA in the late 1960s and early 1970s that consciousness of the manipulative, restricted, competence of the technocratic planning state was first fully enunciated. And in saying this I am quite aware that I neglect the thought associated with Hayek, Popper and the Friedmanite New Right in the US and elsewhere: atavistic celebrations of laissez-faire capitalism are no substitute for intellectual creativity, as is daily becoming clearer as the present depression continues and deepens.

Within the context of work upon the business of the development of the LDCs a similar pattern can be observed. Where we have at the outset a strong – indeed in retrospect ludicrous – confidence in the skills of the economic planners, we can trace a complex pattern of reconsideration. To be sure a significant element of such a history would be of increasingly subtle and powerful analytical, programming and decision-making strategies. None the less this post-war celebration of authoritative intervention has been based upon what seems to me to be an eventually untenable conception of the relationship of social scientifically informed experts to their social world. A belief in the real possibility of a 'science of the social' goes hand in hand, on historical evidence, with a disposition to force recalcitrant social reality into pre-expected forms when plan schemes go awry. Authoritative planning can quickly collapse into authoritarian politics. This is undoubtedly a part of the message of the First World New Left. Within the context of development studies these doubts have moved in two areas – related but distinct. In the first place, doubt has crept in in respect of the claims of the planners; claims have been modified, sights lowered, expectations brought under control. All these in respect of the business of planning development. The related area, and one suspects the place where doubt first arose, centres upon the perceived 'interference' of First World and international agencies – notoriously, IMF and World Bank – in the affairs of putatively sovereign nation states.

Paradoxically it can be, and has been, argued that this sensitivity to outside interference has occasioned responses which serve to render practical development theorizing (i.e. concrete, circumstance-specific rather than academic or legalistic general) only more remote from its context and less effective. Thus the shift of complex patterns of bilateral discussions of aid/development up to the UN level, and the extent to which Third World solidarity actually has been, or could be, achieved and what thereafter might be expected, has been subject to much debate. The endless UN conferences must have had some impact on development processes, but Quite what? would not be an easy question to answer.

Shifting now from direct review of the notion of planning, I can present another element to add to the thread of assumed responsibility. This point is related to the last one. Alongside ideas of planning (authoritative, central, expert direction) have gone, in the First World at least, schemes of ethics we can label 'liberal good will'. Above, I cited growth and modernization theory as emphatically authoritative interventionist, in the present context it is probably safe to cite, as 'best example' of liberal good will, the work of the neo-institutionalists. More than a few commentators have remarked that it is here – in the work of Myrdal especially – that the orthodox line presents itself in its most pleasing guise.

I have analysed the character of the neo-institutionalist effort elsewhere,[15] and do not propose to repeat those observations here. Suffice it to say that with that line we find the clearest coincidence of the regulative state control of business with an ethic of ordered social reform. Power is to pass to the 'reasonable men' in control of the state machine and progress is conceived in what Passmore[16] calls 'governmentalist' terms. In this tradition what is to count as development is read as specifiable in terms of the enlightened role of government programmes of reforms. However, this supposition of the general specifiability of what is to count as development must be called into question. As I argued in chapter 6, notions of progress must, in the light of the marxian-associated rediscovery of specificity in social-theoretic engagement, be locally determined. What is to count as development in any particular situation will depend precisely upon the future possibilities of that situation – an apriori ethic is not helpful. At this point, then, I echo the marxian dismissal of 'bourgeois morals'.

These two elements come together in the injunction, expressing my motif of the assumption of responsibility, that 'we should do something for them'. Indeed there is evidence that this attitude has been taken on board by Third World thinkers and leaders – the claim that First Worlders owe the Third World for past incursions. It seems to me to be an untenable position, and I shall come to it later in the context of a note on 'nationalist developmentalism'. For the moment, it is enough to note that while that attitude was widely shared (by First and Third Worlders) early in the career of development studies, clearly it is of little practical use to invoke such an ethic today. Thus we could plausibly claim that continued discussion about 'resource transfers' is, at the general level, not much more than ritual.

It might be objected at this point that this discussion is flawed by an apparent contradiction: on the one hand I am pointing to the way in which capitalism has changed from 'competitive liberal' to 'monopoly' with the associated system-engendered extension of regulative planning which must be presumed to have been successful to some extent, as the system survives; while on the other hand I am insisting on the extent to which the notion of authoritative intervention, planning, has been over-stressed. More strongly I have said that the idea upon which it rests, a genuine science of the social, is untenable.

Now it is true that the fundamental root of authoritative interventionist schemes of planning is incoherent – there can be no natural science of the social – but the wider debate about just what has been going on in fact under the rubric of planning is less a matter of debate about the nature of social science than a question of how that wrong conception has found extension in the social world. Real world planning systems are ambiguous phenomena; more particularly they have, properly, to be regarded as political phenomena. Planning systems are, it seems to me, central to our modern polities, and their usual technocratic ideology is, as Habermas has pointed out, a most subtle false consciousness.[17]

This general issue can be illustratively pursued by asking, just how effective has interventionist planning been in securing major change? The complex problems of development can here be set aside; we can look instead at change within the DCs, an inherently more simple task, one would think.

If one casually reviews the twentieth-century history of the DCs, the striking thing is that major change seems to have been systemic-historical, so to say, and not the result of planning-type political initiatives: more particularly, change has coalesced around the nexus of war. Thus we see that the dissolution of formal empires flowed from the disintegrating impact of World War II (and, in not a few cases, required a local war to secure). Similarly, associated with the two World Wars is the matter of German liberal democracy – that system was implanted in (West) Germany only as a result of the wars. Or, again, one can call attention to the rise of the modern USSR in the wake of the collapse of Tsarist Russia. In the realm of economics – where we start to meet what are routinely taken as systemic matters (or familiar patterns of evidence routinely taken as fairly directly related thereto) – the shift in the balance of economic power, within the First World, in favour of the USA is clearly related to the disturbances of war. It was World War II that enabled Keynesian remedies to the systemic collapse of liberal capitalism to be brought into effect. In the UK, for example, the whole edifice of the 'Welfare State' owes its emergence to the social upheaval that attended the war.

The general point seems to be this: social systems, patterns of life, have massive inertia. Myrdal has noted this.[18] So too has Allen,[19] who speaks of social change being intermittent; progressive advance is irregular and, in the absence of overriding reasons (cf. Myrdal's insistence upon the idea of crisis[20]), actually contriving a constituency for a major change within society seems to be extraordinarily difficult.

So, to return to the point at issue – the important place in development studies work of authoritative intervention, planning – it would seem that if the extent of the effectiveness of planning initiatives are in doubt in DCs, then there seems to be less reason to rely upon them in LDCs where the whole business of contriving development is a hugely complex matter. I would say that it seems as if three difficulties are being compounded: (a) the intrinsic difficulty of theorizing development; (b) the problems of dubiously effective machineries; (c) the problems of the shift of context between 'forms of life' when it is insisted that 'we ought to do something for them'. In general, then, it seems as if this mental set might well have resulted in claims and proposals which are only poorly intellectually grounded as well as being paternalistic.

Perhaps we should now regard this orthodoxy as the product of a particular concatenation of circumstances, politics and ideas specific to the post-World War II period: a particular 'historical juncture' now past. Further than this, and in line with the arguments thus far presented in these essays, the position could be abandoned in favour of an insistence upon specificity of enquiry. Thus we focus upon the particular patterns of action/interaction within a given social form. We ask just what is going on and what might be done and by whom. Enquiry within development studies must identify particular lines of responsibility – resting content with prescriptions made within the framework of a 'generalized presumption of responsibility' seems to me to be an untenable position.

2.2 What I have claimed above can be represented thus: the habit of thought of interventionism engenders an overgeneral style of enquiry. The complexity of the process of development is obscured and, more crucially (because here we shift out of the frame of identifying factors which can, usually wrongly, be taken as technical complexities), the variety of particular interests in the process is obscured, as is, finally, the variety of ways of making sense of it, of engaging with it. I have argued in chapter 6 that the idea of development is an ethico-political one: the interventionists rather seem to suppose either (a) that the rest of the world shares their view or (b) that if they don't, it is all so self-evidently 'correct' that simple informative exercises will suffice to secure adherence. I think the world is rather more complex than this.

Closely related to the interventionist line is a 'spirit of optimism': my slogan summary can be reworked as follows. To the injunction 'we ought to do something' is added the phrase 'and we can'. Now in this section I am going over ground that has been covered already. What I want to bring out is the optimism of the orthodox line at this time. (The marxian line, to anticipate, was also optimistic – they too were wrong.) This optimism was very strong; so Brookfield[21] can remark, of modernization theory in particular, that the confidence shown in the possibility of securing growth is now (i.e. in the late 1970s) hard to credit. Streeten, writing in 1981, observes: 'It is not easy to convey, in the present atmosphere of gloom, boredom and indifference surrounding discussions of development problems, what an exciting time of ferment these early years were.'[22]

Now the stances taken up by the theorists of modernization and the neo-institutionalists were not of course identical. The former I have argued were essentially manipulative in a rather crude (maybe even cynical, e.g. Rostow?) way, whereas the latter, even if their efforts did eventually run into the intellectual sand, certainly adopted a 'posture of helpfulness', so to say.

The decline of optimism is, at least in part, a result of a dawning appreciation of the ambiguity of planning machineries.[23] The other reasons derive from the lack of any obvious success – a nascent appreciation of the multiplicity of interests in development and the unevenness of social advance.

In summary it can be said that both bourgeois and radical, whom I will look at below, have been optimistic. It would seem sensible to root out such optimism in discussions of issues of development. A sceptical stance seems to be indicated in respect of the claims made by theorists and practitioners, and in respect of expectations of rapid change in LDCs or in the relative positions of DCs and LDCs. Social change is slow: Marx observed, famously, that 'men make their own history but not as they choose'. To this we might usefully add – 'nor at the pace they might desire'. In theorizing development, areas of effective action and specific (restricted) expectations need to be indicated.

2.3   I want now to add a brief note on the work of those whom Hoogevelt[24] labels as 'marxist'. It is difficult to label these people reliably as either optimistic or pessimistic, but bearing in mind the early neo-marxian activism it seems appropriate to call them optimists and then tackle the problem of squeezing and fitting the body of their work into that view. Their optimism resides in what has been pejoratively dubbed their 'Third Worldism' – the view that it is the peripheral areas of the world capitalist system that will provide the next 'world historical' step in the direction of communism. Thus A. G. Frank, for example, insists that a prerequisite for development is socialist revolutionary disengagement from the world capitalist system. And here, of course, we meet their pessimism: it resides, it has been cogently argued, in the view of peripheral capitalism as both deformed and static.

Above I remarked that bourgeois and marxian lines come together (at least in one area) in a reconsideration of their respective intellectual antecedents. It seems to me that they also both display – unevenly – a shift towards specificity of enquiry/engagement.

The work of the marxists re-enters social science, or achieves intellectual respectability, only in the 1960s with the rise of the New Left. Before then, marxism had been largely, but *not* entirely, confined to the ghettos of various communist parties. In the realm of issues of development, the 'rediscovery of Marx' had been anticipated, by a few years, by Paul Baran. The work of the trio of Baran, Frank and Wallerstein is now accorded the status of the label 'neo-marxism'.[25]

This reworking of the marxian tradition has been the subject of much criticism both from the 'right' and from the 'left'. Setting aside criticisms from the 'right', which, *in nuce*, reduce to the observation that politically motivated sloganeering is no substitute for level-headed objective analysis, we can focus upon those of the 'left'. Here we find that the value of neo-marxian work – its popularizing trenchantness and political engagement – is almost wholly dismissed in favour of the claims that: (a) the neo-marxists have offered only polemical inversions of the bourgeois orthodoxy; and (b) that any study of development must be rigorous and centre on the idea of modes of production. This view represents what we can call the 'scientistic left', but others, who are more to my intellectual taste and who centre their reading of Marx on the idea of political economic enquiry rather than modes of production, have offered analogous criticisms. There is, it seems, a coincidence of opinion which would have it that those claiming to operate within the marxian line should pay detailed attention to patterns of class dynamics within peripheral societies, and that A. G. Frank *et al.* have not, generally, done this. Well, the injunction is unobjectionable, but quite whether the neo-marxists are being fairly treated in the still continuing debate is a rather more open question. However, for the present, I shall rest content with recalling Colin Leys's remark to the effect that it should be remembered just what 'intellectual deserts the neo-marxists rescued us from'.[26]

In brief it is my view that the valuable elements of these various 'left' objections to the neo-marxian formulations are to be found in their insistence upon precision and specificity in theorizing. The strategy of political economic enquiry – the 'intellectual reconstruction of the real', Marx's argument strategy – bids us identify the possibilities for the future lodged in the present. This sort of enquiry has to be specific: to time, place, groups, economies, etc. If it is not, it slides toward a general invocation of the historical inevitability of socialism, and so on. In contrast to what is implied here by way of a 'proper procedure', much marxian work, especially I think the Althusserian-inspired material, has been Panglossian in its generality and enthusiasm. It can be caricatured thus: 'all's for the revolution in this revolutionary world' – but, maybe, the world is not quite so revolutionary.

3.0 Above, I remarked that it seemed to be wrong to take for granted – as both bourgeois and marxians do, although in differently stressed ways – the claims of nationalist developmentalism which is seen as an ideology that is both coherent and legitimate. I said above that I would pursue this matter. I do so here *via* a review of those 'gross changes' in the politics and economics of the postwar period that are (routinely taken as) of interest to students of development.

3.1 I think we can pick out four elements of 'gross change' that are relevant to enquiry within the area of studies of development. Of these four the first is population growth. In the nearly forty years that theorists have been addressing issues of development, the world's population growth has been a repeated source of concern. Quite how population growth should be taken into social theorizing has long been a source of debate – Marx, for example, scorned the Malthusian arguments about the socially debilitating effects of population growth. However, for authoritative planners, rapid population growth is really rather like rapid inflation – it just makes the whole business more difficult. Related to population growth there has been general concern for the capacity of the human ecosystem, that is, the planet, to accept the demands made of it both in terms of provision of resources and absorption of the waste products of human civilization – and these latter are not only getting larger in volume terms but also distinctly more dangerous.[27]

The second area of 'gross change' relates to the matter of withdrawal from formal empires. In the wake of World War II, over a period of about fifteen to twenty years, we have seen the formal establishment of a host of nation states. Many of these belong to the Third World. This, coupled with their historical backgrounds, has strongly fuelled the impetus to development theorizing. They above all are the 'clients' for whom theorists have toiled.

Much could be said about the creeds they espouse, but here I shall note just two points. First, that their politico-social creeds have been shaped, in part, by their patterns of emergence from colonial status. This fact cuts across all the other manifold differences; and it is repeated and reinforced by their present status as members of the Third World. Thus, second, there is a continuing pursuit of Third World solidarity – recalling section 2, we here find yet more pressure that shifts theorizing towards the general. This I return to below.

The third change is economic. Here the pattern of change to note is tripartite. We have intra-First World change which sees conflict between the USA and the UK resolved in favour of the former, and lately, new conflicts between Western Europe, USA and Japan. There is change also in relations between First and Second Worlds: notwithstanding the rhetoric of 'cold war', trading links are extensive and growing. Then we have the exchanges between the Third World and the rest – noticeably a general absence of relative advance[28] and a burgeoning debt problem. It seems safe to sum up these complex matters by pointing to a process of shifts and readjustments within an essentially rather static system: by this I mean that while there may have been economic growth and technological advance, we still inhabit an inegalitarian essentially capitalist world system. The 'base line' of activity may have been raised, but, generally, there has been precious little systemic change.

It is in the matter of the fourth change that we meet what for my present purposes is an interesting and relevant issue. The political changes of the post-World War II period include, among other things, the presentation of the ideology of nationalist developmentalism. Nationalist developmentalism has been a common part of the experience of the new nations of the Third World. It has also, more crucially, been a taken-for-granted element of the experience of students of development. It is to the nature of this ideology that I now turn: nationalist developmentalism is, arguably, the Third World counterpart to First World ideologies of authoritative planning: the way the view 'we should do something to help them' is taken on board by those to whom help is thought necessary.

3.2   Nationalist developmentalism is now, it seems to me, an utterly routine element of the common sense of development studies. Clearly, like any element identified as a part of a 'residual common sense', the extent and character of its ready acceptance would vary. Thus, simplifying, for example, the neo-institutionalists would embrace the position as wholly unproblematical, whereas I think 'positivists' and 'marxists' (to revert to my simple labelling of chapter 1) would adopt more cautious positions. The former, perhaps, see potential sources of disturbance to free market exchanges and the latter perhaps see in the element of 'nationalism' a source of potential distortion to the historical progress anticipated by the marxian line.

There must also, rather more importantly, be a series of ways in which the general position has been advanced in political proposals in various states/groups. The understanding of nationalist develop-

169

mentalism held by, say, Nyerere would have been different from that of his neighbour Kenyatta. Again, one could offer comparisons across continents: Allende, Begin, Pol Pot, etc. However, for the present I shall set these refinements/complications aside and rest content with the simpler claim about the pervasive impact of nationalist developmentalism upon development studies.

The claims embodied in the position can be presented by recalling Gellner's work – although I think this is one of those cases where the meaning of the position, in general, is right up on the surface, that is, the substantive concerns which the label encompassed have not been subject to manifold revision as have, say, the notions of 'democracy'. Gellner[29] reports that a society today is legitimate in the eyes of its citizens if it is nationalist and if it is industrial (or industrializing). The fact that Gellner presents his argument as an attempt to ground revised modernization theory securely and that his position includes, among other things, the claim that the term industrial must now replace socialism, capitalism, etc., must give us pause for thought. Not merely in respect of Gellner's arguments but, more importantly, in respect of the claims made by the ideology in question. In the context of this essay we cannot pursue these issues in any detail but we can usefully make a couple of points.

So it seems that there are two elements to note: first, the claim that the ideology is coherent, and second, legitimate – which involves the derivative claim that the position does indeed demand attention and action.

The extent of its coherence/legitimacy may be approached by noting that the ideology was as much a product of a particular concatenation of circumstances as was the reformist interventionism criticized above. Now quite evidently merely noting that a particular view of the world was produced at a particular juncture says nothing very much about either the view itself or its continuing relevance – always supposing it had some originality in the first place. However, taking note of the occasion of presentation does suggest some simple questions in respect of initial conditions and subsequent changes (if any).

If we distinguish, following Basil Davidson,[30] between elite and mass, then the ideologies presented at the time of the dissolution of formal empires can be analysed in terms of the elements present and the interests of the groups involved. In the case of African de-colonization south of the Sahara, Davidson offers a jaundiced reading of events which posits a temporary alliance of convenience between the elite, seeking political reform, and the mass, seeking social reform. It is further argued that this alliance, in the main, quickly broke down after formal political independence was achieved. Most of the replacement regimes are seen as neo-colonial. Now quite clearly, to the extent that this sort of view is correct, the assumption made in studies of development of the coherence/legitimacy of nationalist developmentalism must be undermined. In place of a reading of the behaviour of post-colonial regimes which acknowledge their self-proclamations as both (genuinely) nationalist and industrializers we are, it seems, impelled to substitute other views. These other views will rest on detailed enquiry into the actual behaviours of post-colonial regimes – the pattern of internal group, or class, relations and the exchanges between peripheral elites and metropoles. If the 'real world' pattern is more complex than is claimed in nationalist developmentalist ideology, then students of development would surely do well to acknowledge this. Another way of putting this point has been offered above: nationalist developmentalism presents itself in a variety of guises – to proceed in development studies as if this were not the case, or were irrelevant, is wholly unsatisfactory. Once again, it seems to me, we run into areas of discussion which result in the conclusion that enquiry/engagement needs must be specific.

3.3 I want now to add a very brief note on a paper produced by Paul Streeten.[31] It seems to me that he is one of the more sophisticated representatives of what Hoogevelt[32] would call the 'bourgeois' theorists, and his work falls, I think it is fair to say, within what I have called the neo-institutionalist position. In addition to the interest shown by that tradition in the business of producing a sociologized economics adequate to the task of informing a state planning role conceived as crucial to contriving development, Streeten also pays a great deal of attention – in a philosophically knowledgeable way – to the 'nuts and bolts' of argument.

The paper in which I am interested resembles the present text in so far as it offers a general review of the career of development studies. Streeten argues that development studies was occasioned by the circumstances obtaining in the wake of World War II and has subsequently seen the presentation, discussion and discarding of a whole series of ideas about development. Streeten takes note of the detail of the occasion of development studies and reviews some of the more familiar notions that have appeared over the last thirty to forty years.

Now what is interesting, in the context of the claims I have been making, is what Streeten offers by way of 'lessons' for development studies in the light of the various efforts he has reviewed. Thus we find a series of (five) conclusions, all of which stress the manifold, and continually re-created, nature, of the problems the development theorist faces. All these problems are presented as technical, small scale and piecemeal. Further, in the penultimate passage of his paper, Streeten blithely advances the 'basic needs view' as 'The New Strategy'.[33] Now what is my point here? It is this: Streeten is unable to transcend, it seems, either the interventionist assumption of development studies or its liberal reformist ethic. That 'general presumption of responsibility' characterized above is still found in Streeten. It seems to me that he is locked into a compulsive habit of enquiry. Original presumptions of the obviousness of claims of development and their amenability to expert manipulation have not been abandoned in the light of the lessons (which I have pointed to) of the career of studies of development; rather, the area of their application has been shifted and narrowed. Now we must focus on 'basic needs' of 'Fourth World': *their plight is obvious* and *obviously we can do something*. It seems that Streeten balks at seeing the world as 'political', a multiplicity of interests and intentions, and this locks his work into this repetitive pattern.

4.0 I remarked at the outset that I thought it was not unhelpful to 'appropriate' the development studies work of nearly forty years with reference to the motif of reconsideration. Here I offer a few concluding remarks on the lessons to be drawn from the ongoing, and thoroughly informative, disintegration of orthodox lines (bourgeois and marxist). Two areas can appropriately be noted, though it is the second that flows from my presently stated interests. Thus, first, there is the matter of the lessons for social theorizing *per se*; and, second, there are the lessons for enquiry into matters of development. Both these areas are hugely complex, and the matter of their inter-relationships thus far little dealt with within the literature of academic social science: my remarks are, therefore, tentative.

Social theorizing must be understood to be multiple in its guises: the variety of intentions/conceptions is large. I have sketched out three 'roles', theorist, practitioner and interpreter, but the picture could be made more plausbile (accurate) simply by listing the persons/groups involved in social theorizing. Making sense of the world – in terms which would be recognizable as in some measure 'social scientific' – is a routine part of the life of human social groups. It seems to me that academic social theorists must acknowledge both this multiplicity of modes of social theorizing (broad sense, see chapter 2) and the requirement that they be precise about the character to their own modes of engagement. Mapping the field of modes of engagement and locating ourselves within that field seem to me to be prerequisites of coherent scholarly discourse. The attempt to reduce the multiplicity of modes of engagement to a single model, or a narrowly circumscribed set, seems to me to be a gross error. Thus the naturalist positivist orthodoxy of social science must be rejected: 'policy science' is not the social analogue to natural science, and it does not exhaust the range of possible modes of legitimate social-theoretic engagement. This orthodox strait-jacket is now subject to routine, but by no means universal, rejection by social scientists – but I have recorded above my scepticism about the success of efforts to extirpate the influence of this deforming image. Indeed I think it is still powerful. Equally unfortunate for enquiry are the political 'received models' affirmed by more than a few marxists. It seems to me that we have to acknowledge the diversity and specificity of social theorizing: we confront in our academic role (itself context-specific) a series of situation-sensitive and problem-specific efforts at theorizing. They must be judged, in the first place, in terms of how successfully they achieve their own targets, thereafter, on various specifiable grounds, commentators (where this role includes scholars) can decide whether or not the target was clearly seen and, in the end, whether or not it was actually worth aiming at. Human beings are, among other things, value-bestowing – and this, I think, is the wellspring of all social theorizing.

With regard to studies of development, the burden of my con-clusions must, by now, be fairly obvious. Scholarly commentary, concerned at base to 'display the truth', must eschew the pursuit of a 'general strategy of development' – the task is incoherent. Within the post-World War II career of development studies I think it is fairly clear that this sort of image (of a useful product for the role of scholarship) has been in operation. I have attempted to sketch its outlines in terms of the motif of the 'pursuit of autonomy' and I have argued that the attempt failed, albeit instructively. At present there is, arguably, a process of reconsideration in train: the question arises: Can we identify a 'residual common sense' of development studies? It seems that the answer is Yes, and this residuum centres upon the 'presumption of responsibility', the view that expert inter-vention is the key to development theorizing. It should be clear by now that I consider that this is an unhelpful residuum in that it distracts attention from the context-specificity of enquiry and engagement.

My formulable conclusions in respect of a concern with develop-ment flow from my views about social theorizing. There are, it seems safe to assert, a multiplicity of interests in development – scholarly commentary could usefully begin by acknowledging this. The orthodox bourgeois line of development studies seems to have supposed a common interest in development. But this position is wrong. Even within the narrow area of elaborated theories there have been different ideas about what counted as development. Add to this point an appreciation of the multiplicity of interests in

173

development, and the orthodox project collapses as absurd. Arguably, marxian lines have, rather similarly, erred: there has been something of a tendency to oversimplify the business of securing change. None the less, for my part, it is within the ambit of 'post-neo-marxism' that most of the interesting questions are being presented.

To encompass the multiplicity of interests – in a fashion that refers back to social scientific traditions, thus achieving a minimal continuity and coherence for our enquiries/commentaries – it seems that we must focus on the concatenation of socio-historical-economic-political circumstances holding for particular, identifiable, groups in the world system, itself conceived as capitalistic and only slowly changing. This general scale is orientating, an overview, not a sketch of a vast research project conceived in quasi-orthodox terms.[34] Particular enquiries, particular modes of engagement, or styles of commentary for scholars, can be lodged within this frame.

Notes

Introduction

1. Here I paraphrase Gellner (1964).
2. Preston (1982).
3. Giddens (1979). And see chapter 7.
4. Carroll (1980). And see chapter 1.
5. For a general review see Andrew Tudor, *Beyond Empiricism* (1982).
6. See Bernstein (1976).
7. See chapter 4 below.
8. In a 1974 paper, Peter Worsley argues that this reflexive posture is re-presented in post-war social science by C. Wright Mills and Alvin Gouldner. This may well be true, but subsequently I think the legacy of the radical democratic tradition of Marx has been rediscovered and is now of more importance.
9. Bauman (1976a).
10. This is Giddens's term: it is presented in his *Central Problems in Social Theory* (1979).
11. Now, of course, the orthodox 'naturalist-descriptive' theorists are not the wholly passive creatures I have indicated. Social scientists are an active group. The orthodox social scientists make sense (characterize structures) that feeds into structuration (making sense) *via* the policy-makers who base their 'rational decision-making' upon, *inter alia*, social scientific knowledge conceived thus. At this very general, sociology of sociology, level the major objection to the orthodox is that they deny their ideological role and (as an irritating and absurd corollary) urge that all enquiry that is 'social scientific' should be either forced into their mould or dismissed as pseudo-scientific.

    In contrast to this, the implications of a 'reflexive' view of enquiry/ engagement is that social scientific enquiry is a process inspecting other processes. The particular way in which the local enquiry is embedded in the wider process must be carefully specified. The 'received model', affirmed by the orthodox, simply obscures the business of making such specifications.

12 '-type': this lets in lay theorizing/journalism/pamphleteering/novels, etc. We must acknowledge delimited-formal and pervasive-informal ideologies.

13 The exchange between what Giddens refers to as agency and structure is, as he claims, a central problem for social theory. His own proposals – a theory of structuration – do not strike me as impressive. There seems to be a very strong tendency in Giddens's work to recreate precisely that sort of plodding academic sociological orthodoxy from which the recrudescence of imaginative theorizing in the 1960s and 1970s rescued everyone. I cannot see why anyone should want to recreate such an orthodoxy. Indeed, one of the major lessons of a study of the career of development is precisely that the whole business of social theorizing is multiple in form, and practical. Just who needs an academic general theory? And for what?

14 See chapter 7 below.

15 These points all cluster around my view of the diversity and practicality of modes of social-theoretic engagement: they do not constitute a separable series of discrete points. Doubtless also further points could be included.

16 This is Hoogevelt's phrase. See her *The Third World in Global Development* (1982).

17 My paraphrase of Bernstein (1976).

18 Preston (1982).

1 Some notes on the significance of the career of development studies

1 See, for example, Allen (1975), or Hawthorn (1976) or Hollis and Nell (1975). These are the texts I happened to discover; there are *many* others.

2 Dobb (1973).

3 There is an ambiguity here: is the first occurrence of 'problem' to be taken to be designating a theoretician's problem, while the second occurrence of 'problem' designates a problem as ordinarily understood, one general to society or its ruling group? It seems as if Dobb *might* be fusing these two, whereas if we follow Giddens (1976) with his 'double hermeneutic' we would want to distinguish the two occurrences and make two *sorts* of problems, the ordinarily understood problem being the raw material for the theorist.

4 Dobb (1973), p. 16.

5 Dobb (1973), p. 17.

6 Dobb (1973), p. 17.

7 Bauer (1971).

8 Bauer is right that pre-war governments did pay *some* attention to the development of their colonial holdings, but I think it would be disingenuous to present pre-war and post-war efforts in this direction as being basically the same. In the particular case of the UK – which case comes to provide *the* model of the exchange of 'rich' and 'poor' in this connection – the impact of Keynesianism and war-time social change

was crucial. It is quite possible to identify pre-war anticipations of post-war concerns, but I would take them to be quite distinct.

9 Streeten (1972), chapter 16.
10 Fay (1975).
11 Fay (1975), p.19.
12 Harrod (1939).
13 Jones (1975), p.44.
14 See Kurihara (1968), p. 137.
15 Brookfield (1975), p.29.
16 Hindess (1977).
17 Hindess (1977), p.144.
18 Hindess (1977), p.157.
19 Hindess (1977), p.157.
20 United Nations (1951), cited as Lewis *et al.* (1951).
21 Lewis (1955), reprinted in K. Martin and J. Knapp (eds) (1967).
22 Kurihara (1968), pp. 137-8.
23 Preston (1982) chapter 3.
24 I am thinking of H. Bernstein, A.G. Frank and C. Leys, in particular.
25 See Jones (1975), chapter 4.
26 See Bernstein, Hilal and Frank.
27 Hilal (1970).
28 Seers, 'The limitations of the special case', in *Oxford Bulletin of Statistics*, 1963.
29 Streeten (1972).
30 With Myrdal, of course, there is a strong link with India. But this does not, I think, invalidate my argument. However, the treatment should properly be expanded here to accommodate this particular additional complexity.
31 See Gruchy (1973).
32 Myrdal (1970b), p.21.
33 P. Prebisch is the major figure in early (post-war) Latin American work. See DiMarco (ed.) (1972).
34 Girvan (1973).
35 See Girvan (1973), pp.23-24.
36 See Brookfield (1975), pp.54-62.
37 Girvan (1973) and the criticism of this paper by Cumper (1974).
38 Leys (1977).
39 Culley (1978), p.103.
40 See Sutcliffe's Introduction to Baran (1973).
41 For example, H. Bernstein, A. Philips.
42 Brenner (1977).
43 Brenner (1977), p.27.
44 Palma (1978), p.911.
45 Cardoso and Faletto (1979), p.ix.
46 Palma (1978), p.911.
47 It should be noted that I have treated the process of ideology *construction*. I have not treated the complex story of the *decay* of these various efforts.
48 I do not present this as a *straightforward hierarchy* of better and worse

schemes, or ethically simple to ethically rich conceptions. There is a shift from narrow, self-deluding work to broad and reflexive work. But could it not be said that what is good and bad theory depends on *who* you are, *where* you are and *what* you want to do? At the end of the day, social theorizing is practical, and if that is so then it seems as if we must grant that 'criteria of ranking' will to some extent be *internal* to the 'schools' I have identified. If I present this sequence of 'schools' as a simple hierarchy, it seems as though I might just be declaring where I stand. This is quite proper, but if that's all I do, then our grasp of the character of the efforts treated will somehow be impoverished.

49   In the final chapter I speak of orthodox work as 'repetitive' and 'compulsive', that is, as *insisting* upon an approach that stands in need of revision. On this van Nieuwenhuijze (1982), remarking that theorizing development has to be cast in socio-cultural – as opposed to narrowly economic – terms, says: 'This is an important realization. . . It is also significant in view of the current outcry for a new international order, which some incorrigibles maintain should be economic first and foremost' (p. 18). Of the focus on 'poverty' (basic needs) van Nieuwenhuijze speaks of the presentation of a 'dramatic recapitulation of an earlier compassionate concern with backwardness at large' (p.51). This focus has been adopted, he speculates, in response to 'a slackening of public interest in development' (p.50), and a 'disappointment about the demonstrable effect of development work and especially development cooperation' (p.50).

2 The specificity of social-theoretic engagement

1   Unfortunate in two ways: unhelpful analyses and wrong conceptions of how to execute analyses. In the work below I focus upon the second aspect, the 'formal' one. A related point here is that this sort of misconstrual of the nature of theorizing might be less of a problem for the 'orthodox' than the 'left'. The left claim more for their theories – richer, more penetrating, etc. – and construct them in opposition to orthodox views. This being so, their efforts need to be strictly disciplined and consistent. The orthodox argue in line with common sense ideas of the world; if they relax, common sense to some extent still supports them. In *both* cases any intellectual relaxation will entail a regression to common sense. But this has different effects: for the 'left' it must be wholly enfeebling; whereas for the orthodoxy there is a residual, minimum affirmation of their *status quo*. I do not pursue this matter. (All this relates to theorists in developed areas. In the Third World the circumstances of the two groups might be so different as to render this 'collapse to the common sense mean' unlikely.)

2   Clearly this remains a task to be accomplished at some stage. Preliminary enquiries, see Kilminster (1979), Hamilton (1974), Larrain (1979).

3   (1974).

4   Maurice Dobb (1973) treats the creative exchange between the theorist and the circumstances of his theorizing. In my terms there is a double dynamic of the dialectic of theory and the dialectic of society. Explana-

tions are constructed with particular solutions in mind and out of particular sets of resources. Using this schema in a passive voice, so to say, we can analyse extant efforts in terms of their conception (the question of propriety in explanation) and their intent (the question of the use to which enquiry is directed). Using the notions of conception and intent in this fashion, I analyse the efforts of my exemplars.

5 Rockmore (1976).
6 See Carver (1975).
7 Gellner (1964), p.52.
8 Giddens (1979), p.187.
9 This strategy of using exemplars to map the field of modes of engagement with the social world I have used (Preston 1981a) in a study of the post-war history of development studies. The detail of the occasion/character of my two exemplars provided the terms in which a succession of specific ideological departures were analysed.
10 If we wanted a rather more practical reading of this scheme then it could be said that all these posited relationships can be taken as roles that one theorist (or group, or school) might adopt in some combination or sequence. I am picking out emphases in order to build a systematic frame.
11 Compare also Foster-Carter's remark (1964) to the effect that 'neo-marxist' theories of development are, *inter alia*, a response to how Mao *et al.* have changed the world.
12 Recalling the category of 'practitioners' there is an asymmetry in treating their behaviour. Successful practitioners are one thing: their very success attests to their effective grasp of circumstances/problems. But what, we may ask, of a *'failed* practitioner'?
13 Clairmonte (1960), p.21.
14 Clairmonte (1960), p.321.
15 Pollard (1971), pp. 138-9.
16 Young (1977), p.166.
17 Debray (1970), p.22.
18 K. Minogue, 'Che Guevara', in Cranston (1970).
19 Minogue (1970), p.28.
20 Minogue (1970), p.28.
21 Debray (1967), p.27.
22 Debray (1967), p.19.
23 Debray (1967), p.21.
24 Roxborough (1979), p.134.
25 Debray (1970), p.28.
26 Debray (1970), p.33.
27 Debray (1970), p.33.
28 Caute (1970), p. 41.
29 Caute (1970), p. 41.
30 Worsley (1969), p.32.
31 Caute (1975), p.68.
32 Fanon (1967), p.30.
33 Fanon (1967), p.39.
34 Fanon (1967), pp.117-18.

NOTES

35 Baran I here cast in the role of theorist of development, but, along with Sweezy in particular, his work in the marxian left is much wider and more widely known. What I am after here is the broad distinction, which I think can quite properly be drawn, between activists and scholars, even if (as these workers would claim and my general systematic frame would grant) all work with an ultimately practical intent.

36 Jack Woddis (1972).

37 R. Brenner (1977).

38 There is a spin-off question here. If a natural-science-aping general formulation (theory) is not what is wanted, then just what place, if any, do we grant for general theory? Do we abolish it? Do we recast the 'impulse to generality' in *non*-scientistic terms, and, if so, what do we come up with? An answer to this question might be sought, so far as I can presently see, in the ideas that: (a) theorizing is a process and thus has a 'general moment'; (b) general statements are elaborate cashings of particular moral stances. If these two (which I would, in any case, want to link) are run together, we come up with the idea that from time to time, as we theorize about the social world, it will be useful – for theory and/or for practice – to flesh out our moral stance in general and practical terms. This would give 'general theory' a particular and distinctly social-scientific role. But for the present this issue remains open.

39 Taylor (1974).

40 Foster-Carter (1964).

41 Foster-Carter (1964).

42 Taylor's subsequent work *From Modernization to Modes of Production* (1979) addresses the question (which I have characterized as): what is to count as a properly marxian analysis of the Third World? The 'discourses' of the sociology of development (orthodoxy) and the sociology of underdevelopment (neo-marxism) are inspected and found to be inadequately grounded. The alternative offered is an Althusserian-informed use of the idea of historical materialism: the complex interaction of modes of production must be appropriately examined. It is at this point that the whole issue of the nature of the contribution of Althusserian marxism to social theorizing (of both metropolitan and peripheral capitalisms) is opened up. However, it is not a matter that I can pursue here – although, given that I think Taylor has asked the (or at least *a*) right question, it is something that I hope to follow up at a later date. One distinguishing feature of what I label (with no great insistence upon its general adoption) 'post-neo-marxism' is precisely the issue: what is to count as a marxian analysis of the Third World?

43 This is Foster-Carter's phrase. He identifies (1979) the Althusserians' division in the field of neo-marxist treatments of development as revolving round the idea of problematics. To this he counterposes his own scheme, treating the same general field, centring upon the notion of paradigms. My treatment of this same field (to the limited extent that I have formulated it) would revolve round specifying different modes of social-theoretic engagement. (I would not grant the Althusserian distinction between them and the rest – I count them as one element of

the 'post-neo-marxian' debate.) This is what I am pointing to with my 'early' and 'late' Frank: the distinction is *not* a straightforward chronological one.

44 D. Booth, 'Andre Gunder Frank: an introduction and appreciation', in Oxaal, Barnett and Booth (1975).
45 Paul Baran, in particular the work *The Political Economy of Growth* (1973).
46 Frank (1978).
47 Frank (1978), p.xiii.
48 Frank (1978), p.1.
49 Frank (1978), p.1.
50 Frank (1978), p.2.
51 Frank (1978), p.2.

3 Becoming industrialized, being industrial

1 Gellner (1964), p.33.
2 Gellner (1964), p.33.
3 Gellner (1964), p.36.
4 Gellner (1964), p.37.
5 Gellner (1964), p.38.
6 Gellner (1964), p.40.
7 This is a phrase generally associated with the New Left.
8 Gruchy (1973).
9 Preston (1982).
10 Galbraith's insight is given much clearer formulation in the work of the Frankfurt School theorists Habermas and Marcuse. The regulated system disguises its irrationality in the fusion of practical and technical questions. Thus it is clear that consumerism represents the subjection of the supposedly sovereign consumer to the logic of the producer's operations.
11 Napoleoni (1972), chapters 5 and 6.
12 This is Galbraith's version of the 'decomposition of capital' and one of the points on which marxists have criticized him.
13 However, the extent to which Galbraith worries because of the rise of such a corporate state *per se* as against the extent of his worrying because his brand of liberals are not in power is a moot point. It is left open because of the corporatist-type solutions he proposes.
14 At this point it is rather obvious that this group generally, and Galbraith and Gellner more particularly, have resemblances to Max Weber: both in substance, to the extent that they all share a view of the system that involves centrally the idea of rationalization, and in flavour. Picking up this second element, we can note that Weber was a liberal – in the sense of being a cultured person moving in intellectual/political circles – and was involved in, but not of, the political life of his times. The mixture of reluctant acceptance/distaste/concern for the future of modern capitalism has often been remarked in Weber's work: it is there in Galbraith and Gellner also.
15 Galbraith (1967), p.381.

16 Reisman in his text *State and Welfare* (1982) presents a critical exposition of the work of Galbraith, Tawney and Adam Smith. I am interested in Galbraith, and Reisman tackles him in three stages. First we have a presentation of Galbraith's 'convergence thesis': this is criticized as being rather superficially descriptive, politically 'soft' on the Eastern bloc, and as most intelligible when set against the US scene. With regard to this last element Reisman suggests that Galbraith is guilty of an illegitimate generalization of US experience. Confusingly he adds, seemingly approvingly, that Galbraith, against this backdrop, does indeed look like a radical social democrat. Unhappily Reisman's characterization wanders; thus his subject is also called a socialist and a democratic socialist. Clearly this trio are not synonymous. Then, second, Reisman looks at Galbraith's interventionism – arguments for regulation – which, as far as I can see, is indeed the key to Galbraith. The enquiry is conducted in an unhelpful style, which I will come to. Substantively Reisman's apparent myopia is evidenced in his devoting two pages to national economic planning and óne and three-quarter pages to macro economic policy. It won't do. Nor are matters redeemed in the third part of his treatment. To regulation is added support: the positive side, so to say, of state intervention. Reisman considers Galbraith's remarks on the arts, the planning system, the market system and welfare. Again we are told little of any note. The question thus arises: Why not?

The core of the problem is this: Reisman's history of ideas approach has the effect of substituting for a clearly argued case (as I would enjoin) an ethico-literary exegesis. This is oriented, for all three of his subjects, to elucidating the arguments that have led 'sensitive and intelligent thinkers to conclude that society is most successful in attaining its shared objectives when it attempts to do so consciously and collectively' (p.3). Struggling to render Reisman intelligible over-all, the label that one comes to is 'intelligent conservative' – not too much of a step in the right direction as far as I can see. I am not clear what Reisman thinks of Galbraith (or his other cited theorists, come to that), or thinks social theory is/ought to be. At one point (p.149), a sociology-of-knowledge-type enquiry is damned, then *interestingly* pursued: rather like Hawthorn's text *Enlightenment and Despair* (1976), which rejects the approach while simultaneously using it.

Reisman makes great play with Adam Smith, whose approach, rather than substantive theorems, is commended: but we learn little of what this actually *is*. Smith is rescued from his vulgarizers, labelled, surely anachronistically, an 'institutionalist' (p.211), and accredited (?) with a 'haunted intellectuality' at several points (pp. 9, 211, 225). It might have told us much about Reisman's own views if we had been told just what was the nature of the ghost in Smith's intellectual machineries.

17 Preston (1982).

18 Thus in chapters 1 and 2 we have the problem specified; in chapters 3, 4 and 5 the problem is theorized; and in chapters 6, 7 and 8 a series of 'matters arising' are picked up.

19 It is at this point that Gellner suggests that sociology is now the heir to

classical political philosophy. It is so because it asks the right questions: about the nature of industrial society. These questions exercised the 'founding fathers', and present interest in Third World development permits our rediscovery of this task. We are able to learn about industrial society (and, it seems to me, social theorizing) by analysing the attempts/theories of LDCs to become industrial.

20 Preston (1982).
21 Gellner (1964), p.34.
22 Preston (1982).
23 Reflexivity in argument/enquiry can be read narrowly (attention to form) or broadly (attention to form and context of presentation – sociology of knowledge). Gellner seems to slide between the two: a narrow conception establishes scientificity and scientific enquiry is then conceived broadly. That is, his idea of science is legitimated narrowly and then applied broadly. I do not think this will work. Science, and Gellner has natural science in mind pre-eminently, is a complex social process and it includes, *inter alia,* a stress on reflexive enquiry – considering both substantive claims and rules of enquiry. But, surely, so do lots of other modes of thinking – tax lawyers, for example. It seems that Gellner's formal criterion is too general. Thus his 'narrow' notion cannot carry the 'broad' one. Moreover, and this is my third point, this broad scheme is the scheme of critical rationalism – most definitely not a modest report on logics of enquiry, indeed a powerful delimited formal ideology.
24 Gellner presents a variation of Popper's 'critical rationalism'. This last-mentioned scheme is an influential co-mingling of a mitigated positivist epistemology, which, so far as I understand debate in the philosophy of science, is not widely regarded as the emphatic and obvious solution to extant problems that Popper claimed, with a crude politics, and an evolutionist general frame. The whole clearly constitutes a delimited-formal ideology and the scheme has been claimed as a scheme of social democracy (Magee (1973), chapter 6). I think Magee is right to bring out the central importance for understanding Popper's work of Popper's anti-marxian politics. To my mind it is yet another corporatist scheme.

A few more points could usefully be made here. (a) All this might seem a somewhat cavalier treatment of the philosophy of science/social science and general political-social positions of these two thinkers. However for my present purposes – a sketch, for comparative purposes, of a familiar planning mode of social theoretic engagement – I think these simplifications are excusable. (b) It could be pointed out that both Gellner and Popper have been commended/excoriated for, most importantly given my present interests, presenting robustly argued political-social cases. And reading them in this fashion then the fine distinctions which I am eliding do not seem to me to be currently relevant. (c) That I am disposed to admire Gellner and dismiss (as a political and social thinker) Popper must be clear from these essays, but what I would claim is that I appreciate what moves them to write and argue. I can point up this claim by citing the work of John Hall. In his text, *Diagnoses of Our Time* (1981), he offers an exposition of six such 'diagnoses', including the one on offer from Gellner. What is remarkable about Hall's work, for all its subtlety and skill, is the paucity of any economic/political/social/historical material. The 'diagnoses' reviewed are, it seems, to be understood as literary-type artefacts, amenable to even-handed exegesis and occasional (somewhat banal) political comment, and not as specific social-theoretic interventions which admit of – indeed invite – a substantial ideological response. Hall's work does seem to be politically and socially naive: the style of presentation is familiarly 'academic' and this crucially acts to 'flatten out' his subjects. With Gellner we are left with a distinctly two-dimensional figure which hardly does him justice!

25 By way of an afterthought, perhaps we can understand this material by suggesting a deep tension – not a very original motif, I agree – in Gellner's work. On the one hand Gellner is a sophisticated empiricist in respect of his philosophy of science; he follows Popper who, among other things, distinguishes science from ideology (thus destroying, thinks Popper, the pretensions of Marx and Freud). Gellner's philosophy of science sits uneasily, so far as I can see, with his affirmation of the need for a *new ideology* of the transition. His resolution of this dilemma involves him in an elitist scheme of *two sorts* of knowledge. Scientific for those who rule, and ideological (in a familiar sense) for those who are ruled. Gellner ends up arguing on behalf of the authoritative planners – the experts who know what's best for us! Reading Gellner, I have the strong impression of a sophisticated social theorist whose work is deformed by the presence of large chunks of indigestible Popper.

26 Gellner (1964), pp.120-5 passim.

27 See Passmore (1970), chapters 8 and 9, and chapter 6 in this collection.

28 For example, see the essay 'Technology and Science as Ideology' in Habermas (1971b).

29 I take this distinction from Bauman's *Towards a Critical Sociology* (1976a), although I'm not sure that in offering this expository formulation Bauman does not make the error of conceding too much to orthodox ideas of social scientific explanation. The split between (knowledgeable) theorist and social world is reintroduced, and authentication is presented as an extra stage in the whole business. The essential unity of theory and practice that was, however unsatisfactorily, insisted upon by the Frankfurt School seems to have gone.

30 To recap: compare Habermas's open, dialogic scheme with that of Gellner *et al*. These theorists comprehend social knowledge on the analogy of natural scientific knowledge – essentially knowledge is causally effective knowledge. Things may be a little awkward in the social sciences, but essentially they are the same. Knowledge is thus non-obvious, technical and difficult of acquisition. The institutional location of the effective deployment of this knowledge is the sphere of the expert – thus we have planners and policy science. It might also be compared with Bauman's scheme of validation/authentication noted above. It is not clear in my mind that Bauman is not distorting Habermas at this point such that the therapeutic exchange becomes merely a *link*

between theorizing and practical activity rather than, as I see it, being *central* to a way of conceiving social-theoretic praxis.

31 Throughout this paper I have made reference to the idea of corporatism: now this is a term which has, after the taint of fascism, recently made something of a comeback within the realm of political science. These debates I am now in the process of reviewing, and I hope to adopt an appropriately revised usage in later work – in particular treating the development strategies of Singapore – however, for the present, I would note that my understanding of corporatism is that it is a system tendency of monopoly capitalism and that, nationalistic militarism and racism aside, it did indeed find its clearest statement in those European states of Germany, Italy, Spain and Portugal in the 1930s and 1940s, and indeed longer in Spain and Portugal.

4 The impact of the 'received model' of natural science upon social theorizing

1 Giddens (1979).
2 Giddens (1979), p.235.
3 Giddens (1979), p.259 (his emphasis).
4 Preston (1982).
5 If I am going to argue that social theorizing is about constructing arguments, then I am obliged (it seems to me) to be careful to display the detail of my own arguments so far as I am able, and indicate the sources for the elements I present. This is not simply a stylistic quirk, although it could be grasped with an architectural metaphor: thus my texts are like those modern buildings which reveal all their plumbing, etc. It is, rather, an attempt to make the presentation of my texts consistent with the claims made in them.
6 Hawthorn (1976).
7 Crick (1980).
8 See Kilminster (1975).
9 The anti-positivist line of enquiry into the nature of explanation, in natural and social sciences, is the principal source of my thinking. Otherwise I have picked up *bits* from discussions of social science methodology, from philosophy of science, and from philosophy (language/epistemology).
10 Hawthorn (1976).
11 Allen (1975).
12 Allen (1975), p.5.
13 Allen (1975), p.15.
14 Benton (1977).
15 Benton (1977), p.46.
16 Benton (1977).
17 Benton (1977).
18 Fay (1975).
19 These remarks on economics do not imply a programme for the 'abolition of economics'. They do involve a rejection of orthodox economics as a *positive science:* I see them as one (among very many)

style of ideology-making. Quite what an economics (dealing with the area presently dealt with by orthodox economics) which *reflexively* displayed its philosophical assumptions would look like, I do not know. It might be that all I could reasonably look to was (a) the analysis of orthodox economics, as it is, as one particular mode of social-theoretical engagement (making a particular sort of sense, in a particular context, for particular 'clients'), or (b) the substitution for the orthodoxy of a refurbished political economy.

20 For a further discussion see Preston (1982), chapter 3.
21 Joan Robinson spoke of Mr Harrod's 'ingenious manipulations' and of the economists' vice of shifting from the very abstract and general down to the policy level without too much concern for the propriety of the switch (see *Economic Journal*, March 1949).
22 It might be objected that there is an important difference between 'deductive empiricism' in the style of Robbins and neo-classical work of a later period. The claims made for assumptions are dropped in later work -- it is the usefulness of hypotheses that is the key, and their truthful correspondence to the facts. I am not equipped to pursue this, but two points occur: (a) while there are undoubtedly distinctions to be drawn between logical empiricism, logical positivism, deductive empiricism and the softened naturalism of writers like Nagel or the revisions of Popper, these differences are *of degree, not kind*; (b) the theorists Hollis and Nell (1975) have argued that a plausible economics *must* have a base in real definitions. The positivist prop of the orthodox is useless and their assumptions fantastic – a classical marxian approach (rationalist) is advocated.
23 Lewis (1955).
24 Lewis (1955), p.9.
25 Lewis (1955), p.11.
26 Bernstein (1976), p. 90.
27 Bernstein (1976).
28 Bernstein (1976), p.98.
29 See chapter 20.
30 Ehrensaft (1971).
31 Ehrensaft (1971), p.40.
32 Ehrensaft (1971).
33 Ehrensaft (1971), p.41.
34 Girvan (1973) and Cumper (1974).
35 Girvan (1973), pp. 23-4.
36 Bernstein (1976), p.59.

5 Comparative ranking

1 I take this phrase from Bernstein (1976), p.114.
2 In chapter 2, p. 35, I distinguished a 'wide' and a 'restricted' sense of social theorizing. It is the restricted sense, the production of texts, that concerns me now. The restricted sense involves, crudely, producing texts: and institutionalized social science does this. More broadly institutionalized social science can be seen as one, among many, modes

of social-theoretic engagement. Here I begin with social science – but the remarks hold for any mode of engagement that is centrally concerned with texts. The issue gets a little cloudy because with the Frankfurt School line the criticism of ideology (initially the business of technical social science) is a prerequisite of effecting social change and thus to be regarded *in toto* as social theorizing in the broad sense. It seems to me that the business of social theorizing entails adopting, from time to time, a variety of 'roles' – this present paper focuses on the production of texts, a narrow notion of social theorizing.

3 We can elucidate this by invoking the distinction between validation/ authentication. What counts as 'the truth' is a mixture of self-consciousness in argument making (and one way of checking this is the task of this paper) and demonstrated relevance to society conceived as democratic (here is my irreducible value engagement). For social scientific critique I lay the stress on the technical aspect of argument-crafting: for political critique both elements come into play.

A further elucidation *via* the distinction between deployment/ grounding can be presented. Thus my notion of social theorizing centres on its practicality, and so deployment comes first; it is only thereafter that we look to the effort's grounding. The particular practicality of social science is the commentator's role in social theorizing: the way the effort is grounded is a 'matter arising'. At the end of the day I affirm a Habermas-style scheme that grounds truth in the way language works in rational discourse.

4 Now as different actors construct arguments for different purposes, we can allow these efforts to be well or not so well crafted according to their own targets. Social science judges arguments according to the discipline's target: 'displaying the truth'. (Recall Giddens (1976) with his 'double hermeneutic' of common and disciplinary sense.)

5 Bernstein (1976).

6 Bernstein (1976), p.114.

7 Preston (1982).

8 Bernstein (1976), pp.108-9.

9 Gellner (1964).

10 Dobb (1973).

11 Dobb (1973), p.16.

12 Dobb (1973), p.17.

13 Dobb (1973), p.17.

14 Dobb (1973), p.18.

15 Dobb (1973), p.18.

16 Cf. with Lukes on 'relativism' – 'On the social determination of truth' in *Essays in Social Theory* (1977).

17 Goldmann (1969), p.23, his emphasis.

18 Goldmann (1969), p.36.

19 Goldmann (1969), p. 35, his emphasis.

20 Goldmann (1969), p.36.

21 Goldmann (1969), p.51.

22 Goldmann (1969), p.52, his emphasis.

23 Goldmann (1969), pp.57-62.

24 Goldmann (1969), pp.117-18, his emphasis.
25 This has been a straightforward treatment of Goldmann, yet there are
   problems both for Goldmann and for my borrowings from him. In
   respect of the former see Hamilton (1974) and Larrain (1979). With
   regard to the latter, there are two rather obvious points: (a) his concern
   for the orthodox is not free of orthodox views. His position on the
   relation of fact/value is confused: first granting the orthodox view of a
   disjunction and then denying this view. Similarly, he sometimes seems to
   accept a split between science and ideology and then talks unexpectedly
   of value judgments impacting upon scientific thought in different
   fashions. He talks about perspectives, ideologies, and sociologies as if
   they were all the same sort of thing. Are they all to be contrasted with
   science? Or are they all more or less scientific? (b) His concern with
   orthodox social science *versus* marxism is couched in terms redolent of
   early work in the 'humanist marxian school': thus we have discussions of
   material reality and consciousness, and this is just confusing.
26 Dobb (1973), p.19.
27 Dobb (1973), p.19, his emphasis.
28 Dobb (1973), p.20.
29 Dobb (1973), p.28.
30 Dobb (1973), p.36.
31 Preston (1982).
32 Giddens (1979), p.175.
33 Girvan (1973), p.12, my emphasis.
34 Preston (1981a).
35 See chapter 3.
36 Preston (1981b).
37 Gellner (1964).
38 Galbraith (1975). Also *The Affluent Society* (1970) and *The New
   Industrial State* (1967).
39 Galbraith (1975), p.215.
40 Carver (1975), pp. 40-1.
41 See chapter 1.
42 See Preston (1982), ch. 6.
43 Baran (1973).
44 See Preston (1982), ch. 6.
45 Palma (1978).
46 But, it might be asked, does not the economic form bourgeois
   capitalism provide an economics that can grasp the nature of all other
   economies? In principle, the answer would seem to be Yes. But political
   economy was, and is, practical and as politics is specific it seems as if the
   role of theorist must devolve upon the Third World theorist. Those
   based in the 'West' can reasonably offer only comment – their situation
   is very different and their practical concerns will be different, too. We
   must avoid 'slides to the general' and Third Worldism.
47 Hindess (1977).
48 This is Fay's term.
49 Shaw (1975), p.viii.
50 Hindess's (1977) phrase.

51 Palma (1978).
52 See chapter 2.
53 See Jay (1973).
54 And Habermas presents a particular role for discourse – critical enquiry, as we see below. The role of scholar I take to be a variation of the role of commentator, in my scheme.
55 Giddens (1979), p.175.
56 Bauman (1976a).
57 Bernstein (1976), p.211, his emphasis.

6 The ethico-political notion of development

1 A very much condensed version of this material appeared in my *Theories of Development* (1982), chapter 2.
2 The psychologist Liam Hudson has observed that 'human thought, before it is squeezed into its Sunday best, for purposes of publication, is a nebulous and intuitive affair: in place of logic there brews a stew of hunch and partial insight, half submerged. And although we accept that our mind's products must eventually be judged by the puritan rules of evidence and insight. . . we seem in practice to draw what inspiration we possess from a hidden stockpile of images, metaphors and echoes, ancient in origin but fertile and still growing' (1972), p.13.
3 Winch (1958).
4 Lukes (1977), Giddens (1976) and (1979), Bernstein (1976).
5 Hawthorn (1976).
6 '[T]he central problem of sociology, that of giving an account of the nature of social phenomena in general, itself belongs to philosophy. In fact, not to put too fine a point on it, this part of sociology is really misbegotten epistemology. I say "misbegotten" because its problems have been largely misconstrued, and therefore mishandled, as a species of scientific problem' (1958), p.42.
7 Giddens (1976), pp.17-18, for example.
8 Gellner (1964).
9 Gellner can be regarded as a sophisticated theorist of modernization.
10 Gellner (1964), p.1.
11 Gellner (1964), p.52.
12 Gellner (1964), p.34.
13 Gellner (1964), p.34.
14 Gellner (1964), p.34.
15 Hilal (1970).
16 Hawthorn (1976), p.86. On the matter of the relationship between, on the one hand, *models of man,* and on the other, *schemas in respect of society,* there is a simple link (even if it requires complex unpacking). Hollis ((1977); all citations p.1) introduces his interest by speaking of 'Recipes for the good society' – a mix of essences and 'socialising syrup': the mix varies. 'In particular the magic formula for the socialising syrup varies with the analysis of human nature. For instance, if men are essentially greedy egoists in pursuit of riches, fame and honour, then the syrup will be a blend of repression through fear and reward for

cooperation. If men are born free, equal and good, they need only be stewed in Enlightened education amid democratic institutions. If men are by nature the sinful children of God, then a conservative chef will distil his brew from notions like law, authority, tradition, property and patriotism, tinged with distrust of reason. . . there is always an essence of man and a consequent syrup.'

17 I think this can best be seen as a piece of moral psychology and might best be developed by looking at the idea of integrity. This can be taken to comprise two elements: one being the demand for consistency in formulation of moral statements; and the other being the requirement of continuity of personal identity. The requirement of consistency in statement is general to intellectual discourse, but the necessary link to personal self-image is novel to moral discourse. That a person is thoroughly involved in what is being said is not a defect to be regretted or minimized; it is, rather, a necessary condition of that discourse being moral discourse.

18 Hawthorn (1976), p.6.

19 See the essay on Fanon and Debray.

20 Hawthorn, biting the hand that feeds him, remarks of his history of social thought: 'If the history is to be rational, it must presume rationality in its subjects, and forswear sociology' (1976), p.6.

21 Vic Allen (1975) argues that theorizing is about making sense of the world and captures the practicality (ordinarily understood) of the business rather well.

22 Hollis (1977), p.3.

23 Gellner (1964), p.3.

24 Passmore (1970).

25 Pollard (1971).

26 It is 'naive' in the sense that he is a historian who constructs his history upon a base which takes a marxian sociology of knowledge entirely for granted. This paper, where it is a 'history', is 'naive' in the same way.

27 Macpherson (1973).

28 See Passmore (1970), especially chapter 1.

29 Passmore (1970), p.158.

30 Passmore (1970), p.169.

31 Bauman (1976b), p.20.

32 Passmore (1970), p.208.

33 Pollard (1971), p.26.

34 Pollard (1971), p.30.

35 MacIntyre (1967).

36 Pollard (1971), p.49.

37 Passmore (1970), p.193.

38 Pollard (1971), p.104.

39 See for example A.G. Frank's work.

40 Passmore (1970), p.238.

41 Avineri (1968), p.153.

42 Pollard (1971), p.139.

43 Berlin, 'Two Concepts of Liberty' in (1969), p.131.

44 Macpherson (1973).

45 Goldmann (1973), p.25.
46 Macpherson (1973), p.3.
47 Galbraith does not take these claims at face value. The claim that the liberal capitalist economy maximizes equitably individual utilities rests upon the theory of consumer demand. The notion of consumer demand posits that the consumer knows his wants best and that the market efficiently meets such needs: the consumer is sovereign. This line of argument is based, Galbraith argues, on two broad propositions. The first is that the urgency of wants does not diminish appreciably as more of them are satisfied (postulate of infinite desirousness). And second, that these wants originate in the person of the consumer (postulate of individualism).

Galbraith analyses these two postulates and finds their root in the old problem of price determination. Water has no price and yet it is vital to life, whereas diamonds command a high price and are far from being vital. The explanation of this came with the concept of marginal utility so that the urgency of desire is a function of the quantity of goods available to the individual. However, this seemingly puts economics firmly on the side of the view that production was of diminishing importance in an affluent society. And this claim cuts against the stress on production as an evasion/resolution of the problem of inequality in society.

So how was the position retrieved? Galbraith reports that a distinction between fact and value is invoked – the better to make economics 'scientific'. Any judgments on the satisfactions derived from various goods is ruled out. An infinite variety of rather similar goods could then be presented to the consumer and thus the importance of production was secured.

Galbraith comments: 'This position ignores the obvious fact that some things are acquired before others. . . this. . . implies a declining urgency of need' (1970), p.145. This evasion of the problem of diminishing marginal utility is pursued by Galbraith in the area of the supposed origins within the consumer of his wants in the light of the existence of the advertising industry: the system generates the wants it then claims to satisfy.

If we couple Galbraith and Macpherson, we can present the economic orthodoxy with a dilemma. Thus, if we *cannot compare* the satisfactions of persons with various goods, we cannot sustain a claim that the set of utilities produced under capitalism is the best set that could be produced under any system of production. If, however, we grant that we *can compare* the satisfactions people derive from various utilities, we are faced with the problem indicated by the notion of diminishing marginal utility. That is, the declining importance of production *per se*, and the concomitant importance of the *actual sort* of production undertaken – this opens up the issues of inequality which are suppressed ordinarily. Either way, the claims of liberal-democratic theory to maximize equitably individual utilities cannot be sustained.

48 Lukes (1974).
49 Macpherson (1973), p.18.
50 Macpherson (1973), p.20.

NOTES

51 In slogan form, this complex argument can be summarized as follows. That there are two quite distinct schemes of social progress: that is, what is to count as progress. The one is *intellectually coherent and ethically rich* – it is also the calumnied, submerged, counter tradition to the other. This is the orthodox scheme – *intellectually incoherent and ethically impoverished*.
52 Ehrensaft (1971).
53 Fay (1975).
54 Clark (1957).
55 Harrod (1939).
56 Solow (1956).
57 Huntington (1971).
58 Rostow (1960).
59 Brookfield (1975), p.77.
60 Sachs (1976).
61 Sachs (1976), p.30.
62 Hetherington (1978).
63 Hetherington (1978), p.104.
64 Davidson (1978), pp.182-3.
65 This is the sort of line presented by British theorists in the late nineteenth century with respect to international specialization and exchange when, to a large extent, the UK was the only industrial nation.
66 Gellner (1964), p.36, remarks that there are 'now very nearly only two kinds of politics. . . the politics of getting industrialised, and there are the politics of affluence.' With respect to the former he mentions Myrdal, and to the latter, Galbraith.
67 Ehrensaft (1971).
68 Streeten, see his introductory remarks to Myrdal (1958).
69 Palma (1978).
70 Palma (1978), p.885.
71 The work of Furtado I have already looked at, and Palma's presentation of Cardoso as preferable to Baran *et al*. I shall not discuss as it opens up intra-marxian debates that are too complex for any summary treatment here. These debates are also, given the scale and comparative strategy of this chapter, arguably over-subtle and thus not directly relevant.
72 Palma (1978), p.900.
73 I have made some preliminary remarks on this matter in Preston (1981a), and the gist of my remarks can be presented as follows. The left critics of Baran *et al*. suggested that what we have in the neo-marxian line is an aggregative left Keynesianism. I granted their critique some force in respect of the moral basis of neo-marxism. I acknowledged that Baran *et al*. do not resemble very closely Marx's political economy. However, I suggested that (a) the Althusserians' dismissal of valuation in theorizing was wrong, and that (b) whether Baran *et al*. were, or were not, 'really' marxist was less interesting than the issue of how good they were at political economy.

Looking at Cardoso, after Palma's suggestion, I found a 'sociologists' political economy': much discussion of class dynamics through history, but no apparent treatment of economics. There the matter rested and I

192

presented two interim conclusions: (a) that discussion of Baran *et al.*
should remember to pay attention to its circumstances of manufacture
and its objectives. We cannot judge all theorizing by one model of
'properly marxian revolution-making', which is what these critics seemed
to be doing. Then (b) that the precise mix of 'sociology' and 'economics'
was an open question – neither Baran *et al.* nor Cardoso seemed to have
solved it.
74 C. Taylor (1967).

7 The common sense of development studies

1 We can date the start of a concern with development studies as 1940 –
the Colonial Development Act in UK; or 1941 – the Atlantic Charter; or
1945 – the end of World War II; or 1951 – the UN report of Lewis *et al.*
Thus we have a period of between 32 and 43 years.
2 Preston (1982).
3 Lewis *et al.* (1951).
4 Merton's phrases in his *Social Theory and Social Structure*.
5 Seers, 'The limitations of the special case', *Oxford Bulletin of Statistics*
1963.
6 Streeten (1972) and (1981).
7 Brookfield (1975).
8 Kitching (1982).
9 Preston (1982).
10 Accepting provisos here about *which* 'received model'.
11 Preston (1982).
12 Streeten (1981).
13 For example my own work flows out of the radical democratic traditions
of Europe, but it is certainly not clear, notwithstanding the (almost)
universal protestations of democratic status made by nation states, that
these values are widely affirmed. Nor is it clear that the denials
identifiable are all examples of 'falling away'. Clearly the crypto-fascist
regimes of Central America presently being re-embraced by Reagan do
represent degenerate polities. But this is certainly not the general case;
in the Islamic world a different non-democratic ethic is affirmed. So too
in parts of Asia: here the situation is differently ambiguous; Western
models of liberal democracy are doubted sometimes, it seems, in favour
of ethics drawn from indigenous traditions such as confucianism,
sometimes in favour of what seems to me to be a vulgar and spurious
pragmatism.
14 Clairmonte (1960).
15 Preston (1982).
16 Passmore (1970).
17 Habermas (1971b).
18 Myrdal's scheme of 'cumulative circular causation' embraces the idea of
inertia.
19 Allen (1975).
20 The notion of 'crisis' permits the claim that dissensus has been
temporarily overcome – a 'constituency' is created by pressure of events.

21 Brookfield (1975), pp. 76-7.
22 Streeten (1981), pp. 61-2.
23 The rise of technocratic politics in the First World is of long-standing concern for social scientists. For example Max Weber and his 'iron cage of bureacratic rationality', and recently all the work surrounding the Frankfurt School. Now the way in which this idea, or area of concern, can be shifted to the context of the Third World is problematic. Oversimplifying matters radically, we could present an image of *entrenched class groupings* on the one hand *versus fluid groupings* – ethnic, religious, linguistic, etc. – on the other. Given these different political, economic and social circumstances, it is not too surprising that the institution or implantation of technocratic systems in the Third World has produced novel forms of polities.
24 Hoogevelt (1982).
25 But see also A.G. Frank and G. Palma; who goes into which box is debated.
26 Leys (1977).
27 One can speculate about whether or not – in the medium and long term – it would not have been better for us all if Three Mile Island actually had blown up. Some lessons need, it seems, to be made absolutely obvious before vested interests will acknowledge them.
28 Save for OPEC nations and the NICs.
29 Gellner (1964).
30 Davidson (1978).
31 'Development ideas in historical perspective', in Streeten (1981).
32 Hoogevelt (1982).
33 Streeten (1981), p.124.
34 One issue that I have not thus far satisfactorily presented, let alone resolved, is that of the precise role of 'general theories' in social theorizing. It seems as though I must regard them as 'preliminary cashings of moral stances' – they make sense of the world in a practical fashion. Moreover they achieve their task in this form. Subsequently we can posit two stages of revision: an initial 'polishing process' which sees the removal of gross errors, provision of examples, etc., and then the business of being taken up into elaborate academic discourse. This last step seems to me to be secondary and often misconceived in the light of the 'received model' – thus 'preliminary cashings' are misunderstood as research project outlines.

Bibliography

ALLEN, V. L. (1975) *Social Analysis: a Marxist Critique and Alternative*, London, Longman.

AVINERI, S. (1968) *The Social and Political Thought of Karl Marx*, Cambridge University Press.

BARAN, P. (1973) *The Political Economy of Growth*, Harmondsworth, Pelican.

BAUER, P. T. (1971) *Dissent on Development*, London, Weidenfeld & Nicolson.

BAUMAN, Z. (1972) 'Praxis: the controversial culture-society paradigm' in T. Shanin (ed.), *The Rules of the Game: Cross Disciplinary Essays on Models in Scholarly Thought*, London, Tavistock.

BAUMAN, Z. (1976a) *Towards a Critical Sociology*, London, Routledge & Kegan Paul.

BAUMAN, Z. (1976b) *Socialism: the Active Utopia*, London, George Allen & Unwin.

BENTON, T. (1977) *The Philosophical Foundations of the Three Sociologies*, London, Routledge & Kegan Paul.

BERLIN, I. (1969) *Four Essays on Liberty*, Oxford University Press.

BERNSTEIN, H. (1971) 'Modernization theory and the sociological study of development' in *Journal of Development Studies*, No. 7.

BERNSTEIN, H. (1979) 'Sociology of underdevelopment versus sociology of development'in D. Lehman (ed.), *Development of Theory*, London, Cass.

BERNSTEIN, R. (1976) *The Restructuring of Social and Political Theory*, Oxford, Blackwell.

BLACK, C. E. (ed.) (1976) *Comparative Modernization*, London, Collier Macmillan.

BLACKBURN, R. (1970) *see* Debray (1970).

BRENNER, R. (1977) 'The origins of capitalist development: a critique of neo-Smithian marxism', *New Left Review*, 104.

BROOKFIELD, H. (1975) *Interdependent Development*, London, Methuen.

CARDOSO, F. H. and FALETTO, E. (1979) *Dependency and Development in Latin America*, University of California Press.

195

BIBLIOGRAPHY

CARROLL, J. (1980) *Sceptical Sociology*, London, Routledge & Kegan Paul.
CARVER, T. (1975) *Karl Marx: Texts on Method*, Oxford, Blackwell.
CAUTE, D. (1970) *Fanon*, London, Fontana.
CLAIRMONTE, F. A. (1960) *Economic Liberalism and Underdevelopment*, Bombay, Asia Publishing House.
CLARK, C. (1957) *The Conditions of Economic Progress*, 3rd edn., London, Macmillan.
CRANSTON, M. (ed.) (1970) *The New Left*, London, Bodley Head.
CRICK, B. (1980) *Guardian*, 9 October.
CULLEY, L. (1978) 'Economic development in neo-marxist theory', in B. Hindess (ed.) (1978).
CUMPER, G. (1974) 'Dependence, development, and the sociology of economic thought', *Social and Economic Studies*, vol. 23.
DAVIDSON, B. (1978) *Africa in Modern History*, London, Allen Lane.
DEBRAY, R. (1967) *Revolution in the Revolution*, London, Monthly Review Press.
DEBRAY, R. (1970) *Strategy for the Revolution* (ed. R. Blackburn), London, Cape.
DiMARCO, L. E. (ed.) (1972) *International Economics and Development: Essays in Honor of Paul Prebisch*, London, Academic Press.
DOBB, M. (1973) *Theories of Value and Distribution since Adam Smith*, Cambridge University Press.
EAGLY, R. V. (ed.) (1968) *Events, Ideology and Economic Theory*, Wayne State University Press.
EHRENSAFT, P. (1971) 'Semi-industrial capitalism in the Third World: implications for social research in Africa', *Africa Today*, January.
FANON, F. (1967) *The Wretched of the Earth*, Harmondsworth, Penguin.
FAY, B. (1975) *Social Theory and Political Practice*, London, Allen & Unwin.
FOSTER-CARTER, A. (1964) 'Neo-marxist approaches to development and underdevelopment', in E. DeKadt and G. Williams (eds), *Sociology and Development*, London, Tavistock.
FOSTER-CARTER, A. (1979) 'Marxism versus dependency theory? A polemic', *Leeds Occasional Papers in Sociology*, no. 8.
FRANK, A. G. (1969a) *Capitalism and Underdevelopment in Latin America*, New York, Monthly Review Press.
FRANK, A. G. (1969b) *Latin America: Underdevelopment or Revolution*, New York, Monthly Review Press.
FRANK, A. G. (1972) *Lumpenbourgeoisie-Lumpendevelopment*, New York, Monthly Review Press.
FRANK, A. G. (1975) *On Capitalist Underdevelopment*, Bombay, Oxford University Press.
FRANK, A. G. (1978) *Dependent Accumulation and Underdevelopment*, London, Macmillan.
FURTADO, C. (1964) *Development of Underdevelopment*, University of California Press.
FURTADO, C. (1965) *Diagnosis of the Brazilian Crisis*, University of California Press.
FURTADO, C. (1970) *Economic Development of Latin America: a Survey*

from Colonial Times to the Cuban Revolution, Cambridge University Press.

GALBRAITH, J. K. (1967) *The New Industrial State*, Harmondsworth, Pelican.

GALBRAITH, J. K. (1970) *The Affluent Society*, Harmondsworth, Pelican.

GALBRAITH, J. K. (1975) *Economics and the Public Purpose*, Harmondsworth, Pelican.

GELLNER, E. (1964) *Thought and Change*, London, Weidenfeld & Nicolson.

GELLNER, E. (1974) *Legitimation of Belief*, Cambridge University Press.

GIDDENS, A. (1976) *New Rules of Sociological Method*, London, Hutchinson.

GIDDENS, A. (1979) *Central Problems in Social Theory*, London, Macmillan.

GIRVAN, N. (1973) 'The development of dependency economics in the Caribbean and Latin America: review and comparison', *Social and Economic Studies*, vol. 22.

GOLDMANN, L. (1969) *The Human Sciences and Philosophy*, London, Cape.

GOLDMANN, L. (1973) *The Philosophy of the Enlightenment*, London, Routledge & Kegan Paul.

GRUCHY, A. (1973) *Contemporary Economic Thought: the Contribution of Neo-institutional Economics*, London, Macmillan.

HABERMAS, J. (1971a) *Knowledge and Human Interest*, Boston, Beacon Press.

HABERMAS, J. (1971b) *Towards a Rational Society*, London, Heinemann.

HABERMAS, J. (1974) *Theory and Practice*, London, Heinemann.

HALL, J. (1981) *Diagnoses of Our Time*, London, Heinemann.

HAMILTON, P. (1974) *Knowledge and Social Structure*, London, Routledge & Kegan Paul.

HARROD, R. (1939) 'An essay in dynamic theory', *Economic Journal*, March.

HAWTHORN, G. (1976) *Enlightenment and Despair*, Cambridge University Press.

HETHERINGTON, P. (1978) *British Paternalism in Africa: 1920-1940*, London, Cass.

HILAL, J. (1970) 'Sociology and Underdevelopment', Durham University, mimeo.

HINDESS, B. (1977) *Philosophy and Methodology in the Social Sciences*, Hassocks, Harvester.

HINDESS, B. (ed.) (1978) *Sociologocal Theories of the Economy*, London, Macmillan.

HOLLIS, M. (1977) *Models of Man*, Cambridge University Press.

HOLLIS, M. and NELL, E. J. (1975) *Rational Economic Man*, Cambridge University Press.

HOOGEVELT, A. (1982) *The Third World in Global Development*, London, Macmillan.

HUDSON, L. (1972) *The Cult of the Fact*, London, Cape.

HUNTINGTON, S. (1971) 'The change to change: modernization, development, and politics', in Black (ed.) (1976).

JAY, M. (1973) *The Dialectical Imagination*, Boston, Little Brown.

JONES, H. (1975) *An Introduction to Modern Theories of Economic Growth*, London, Nelson.

197

KAY, G. (1975) *Development and Underdevelopment: a Marxist Analysis,* London, Macmillan.

KILMINSTER, R. (1975) 'On the structure of critical thinking', *Leeds Occasional Papers in Sociology,* no. 2.

KILMINSTER, R. (1979) *Praxis and Method,* London, Routledge & Kegan Paul.

KITCHING, G. (1982) *Development and Underdevelopment in Historical Perspective,* London, Methuen.

KURIHARA, K. (1968) 'The dynamic impact of history on Keynesian theory', in Eagly (ed.) (1968).

LARRAIN, G. (1979) *The Concept of Ideology,* London, Hutchinson.

LÉVI-STRAUSS, C. (1968) *Structural Anthropology,* London, Allen Lane.

LEWIS, W. A. (1955) *The Theory of Economic Growth,* London, Allen & Unwin.

LEWIS *et al.* (1951) *see* United Nations (1951).

LEYS, C. (1977) 'Underdevelopment and dependency: critical notes', *Journal of Contemporary Asia,* vol. 7.

LUKES, S. (1974) *Power: a Radical View,* London, Macmillan.

LUKES, S. (1977) *Essays in Social Theory,* London, Macmillan.

MACINTYRE, A. A. (1967) *A Short History of Ethics,* London, Routledge & Kegan Paul.

MACPHERSON, C. B. (1964) *The Political Theory of Possessive Individualism,* Oxford University Press.

MACPHERSON, C. B. (1966) *The Real World of Democracy,* Oxford University Press.

MACPHERSON, C. B. (1973) *Democratic Theory: Essays in Retrieval,* Oxford University Press.

MAGEE, B. (1973) *Popper,* London, Fontana.

MARTIN, K. and KNAPP, J. (eds) (1967) *The Teaching of Development Economics,* London, Cass.

MARX, KARL (1973) *Grundrisse,* Harmondsworth, Pelican.

MERTON, R. K. (1968) *Social Theory and Social Structure,* New York, Free Press.

MYRDAL, G. (1957) *Economic Theory and Underdeveloped Regions,* London, Duckworth.

MYRDAL, G. (1958) *Value in Social Theory* (ed. Paul Streeten), London, Routledge & Kegan Paul.

MYRDAL, G. (1970a) *Objectivity in Social Research,* London, Duckworth.

MYRDAL, G. (1970b) *The Challenge of World Poverty,* London, Allen Lane.

NAPOLEONI, C. (1972) *Economic Thought of the Twentieth Century,* London, Martin Robertson.

OXAAL, I., BARNETT, T. and BOOTH, D. (eds) (1975) *Beyond the Sociology of Development,* London, Routledge & Kegan Paul.

PALMA, G. (1978) 'Dependency: a formal theory of underdevelopment or a methodology for the analysis of concrete situations of underdevelopment', *World Development,* 6.

PASSMORE, J. (1970) *The Perfectibility of Man,* London, Duckworth.

POLLARD, S. (1971) *The Idea of Progress,* Harmondsworth, Penguin.

PRESTON, P. W. (1981a) 'An Analytical and Historical Survey of Theories of

Development in the Period 1945-1975,' Leeds, PhD dissertation.

PRESTON, P. W. (1981b) 'Theory and practice in development studies: neo-institutionalism in the late 1950s and 1960s', *Leeds Occasional Papers in Sociology*, no. 11.

PRESTON, P. W. (1982) *Theories of Development*, London, Routledge & Kegan Paul.

REISMAN, D. (1982) *State and Welfare*, London, Macmillan.

ROBINSON, J. (1962) *Economic Philosophy*, Harmondsworth, Pelican.

ROCKMORE, T. (1976) 'Radicalism, science and philosophy in Marx,' *Cultural Hermeneutics*, 3.

ROSTOW, W. W. (1960) *The Stages of Economic Growth*, Cambridge University Press.

ROXBOROUGH, I. (1979) *Theories of Underdevelopment*, London, Macmillan.

SACHS, I. (1976) *The Discovery of the Third World*, London, M.I.T. Press.

SHAW, M. (1975) *Marxism and Social Science: the Roots of Social Knowledge*, London, Pluto Press.

SOLOW, R. (1956) 'A contribution to the theory of economic growth', *Quarterly Journal of Economics*.

STREETEN, P. (ed.) (1970) *Unfashionable Economics: Essays in Honour of Lord Balogh*, London, Weidenfeld & Nicolson.

STREETEN, P. (1972) *The Frontiers of Development Studies*, London, Macmillan.

STREETEN, P. (1981) *Development Perspectives*, London, Macmillan.

SUTCLIFFE, R. (1973) Introduction to Baran (1973).

TAYLOR, C. (1967) 'Neutrality in political science' in P. Laslett and W. G. Runciman (eds), *Philosophy, Politics and Society*, 3rd series, Oxford, Blackwell.

TAYLOR, J. (1974) 'Neo-marxism and underdevelopment: a sociological phantasy', *Journal of Contemporary Asia*, vol. 4.

TAYLOR, J. (1979) *From Modernization to Modes of Production*, London, Macmillan.

TUDOR, A. (1982) *Beyond Empiricism: Philosophy of Science in Sociology*, London, Routledge & Kegan Paul.

UNITED NATIONS (1951) *Measures for the Economic Development of Underdeveloped Countries*, E/1986 ST/ECA/10.

VAN NIEWENHUIJZE, C. A. O. (1982) *Development Begins at Home*. Oxford, Pergamon.

WINCH, P. (1958) *The Idea of a Social Science and its Relation to Philosophy*, London, Routledge & Kegan Paul.

WODDIS, J. (1972) *New Theories of Revolution: A Commentary on the Views of Franz Fanon, Régis Debray and Herbert Marcuse*, London, Lawrence & Wishart.

WORSLEY, P. (1964) *The Third World*, London, Weidenfeld & Nicolson.

WORSLEY, P. (1969) 'Revolutionary theories', *Monthly Review Press*, May.

WORSLEY, P. (1974) 'The state of theory and the status of theory', *Sociology*, vol. 8.

YOUNG, N. (1977) *An Infantile Disorder? the Crisis and Decline of the New Left*, London, Routledge & Kegan Paul.

Index

Routledge Social Science Series

Routledge & Kegan Paul
London, Boston, Melbourne and Henley

39 Store Street, London WC1E 7DD
9 Park Street, Boston, Mass 02108
296 Beaconsfield Parade, Middle Park,
Melbourne, 3206 Australia
Broadway House, Newtown Road,
Henley-on-Thames, Oxon RG9 1EN

Contents

*Authors wishing to submit manuscripts for any series
in this catalogue should send them to the Social Science Editor,
Routledge & Kegan Paul plc, 39 Store Street,
London WC1E 7DD.*
● *Books so marked are available in paperback also.*
○ *Books so marked are available in paperback only.*
*All books are in metric Demy 8vo format (216 × 138mm approx.)
unless otherwise stated.*

International Library of Sociology
General Editor John Rex

GENERAL SOCIOLOGY

Alexander, J. Theoretical Logic in Sociology.
  Volume 1: Positivism, Presuppositions and Current Controversies. *234 pp.*
  Volume 2: The Antinomies of Classical Thought: *Marx and Durkheim.*
  Volume 3: The Classical Attempt at Theoretical Synthesis: *Max Weber.*
  Volume 4: The Modern Reconstruction of Classical Thought: *Talcott Parsons.*
Barnsley, J. H. The Social Reality of Ethics. *464 pp.*
Brown, Robert. Explanation in Social Science. *208 pp.*
● Rules and Laws in Sociology. *192 pp.*
Bruford, W. H. Chekhov and His Russia. *A Sociological Study. 244 pp.*
Burton, F. and **Carlen, P.** Official Discourse. *On Discourse Analysis, Government Publications, Ideology. 160 pp.*
Cain, Maureen E. Society and the Policeman's Role. *326 pp.*
● **Fletcher, Colin.** Beneath the Surface. *An Account of Three Styles of Sociological Research. 221 pp.*
Gibson, Quentin. The Logic of Social Enquiry. *240 pp.*
Glassner, B. Essential Interactionism. *208 pp.*
Glucksmann, M. Structuralist Analysis in Contemporary Social Thought. *212 pp.*
Gurvitch, Georges. Sociology of Law. *Foreword by Roscoe Pound. 264 pp.*
Hinkle, R. Founding Theory of American Sociology 1881–1913. *376 pp.*
Homans, George C. Sentiments and Activities. *336 pp.*
Johnson, Harry M. Sociology: *A Systematic Introduction. Foreword by Robert K. Merton. 710 pp.*
● **Keat, Russell** and **Urry, John.** Social Theory as Science. *Second Edition. 278 pp.*
Mannheim, Karl. Essays on Sociology and Social Psychology. *Edited by Paul Kecskemeti. With Editorial Note by Adolph Lowe. 344 pp.*
Martindale, Don. The Nature and Types of Sociological Theory. *292 pp.*
● **Maus, Heinz.** A Short History of Sociology. *234 pp.*
Merquior, J. G. Rousseau and Weber. *A Study in the Theory of Legitimacy. 240 pp.*
Myrdal, Gunnar. Value in Social Theory: *A Collection of Essays on Methodology. Edited by Paul Streeten. 332 pp.*
Ogburn, William F. and **Nimkoff, Meyer F.** A Handbook of Sociology. *Preface by Karl Mannheim. 656 pp. 46 figures. 35 tables.*
Parsons, Talcott and **Smelser, Neil J.** Economy and Society: *A Study in the Integration of Economic and Social Theory. 362 pp.*
Payne, G., Dingwall, R., Payne, J. and **Carter, M.** Sociology and Social Research. *336 pp.*
Podgórecki, A. Practical Social Sciences. *144 pp.*
Podgórecki, A. and **Łos, M.** Multidimensional Sociology. *268 pp.*
Raffel, S. Matters of Fact. *A Sociological Inquiry. 152 pp.*
● **Rex, John.** Key Problems of Sociological Theory. *220 pp.*
  Sociology and the Demystification of the Modern World. *282 pp.*
● **Rex, John.** (Ed.) Approaches to Sociology. *Contributions by Peter Abell, Frank Bechhofer, Basil Bernstein, Ronald Fletcher, David Frisby, Miriam Glucksmann, Peter Lassman, Herminio Martins, John Rex, Roland Robertson, John Westergaard and Jock Young. 302 pp.*
Rigby, A. Alternative Realities. *352 pp.*
Roche, M. Phenomenology, Language and the Social Sciences. *374 pp.*
Sahay, A. Sociological Analysis. *220 pp.*
Strasser, Hermann. The Normative Structure of Sociology. *Conservative and Emancipatory Themes in Social Thought. 286 pp.*

Strong, P. Ceremonial Order of the Clinic. *267 pp.*
Urry, J. Reference Groups and the Theory of Revolution. *244 pp.*
Weinberg, E. Development of Sociology in the Soviet Union. *173 pp.*

FOREIGN CLASSICS OF SOCIOLOGY

● Gerth, H. H. and Mills, C. Wright. From Max Weber: *Essays in Sociology.*
502 pp.
● Tönnies, Ferdinand. Community and Association (*Gemeinschaft und Gesell-schaft*). *Translated and Supplemented by Charles P. Loomis. Foreword by Pitirim A. Sorokin. 334 pp.*

SOCIAL STRUCTURE

Andreski, Stanislav. Military Organization and Society. *Foreword by Professor A. R. Radcliffe-Brown. 226 pp. 1 folder.*
Bozzoli, B. The Political Nature of a Ruling Class. *Capital and Ideology in South Africa 1890–1939. 396 pp.*
Bauman, Z. Memories of Class. *The Prehistory and After life of Class. 240 pp.*
Broom, L., Lancaster Jones, F., McDonnell, P. and Williams, T. The Inheritance of Inequality. *208 pp.*
Carlton, Eric. Ideology and Social Order. *Foreword by Professor Philip Abrahams. 326 pp.*
Clegg, S. and Dunkerley, D. Organization, Class and Control. *614 pp.*
Coontz, Sydney H. Population Theories and the Economic Interpretation. *202 pp.*
Coser, Lewis. The Functions of Social Conflict. *204 pp.*
Crook, I. and D. The First Years of the Yangyi Commune. *304 pp., illustrated.*
Dickie-Clark, H. F. Marginal Situation: *A Sociological Study of a Coloured Group. 240 pp. 11 tables.*
Fidler, J. The British Business Elite. *Its Attitudes to Class, Status and Power. 332 pp.*
Giner, S. and Archer, M. S. (Eds) Contemporary Europe: *Social Structures and Cultural Patterns. 336 pp.*
● Glaser, Barney and Strauss, Anselm L. Status Passage: *A Formal Theory. 212 pp.*
Glass, D. V. (Ed.) Social Mobility in Britain. *Contributions by J. Berent, T. Bottomore, R. C. Chambers, J. Floud, D. V. Glass, J. R. Hall, H. T. Himmelweit, R. K. Kelsall, F. M. Martin, C. A. Moser, R. Mukherjee and W. Ziegel. 420 pp.*
Kelsall, R. K. Higher Civil Servants in Britain: *From 1870 to the Present Day. 268 pp. 31 tables.*
● Lawton, Denis. Social Class, Language and Education. *192 pp.*
McLeish, John. The Theory of Social Change. *Four Views Considered. 128 pp.*
● Marsh, David C. The Changing Social Structure of England and Wales, 1871–1961. *Revised edition. 288 pp.*
Menzies, Ken. Talcott Parsons and the Social Image of Man. *206 pp.*
● Mouzelis, Nicos. Organization and Bureaucracy. *An Analysis of Modern Theories. 240 pp.*
● Ossowski, Stanislaw. Class Structure in the Social Consciousness. *210 pp.*
● Podgórecki, Adam. Law and Society. *302 pp.*
Ratcliffe, P. Racism and Reaction. *A Profile of Handsworth. 388 pp.*
Renner, Karl. Institutions of Private Law and Their Social Functions. *Edited, with an Introduction and Notes, by O. Kahn-Freud. Translated by Agnes Schwarzschild. 316 pp.*
Rex, J. and Tomlinson, S. Colonial Immigrants in a British City. *A Class Analysis. 368 pp.*
Smooha, S. Israel. *Pluralism and Conflict. 472 pp.*
Strasser, H. and Randall, S. C. An Introduction to Theories of Social Change. *300 pp.*

Wesolowski, W. Class, Strata and Power. *Trans. and with Introduction by G. Kolankiewicz. 160 pp.*

Zureik, E. Palestinians in Israel. *A Study in Internal Colonialism. 264 pp.*

SOCIOLOGY AND POLITICS

Acton, T. A. Gypsy Politics and Social Change. *316 pp.*

Burton, F. Politics of Legitimacy. *Struggles in a Belfast Community. 250 pp.*

Crook, I. and D. Revolution in a Chinese Village. *Ten Mile Inn. 216 pp., illustrated.*

de Silva, S. B. D. The Political Economy of Underdevelopment. *640 pp.*

Etzioni-Halevy, E. Political Manipulation and Administrative Power. *A Comparative Study. 228 pp.*

Fielding, N. The National Front. *260 pp.*

● Hechter, Michael. Internal Colonialism. *The Celtic Fringe in British National Development, 1536–1966. 380 pp.*

Levy, N. The Foundations of the South African Cheap Labour System. *367 pp.*

Kornhauser, William. The Politics of Mass Society. *272 pp. 20 tables.*

● Korpi, W. The Working Class in Welfare Capitalism. *Work, Unions and Politics in Sweden. 472 pp.*

Kroes, R. Soldiers and Students. *A Study of Right- and Left-wing Students. 174 pp.*

Martin, Roderick. Sociology of Power. *214 pp.*

Merquior, J. G. Rousseau and Weber. *A Study in the Theory of Legitimacy. 286 pp.*

Myrdal, Gunnar. The Political Element in the Development of Economic Theory. *Translated from the German by Paul Streeten. 282 pp.*

Preston, P. W. Theories of Development. *296 pp.*

Varma, B. N. The Sociology and Politics of Development. *A Theoretical Study. 236 pp.*

Wong, S.-L. Sociology and Socialism in Contemporary China. *160 pp.*

Wootton, Graham. Workers, Unions and the State. *188 pp.*

CRIMINOLOGY

Ancel, Marc. Social Defence: *A Modern Approach to Criminal Problems. Foreword by Leon Radzinowicz. 240 pp.*

Athens, L. Violent Criminal Acts and Actors. *104 pp.*

Cain, Maureen E. Society and the Policeman's Role. *326 pp.*

Cloward, Richard A. and Ohlin, Lloyd E. Delinquency and Opportunity: *A Theory of Delinquent Gangs. 248 pp.*

Downes, David M. The Delinquent Solution. *A Study in Subcultural Theory. 296 pp.*

Friedlander, Kate. The Psycho-Analytical Approach to Juvenile Delinquency: *Theory, Case Studies, Treatment. 320 pp.*

Glueck, Sheldon and Eleanor. Family Environment and Delinquency. *With the statistical assistance of Rose W. Kneznek. 340 pp.*

Lopez-Rey, Manuel. Crime. *An Analytical Appraisal. 288 pp.*

Mannheim, Hermann. Comparative Criminology: *A Text Book. Two volumes. 442 pp. and 380 pp.*

Morris, Terence. The Criminal Area: *A Study in Social Ecology. Foreword by Hermann Mannheim. 232 pp. 25 tables. 4 maps.*

Rock, Paul. Making People Pay. *338 pp.*

● Taylor, Ian, Walton, Paul and Young, Jock. The New Criminology. *For a Social Theory of Deviance. 325 pp.*

● Taylor, Ian, Walton, Paul and Young, Jock. (Eds) Critical Criminology. *268 pp.*

SOCIAL PSYCHOLOGY

Bagley, Christopher. The Social Psychology of the Epileptic Child. *320 pp.*
Brittan, Arthur. Meanings and Situations. *224 pp.*
Carroll, J. Break-Out from the Crystal Palace. *200 pp.*
● **Fleming, C. M.** Adolescence: Its Social Psychology. *With an Introduction to recent findings from the fields of Anthropology, Physiology, Medicine, Psychometrics and Sociometry. 288 pp.*
● The Social Psychology of Education: *An Introduction and Guide to Its Study. 136 pp.*
Linton, Ralph. The Cultural Background of Personality. *132 pp.*
● **Mayo, Elton.** The Social Problems of an Industrial Civilization. *With an Appendix on the Political Problem. 180 pp.*
Ottaway, A. K. C. Learning Through Group Experience. *176 pp.*
Plummer, Ken. Sexual Stigma. *An Interactionist Account. 254 pp.*
● **Rose, Arnold M.** (Ed.) Human Behaviour and Social Processes: *an Interactionist Approach. Contributions by Arnold M. Rose, Ralph H. Turner, Anselm Strauss, Everett C. Hughes, E. Franklin Frazier, Howard S. Becker et al. 696 pp.*
Smelser, Neil J. Theory of Collective Behaviour. *448 pp.*
Stephenson, Geoffrey M. The Development of Conscience. *128 pp.*
Young, Kimball. Handbook of Social Psychology. *658 pp. 16 figures. 10 tables.*

SOCIOLOGY OF THE FAMILY

Bell, Colin R. Middle Class Families: *Social and Geographical Mobility. 224 pp.*
Burton, Lindy. Vulnerable Children. *272 pp.*
Gavron, Hannah. The Captive Wife: *Conflicts of Household Mothers. 190 pp.*
George, Victor and **Wilding, Paul.** Motherless Families. *248 pp.*
Klein, Josephine. Samples from English Cultures.
    1. Three Preliminary Studies and Aspects of Adult Life in England. *447 pp.*
    2. Child-Rearing Practices and Index. *247 pp.*
Klein, Viola. The Feminine Character. *History of an Ideology. 244 pp.*
McWhinnie, Alexina M. Adopted Children. *How They Grow Up. 304 pp.*
● **Morgan, D. H. J.** Social Theory and the Family. *188 pp.*
● **Myrdal, Alva** and **Klein, Viola.** Women's Two Roles: *Home and Work. 238 pp. 27 tables.*
Parsons, Talcott and **Bales, Robert F.** Family: Socialization and Interaction Process. *In collaboration with James Olds, Morris Zelditch and Philip E. Slater. 456 pp. 50 figures and tables.*

SOCIAL SERVICES

Bastide, Roger. The Sociology of Mental Disorder. *Translated from the French by Jean McNeil. 260 pp.*
Carlebach, Julius. Caring for Children in Trouble. *266 pp.*
George, Victor. Foster Care. *Theory and Practice. 234 pp.*
  Social Security: *Beveridge and After. 258 pp.*
George, V. and **Wilding, P.** Motherless Families. *248 pp.*
● **Goetschius, George W.** Working with Community Groups. *256 pp.*
Goetschius, George W. and **Tash, Joan.** Working with Unattached Youth. *416 pp.*
Heywood, Jean S. Children in Care. *The Development of the Service for the Deprived Child. Third revised edition. 284 pp.*
King, Roy D., Ranes, Norma V. and **Tizard, Jack.** Patterns of Residential Care. *356 pp.*
Leigh, John. Young People and Leisure. *256 pp.*
● **Mays, John.** (Ed.) Penelope Hall's Social Services of England and Wales. *368 pp.*

Morris Mary. Voluntary Work and the Welfare State. *300 pp.*
Nokes. P. L. The Professional Task in Welfare Practice. *152 pp.*
Timms, Noel. Psychiatric Social Work in Great Britain (1939–1962). *280 pp.*
● Social Casework: *Principles and Practice. 256 pp.*

SOCIOLOGY OF EDUCATION

Banks, Olive. Parity and Prestige in English Secondary Education: a Study in Educational Sociology. *272 pp.*
● Blyth, W. A. L. English Primary Education. *A Sociological Description.* 2. Background. *168 pp.*
Collier, K. G. The Social Purposes of Education: *Personal and Social Values in Education. 268 pp.*
Evans, K. M. Sociometry and Education. *158 pp.*
● Ford, Julienne. Social Class and the Comprehensive School. *192 pp.*
Foster, P. J. Education and Social Change in Ghana. *336 pp. 3 maps.*
Fraser, W. R. Education and Society in Modern France. *150 pp.*
Grace, Gerald R. Role Conflict and the Teacher. *150 pp.*
Hans, Nicholas. New Trends in Education in the Eighteenth Century. *278 pp. 19 tables.*
● Comparative Education: *A Study of Educational Factors and Traditions. 360 pp.*
● Hargreaves, David. Interpersonal Relations and Education. *432 pp.*
● Social Relations in a Secondary School. *240 pp.*
School Organization and Pupil Involvement. *A Study of Secondary Schools.*
● Mannheim, Karl and Stewart, W. A. C. An Introduction to the Sociology of Education. *206 pp.*
● Musgrove, F. Youth and the Social Order. *176 pp.*
● Ottaway, A. K. C. Education and Society: An Introduction to the Sociology of Education. *With an Introduction by W. O. Lester Smith. 212 pp.*
Peers, Robert. Adult Education: *A Comparative Study. Revised edition. 398 pp.*
Stratta, Erica. The Education of Borstal Boys. *A Study of their Educational Experiences prior to, and during, Borstal Training. 256 pp.*
● Taylor, P. H., Reid, W. A. and Holley, B. J. The English Sixth Form. *A Case Study in Curriculum Research. 198 pp.*

SOCIOLOGY OF CULTURE

● Eppel, E. M. and M. Adolescents and Morality: *A Study of some Moral Values and Dilemmas of Working Adolescents in the Context of a changing Climate of Opinion. Foreword by W. J. H. Sprott. 268 pp. 39 tables.*
● Fromm, Erich. The Fear of Freedom. *286 pp.*
● The Sane Society. *400 pp.*
Johnson, L. The Cultural Critics. *From Matthew Arnold to Raymond Williams. 233 pp.*
Mannheim, Karl. Essays on the Sociology of Culture. *Edited by Ernst Mannheim in co-operation with Paul Kecskemeti. Editorial Note by Adolph Lowe. 280 pp.*
Structures of Thinking. *Edited by David Kettler, Volker Meja and Nico Stehr. 304 pp.*
Merquior, J. G. The Veil and the Mask. *Essays on Culture and Ideology. Foreword by Ernest Gellner. 140 pp.*
Zijderfeld, A. C. On Clichés. *The Supersedure of Meaning by Function in Modernity. 150 pp.*
Reality in a Looking Glass. *Rationality through an Analysis of Traditional Folly. 208 pp.*

SOCIOLOGY OF RELIGION

Argyle, Michael and **Beit-Hallahmi, Benjamin.** The Social Psychology of Religion. *256 pp.*

Glasner, Peter E. The Sociology of Secularisation. *A Critique of a Concept. 146 pp.*

Hall, J. R. The Ways Out. *Utopian Communal Groups in an Age of Babylon. 280 pp.*

Ranson, S., Hinings, B. and **Bryman, A.** Clergy, Ministers and Priests. *216 pp.*

Stark, Werner. The Sociology of Religion. *A Study of Christendom.*
  Volume II. *Sectarian Religion. 368 pp.*
  Volume III. *The Universal Church. 464 pp.*
  Volume IV. *Types of Religious Man. 352 pp.*
  Volume V. *Types of Religious Culture. 464 pp.*

Turner, B. S. Weber and Islam. *216 pp.*

Watt, W. Montgomery. Islam and the Integration of Society. 230 pp.

Pomian-Srzednicki, M. Religious Change in Contemporary Poland. *Sociology and Secularization. 280 pp.*

SOCIOLOGY OF ART AND LITERATURE

Jarvie, Ian C. Towards a Sociology of the Cinema. *A Comparative Essay on the Structure and Functioning of a Major Entertainment Industry. 405 pp.*

Rust, Frances S. Dance in Society. *An Analysis of the Relationships between the Social Dance and Society in England from the Middle Ages to the Present Day. 256 pp. 8 pp. of plates.*

Schücking, L. L. The Sociology of Literary Taste. *112 pp.*

Wolff, Janet. Hermeneutic Philosophy and the Sociology of Art. *150 pp.*

SOCIOLOGY OF KNOWLEDGE

Diesing, P. Patterns of Discovery in the Social Sciences. *262 pp.*

● **Douglas, J. D.** (Ed.) Understanding Everyday Life. *270 pp.*

● **Hamilton, P.** Knowledge and Social Structure. *174 pp.*

Jarvie, I. C. Concepts and Society. *232 pp.*

Mannheim, Karl. Essays on the Sociology of Knowledge. *Edited by Paul Kecskemeti. Editorial Note by Adolph Lowe. 353 pp.*

Remmling, Gunter W. The Sociology of Karl Mannheim. *With a Bibliographical Guide to the Sociology of Knowledge, Ideological Analysis, and Social Planning. 255 pp.*

Remmling, Gunter W. (Ed.) Towards the Sociology of Knowledge. *Origin and Development of a Sociological Thought Style. 463 pp.*

Scheler, M. Problems of a Sociology of Knowledge. *Trans. by M. S. Frings. Edited and with an Introduction by K. Stikkers. 232 pp.*

URBAN SOCIOLOGY

Aldridge, M. The British New Towns. *A Programme Without a Policy. 232 pp.*

Ashworth, William. The Genesis of Modern British Town Planning: *A Study in Economic and Social History of the Nineteenth and Twentieth Centuries. 288 pp.*

Brittan, A. The Privatised World. *196 pp.*

Cullingworth, J. B. Housing Needs and Planning Policy: *a Restatement of the Problems of Housing Need and 'Overspill' in England and Wales. 232 pp. 44 tables. 8 maps.*

Dickinson, Robert E. City and Region: *A Geographical Interpretation. 608 pp. 125 figures.*
  The West European City: *A Geographical Interpretation. 600 pp. 129 maps. 29 plates.*

Humphreys, Alexander J. New Dubliners: *Urbanization and the Irish Family.* *Foreword by George C. Homans. 304 pp.*

Jackson, Brian. Working Class Community: *Some General Notions raised by a Series of Studies in Northern England. 192 pp.*

● **Mann, P. H.** An Approach to Urban Sociology. *240 pp.*

Mellor, J. R. Urban Sociology in an Urbanized Society. *326 pp.*

Morris, R. N. and **Mogey, J.** The Sociology of Housing. *Studies at Berinsfield. 232 pp. 4 pp. plates.*

Mullan, R. Stevenage Ltd. *438 pp.*

Rex, J. and **Tomlinson, S.** Colonial Immigrants in a British City. *A Class Analysis. 368 pp.*

Rosser, C. and **Harris, C.** The Family and Social Change. *A Study of Family and Kinship in a South Wales Town. 352 pp. 8 maps.*

● **Stacey, Margaret, Batsone, Eric, Bell, Colin** and **Thurcott, Anne.** Power, Persistence and Change. *A Second Study of Banbury. 196 pp.*

RURAL SOCIOLOGY

● **Mayer, Adrian C.** Peasants in the Pacific. *A Study of Fiji Indian Rural Society. 248 pp. 20 plates.*

Williams, W. M. The Sociology of an English Village: *Gosforth. 272 pp. 12 figures. 13 tables.*

SOCIOLOGY OF INDUSTRY AND DISTRIBUTION

Dunkerley, David. The Foreman. *Aspects of Task and Structure. 192 pp.*

Eldridge, J. E. T. *Industrial Disputes. Essays in the Sociology of Industrial Relations. 288 pp.*

Hollowell, Peter G. The Lorry Driver. *272 pp.*

● **Oxaal, I., Barnett, T.** and **Booth, D.** (Eds) Beyond the Sociology of Development. *Economy and Society in Latin America and Africa. 295 pp.*

Smelser, Neil J. Social Change in the Industrial Revolution: *An Application of Theory to the Lancashire Cotton Industry, 1770–1840. 468 pp. 12 figures. 14 tables.*

Watson, T. J. The Personnel Managers. *A Study in the Sociology of Work and Employment, 262 pp.*

ANTHROPOLOGY

Brandel-Syrier, Mia. Reeftown Elite. *A Study of Social Mobility in a Modern African Community on the Reef. 376 pp.*

Dickie-Clark, H. F. The Marginal Situation. *A Sociological Study of a Coloured Group. 236 pp.*

Dube, S. C. Indian Village. *Foreword by Morris Edward Opler. 276 pp. 4 plates.*

India's Changing Villages: *Human Factors in Community Development. 260 pp. 8 plates. 1 map.*

Fei, H.-T. Peasant Life in China. *A Field Study of Country Life in the Yangtze Valley. With a foreword by Bronislaw Malinowski. 328 pp. 16 pp. plates.*

Firth, Raymond. Malay Fishermen. *Their Peasant Economy. 420 pp. 17 pp. plates.*

Gulliver, P. H. Social Control in an African Society: a Study of the Arusha, Agricultural Masai of Northern Tanganykia. *320 pp. 8 plates. 10 figures.* Family Herds. *288 pp.*

Jarvie, Ian C. The Revolution in Anthropology. *268 pp.*

Little, Kenneth L. Mende of Sierra Leone. *308 pp. and folder.*

Negroes in Britain. *With a New Introduction and Contemporary Study by Leonard Bloom. 320 pp.*

Tambs-Lyche, H. London Patidars. *168 pp.*

Madan, G. R. Western Sociologists on Indian Society. *Marx, Spencer, Weber, Durkheim, Pareto. 384 pp.*

Mayer, A. C. Peasants in the Pacific. *A Study of Fiji Indian Rural Society. 248 pp.*

Meer, Fatima. Race and Suicide in South Africa. *325 pp.*

Smith, Raymond T. The Negro Family in British Guiana: *Family Structure and Social Status in the Villages. With a Foreword by Meyer Fortes. 314 pp. 8 plates. 1 figure. 4 maps.*

SOCIOLOGY AND PHILOSOPHY

● Adriaansens, H. Talcott Parsons and the Conceptual Dilemma. *200 pp.*

Barnsley, John H. The Social Reality of Ethics. *A Comparative Analysis of Moral Codes. 448 pp.*

Diesing, Paul. Patterns of Discovery in the Social Sciences. *362 pp.*

● Douglas, Jack D. (Ed.) Understanding Everyday Life. *Toward the Reconstruction of Sociological Knowledge. Contributions by Alan F. Blum, Aaron W. Cicourel, Norman K. Denzin, Jack D. Douglas, John Heeren, Peter McHugh, Peter K. Manning, Melvin Power, Matthew Speier, Roy Turner, D. Lawrence Wieder, Thomas P. Wilson and Don H. Zimmerman. 370 pp.*

Gorman, Robert A. The Dual Vision. *Alfred Schutz and the Myth of Phenomenological Social Science. 240 pp.*

Jarvie, Ian C. Concepts and Society. *216 pp.*

Kilminster, R. Praxis and Method. *A Sociological Dialogue with Lukács, Gramsci and the Early Frankfurt School. 334 pp.*

Outhwaite, W. Concept Formation in Social Science. *255 pp.*

● Pelz, Werner. The Scope of Understanding in Sociology. *Towards a More Radical Reorientation in the Social Humanistic Sciences. 283 pp.*

Roche, Maurice, Phenomenology, Language and the Social Sciences. *371 pp.*

Sahay, Arun. Sociological Analysis. *212 pp.*

● Slater, P. Origin and Significance of the Frankfurt School. *A Marxist Perspective. 185 pp.*

Spurling, L. Phenomenology and the Social World. *The Philosophy of Merleau-Ponty and its Relation to the Social Sciences. 222 pp.*

Wilson, H. T. The American Ideology. *Science, Technology and Organization as Modes of Rationality. 368 pp.*

International Library of Anthropology
General Editor Adam Kuper

● Ahmed, A. S. Millennium and Charisma Among Pathans. *A Critical Essay in Social Anthropology. 192 pp.*
Pukhtun Economy and Society. *Traditional Structure and Economic Development. 422 pp.*

Barth, F. Selected Essays. *Volume 1. 256 pp.* Selected Essays. *Volume II. 200 pp.*

Brown, Paula. The Chimbu. *A Study of Change in the New Guinea Highlands. 151 pp.*

Duller, H. J. Development Technology. *192 pp.*

Foner, N. Jamaica Farewell. *200 pp.*

Gudeman, Stephen. Relationships, Residence and the Individual. *A Rural Panamanian Community. 288 pp. 11 plates, 5 figures, 2 maps, 10 tables.*
The Demise of a Rural Economy. *From Subsistence to Capitalism in a Latin American Village. 160 pp.*

Hamnett, Ian. Chieftainship and Legitimacy. *An Anthropological Study of Executive Law in Lesotho. 163 pp.*

Hanson, F. Allan. Meaning in Culture. *127 pp.*

Hazan, H. The Limbo People. *A Study of the Constitution of the Time Universe Among the Aged. 208 pp.*

Humphreys, S. C. Anthropology and the Greeks. *288 pp.*

Karp, I. Fields of Change Among the Iteso of Kenya. *140 pp.*

Kuper, A. Wives for Cattle. *Bridewealth in Southern Africa. 224 pp.*

Lloyd, P. C. Power and Independence. *Urban Africans' Perception of Social Inequality. 264 pp.*

Malinowski, B. and **de la Fuente, J.** Malinowski in Mexico. *The Economics of a Mexican Market System. Edited and Introduced by Susan Drucker-Brown. About 240 pp.*

Parry, J. P. Caste and Kinship in Kangra. *352 pp. Illustrated.*

Pettigrew, Joyce. Robber Noblemen. *A Study of the Political System of the Sikh Jats. 284 pp.*

Street, Brian V. The Savage in Literature. *Representations of 'Primitive' Society in English Fiction, 1858–1920. 207 pp.*

Van Den Berghe, Pierre L. Power and Privilege at an African University. *278 pp.*

International Library of Phenomenology and Moral Sciences
General Editor John O'Neill

Adorno, T. W. Aesthetic Theory. Translated by C. Lenhardt.

Apel, K.-O. Towards a Transformation of Philosophy. *308 pp.*

Bologh, R. W. Dialectical Phenomenology. *Marx's Method. 287 pp.*

Fekete, J. The Critical Twilight. *Explorations in the Ideology of Anglo-American Literary Theory from Eliot to McLuhan. 300 pp.*

Green, B. S. Knowing the Poor. *A Case Study in Textual Reality Construction. 200 pp.*

McHoul, A. W. How Texts Talk. *Essays on Reading and Ethnomethodology. 163 pp.*

Medina, A. Reflection, Time and the Novel. *Towards a Communicative Theory of Literature. 143 pp.*

O'Neill, J. Essaying Montaigne. *A Study of the Renaissance Institution of Writing and Reading. 244 pp.*

Schutz. A. Life Forms and Meaning Structure. *Translated, Introduced and Annotated by Helmut Wagner. 207 pp.*

International Library of Social Policy
General Editor Kathleen Jones

Bayley, M. Mental Handicap and Community Care. *426 pp.*

Bottoms, A. E. and **McClean, J. D.** Defendants in the Criminal Process. *284 pp.*

Bradshaw, J. The Family Fund. *An Initiative in Social Policy. 248 pp.*

Butler, J. R. Family Doctors and Public Policy. *208 pp.*

Davies, Martin. Prisoners of Society. *Attitudes and Aftercare. 204 pp.*

Gittus, Elizabeth. Flats, Families and the Under-Fives. *285 pp.*

Holman, Robert. Trading in Children. *A Study of Private Fostering. 355 pp.*

Jeffs, A. Young People and the Youth Service. *160 pp.*

Jones, Howard and **Cornes, Paul.** Open Prisons. *288 pp.*

Jones, Kathleen. History of the Mental Health Service. *428 pp.*

11

Jones, Kathleen with Brown, John, Cunningham, W. J., Roberts, Julian and Williams, Peter. Opening the Door. *A Study of New Policies for the Mentally Handicapped. 278 pp.*
Karn, Valerie. Retiring to the Seaside. *400 pp. 2 maps. Numerous tables.*
King, R. D. and Elliot, K. W. Albany: Birth of a Prison—End of an Era. *294 pp.*
Thomas, J. E. The English Prison Officer since 1850. *258 pp.*
Walton, R. G. Women in Social Work. *303 pp.*
● Woodward, J. To Do the Sick No Harm. *A Study of the British Voluntary Hospital System to 1875. 234 pp.*

International Library of Welfare and Philosophy
General Editors Noel Timms and David Watson

○ Campbell, J. The Left and Rights. *A Conceptual Analysis of the Idea of Socialist Rights. About 296 pp.*
● McDermott, F. E. (Ed.) Self-Determination in Social Work. *A Collection of Essays on Self-determination and Related Concepts by Philosophers and Social Work Theorists. Contributors: F. P. Biestek, S. Bernstein, A. Keith-Lucas, D. Sayer, H. H. Perelman, C. Whittington, R. F. Stalley, F. E. McDermott, I. Berlin, H. J. McCloskey, H. L. A. Hart, J. Wilson, A. I. Melden, S. I. Benn. 254 pp.*
● Plant, Raymond. Community and Ideology. *104 pp.*
● Plant, Raymond, Lesser, Harry and Taylor-Gooby, Peter. Political Philosophy and Social Welfare. *Essays on the Normative Basis of Welfare Provision. 276 pp.*
Ragg, N. M. People Not Cases. *A Philosophical Approach to Social Work. 168 pp.*
Timms, Noel (Ed.) Social Welfare. *Why and How? 316 pp. 7 figures.*
● Timms, Noel and Watson, David (Eds) Talking About Welfare. *Readings in Philosophy and Social Policy. Contributors: T. H. Marshall, R. B. Brandt, G. H. von Wright, K. Nielsen, M. Cranston, R. M. Titmuss, R. S. Downie, E. Telfer, D. Donnison, J. Benson, P. Leonard. A. Keith-Lucas, D. Walsh, I. T. Ramsey. 230 pp.*
● Philosophy in Social Work. *250 pp.*
● Weale, A. Equality and Social Policy. *164 pp.*

Library of Social Work
General Editor Noel Timms

● Baldock, Peter. Community Work and Social Work. *140 pp.*
○ Beedell, Christopher. Residential Life with Children. *210 pp. Crown 8vo.*
● Berry, Juliet. Daily Experience in Residential Life. *A Study of Children and their Care-givers. 202 pp.*
○ Social Work with Children. *190 pp. Crown 8vo.*
● Brearley, C. Paul. Residential Work with the Elderly. *116 pp.*
● Social Work, Ageing and Society. *126 pp.*
● Cheetham, Juliet. Social Work with Immigrants. *240 pp. Crown 8vo.*
● Cross, Crispin P. (Ed.) Interviewing and Communication in Social Work. *Contributions by C. P. Cross, D. Laurenson, B. Strutt, S. Raven. 192 pp. Crown 8vo.*
● Curnock, Kathleen and Hardiker, Pauline. Towards Practice Theory. *Skills and Methods in Social Assessments. 208 pp.*
● Davies, Bernard. The Use of Groups in Social Work Practice. *158 pp.*
Davies, Bleddyn and Knapp, M. Old People's Homes and the Production of Welfare. *264 pp.*

● **Davies, Martin.** Support Systems in Social Work. *144 pp.*

    Ellis, June. (Ed.) West African Families in Britain. *A Meeting of Two Cultures. Contributions by Pat Stapleton, Vivien Biggs. 150 pp. 1 map.*

○ **Ford, J.** Human Behaviour. *Towards a Practical Understanding. About 160 pp.*

● **Hart, John.** Social Work and Sexual Conduct. *230 pp.*

    Heraud, Brian. Training for Uncertainty. *A Sociological Approach to Social Work Education. 138 pp.*

    Holder, D. and **Wardle, M.** Teamwork and the Development of a Unitary Approach. *212 pp.*

● **Hutten, Joan M.** Short-Term Contracts in Social Work. *Contributions by Stella M. Hall, Elsie Osborne, Mannie Sher, Eva Sternberg, Elizabeth Tuters. 134 pp.*

    Jackson, Michael P. and **Valencia, B. Michael.** Financial Aid Through Social Work. *140 pp.*

● **Jones, Howard.** The Residential Community. *A Setting for Social Work. 150 pp.*

● (Ed.) Towards a New Social Work. *Contributions by Howard Jones, D. A. Fowler, J. R. Cypher, R. G. Walton, Geoffrey Mungham, Philip Priestley, Ian Shaw, M. Bartley, R. Deacon, Irwin Epstein, Geoffrey Pearson. 184 pp.*

    Jones, Ray and **Pritchard, Colin.** (Eds) Social Work With Adolescents. *Contributions by Ray Jones, Colin Pritchard, Jack Dunham, Florence Rossetti, Andrew Kerslake, John Burns, William Gregory, Graham Templeman, Kenneth E. Reid, Audrey Taylor.*

○ **Jordon, William.** The Social Worker in Family Situations. *160 pp. Crown 8vo.*

● **Laycock, A. L.** Adolescents and Social Work. *128 pp. Crown 8vo.*

● **Lees, Ray.** Politics and Social Work. *128 pp. Crown 8vo.*

● Research Strategies for Social Welfare. *112 pp. Tables.*

○ **McCullough, M. K.** and **Ely, Peter J.** Social Work with Groups. *127 pp. Crown 8vo.*

● **Moffett, Jonathan.** Concepts in Casework Treatment. *128 pp. Crown 8vo.*

    Parsloe, Phyllida. Juvenile Justice in Britain and the United States. *The Balance of Needs and Rights. 336 pp.*

● **Plant, Raymond.** Social and Moral Theory in Casework. *112 pp. Crown 8vo.*

    Priestley, Philip, Fears, Denise and **Fuller, Roger.** Justice for Juveniles. *The 1969 Children and Young Persons Act: A Case for Reform? 128 pp.*

● **Pritchard, Colin** and **Taylor, Richard.** Social Work: Reform or Revolution? *170 pp.*

○ **Pugh, Elisabeth.** Social Work in Child Care. *128 pp. Crown 8vo.*

● **Robinson, Margaret.** Schools and Social Work. *282 pp.*

○ **Ruddock, Ralph.** Roles and Relationships. *128 pp. Crown 8vo.*

● **Sainsbury, Eric.** Social Diagnosis in Casework. *118 pp. Crown 8vo.*

● **Sainsbury, Eric, Phillips, David** and **Nixon, Stephen.** Social Work in Focus. *Clients' and Social Workers' Perceptions in Long-Term Social Work. 220 pp.*

● Social Work with Families. *Perceptions of Social Casework among Clients of a Family Service. 188pp.*

    Seed, Philip. The Expansion of Social Work in Britain. *128 pp. Crown 8vo.*

● **Shaw, John.** The Self in Social Work. *124 pp.*

    Smale, Gerald G. Prophecy, Behaviour and Change. *An Examination of Self-fulfilling Prophecies in Helping Relationships. 116 pp. Crown 8vo.*

    Smith, Gilbert. Social Need. *Policy, Practice and Research. 155 pp.*

● Social Work and the Sociology of Organisations. *124 pp. Revised edition.*

● **Sutton, Carole.** Psychology for Social Workers and Counsellors. *An Introduction. 248 pp.*

● **Timms, Noel.** Language of Social Casework. *122 pp. Crown 8vo.*

● Recording in Social Work. *124 pp. Crown 8vo.*
● **Todd, F. Joan.** Social Work with the Mentally Subnormal. *96 pp. Crown 8vo.*
● **Walrond-Skinner, Sue.** Family Therapy. *The Treatment of Natural Systems. 172 pp.*
● **Warham, Joyce.** An Introduction to Administration for Social Workers. *Revised edition. 112 pp.*
● An Open Case. *The Organisational Context of Social Work. 172 pp.*
○ **Wittenberg, Isca Salzberger.** Psycho-Analytic Insight and Relationships. *A Kleinian Approach. 196 pp. Crown 8vo.*

Primary Socialization, Language and Education
General Editor Basil Bernstein

Adlam, Diana S., *with the assistance of Geoffrey Turner and Lesley Lineker.* Code in Context. *272 pp.*
Bernstein, Basil. Class, Codes and Control. *3 volumes.*
●   1. *Theoretical Studies Towards a Sociology of Language. 254 pp.*
    2. *Applied Studies Towards a Sociology of Language. 377 pp.*
●   3. *Towards a Theory of Educational Transmission. 167 pp.*
Brandis, Walter and **Henderson, Dorothy.** Social Class, Language and Communication. *288 pp.*
Cook-Gumperz, Jenny. Social Control and Socialization. *A Study of Class Differences in the Language of Maternal Control. 290 pp.*
● **Gahagan, D. M.** and **G. A.** Talk Reform. *Exploration in Language for Infant School Children. 160 pp.*
Hawkins, P. R. Social Class, the Nominal Group and Verbal Strategies. *About 220 pp.*
Robinson, W. P. and **Rakstraw, Susan D. A.** A Question of Answers. *2 volumes. 192 pp. and 180 pp.*
Turner, Geoffrey J. and **Mohan, Bernard A.** A Linguistic Description and Computer Programme for Children's Speech. *208 pp.*

Reports of the Institute of Community Studies

Baker, J. The Neighbourhood Advice Centre. *A Community Project in Camden. 320 pp.*
● **Cartwright, Ann.** Patients and their Doctors. *A Study of General Practice. 304 pp.*
Dench, Geoff. Maltese in London. *A Case-study in the Erosion of Ethnic Consciousness. 302 pp.*
Jackson, Brian and **Marsden, Dennis.** Education and the Working Class: *Some General Themes Raised by a Study of 88 Working-class Children in a Northern Industrial City. 268 pp. 2 folders.*
Madge, C. and **Willmott, P.** Inner City Poverty in Paris and London. *144 pp.*
Marris, Peter. The Experience of Higher Education. *232 pp. 27 tables.*
● Loss and Change. *192 pp.*
Marris, Peter and **Rein, Martin.** Dilemmas of Social Reform. *Poverty and Community Action in the United States. 256 pp.*
Marris, Peter and **Somerset, Anthony.** African Businessmen. *A Study of Entrepreneurship and Development in Kenya. 256 pp.*
Mills, Richard. Young Outsiders: *a Study in Alternative Communities. 216 pp.*
Runciman, W. G. Relative Deprivation and Social Justice. *A Study of Attitudes to Social Inequality in Twentieth-Century England. 352 pp.*

14

Willmott, Peter. Adolescent Boys in East London. *230 pp.*
Willmott, Peter and Young, Michael. Family and Class in a London Suburb. *202 pp. 47 tables.*
Young, Michael and McGeeney, Patrick. Learning Begins at Home. *A Study of a Junior School and its Parents. 128 pp.*
Young, Michael and Willmott, Peter. Family and Kinship in East London. *Foreword by Richard M. Titmuss. 252 pp. 39 tables.*
The Symmetrical Family. *410 pp.*

Reports of the Institute for Social Studies in Medical Care

Cartwright, Ann, Hockey, Lisbeth and Anderson, John J. Life Before Death. *310 pp.*
Dunnell, Karen and Cartwright, Ann. Medicine Takers, Prescribers and Hoarders. *190 pp.*
Farrell, C. My Mother Said. . . *A Study of the Way Young People Learned About Sex and Birth Control. 288 pp.*

Medicine, Illness and Society
General Editor W. M. Williams

Hall, David J. Social Relations & Innovation. *Changing the State of Play in Hospitals. 232 pp.*
Hall, David J. and Stacey M. (Eds) Beyond Separation. *234 pp.*
Robinson, David. The Process of Becoming Ill. *142 pp.*
Stacey, Margaret *et al.* Hospitals, Children and Their Families. *The Report of a Pilot Study. 202 pp.*
Stimson, G. V. and Webb, B. Going to See the Doctor. *The Consultation Process in General Practice. 155 pp.*

Monographs in Social Theory
General Editor Arthur Brittan

● Barnes, B. Scientific Knowledge and Sociological Theory. *192 pp.*
Bauman, Zygmunt. Culture as Praxis. *204 pp.*
● Dixon, Keith. Sociological Theory. *Pretence and Possibility. 142 pp.*
The Sociology of Belief. *Fallacy and Foundation. 144 pp.*
Goff, T. W. Marx and Mead. *Contributions to a Sociology of Knowledge. 176 pp.*
Meltzer, B. N., Petras, J. W. and Reynolds, L. T. Symbolic Interactionism. *Genesis, Varieties and Criticisms. 144 pp.*
● Smith, Anthony D. The Concept of Social Change. *A Critique of the Functionalist Theory of Social Change. 208 pp.*
● Tudor, Andrew. Beyond Empiricism. *Philosophy of Science in Sociology. 224 pp.*

Routledge Social Science Journals

The British Journal of Sociology. *Editor – Angus Stewart; Associate Editor – Leslie Sklair. Vol. 1, No. 1 – March 1950 and Quarterly. Roy. 8vo. All back issues available. An international journal publishing original papers in the field of sociology and related areas.*

Community Work. *Edited by David Jones and Majorie Mayo. 1973. Published annually.*

Economy and Society. *Vol. 1, No. 1. February 1972 and Quarterly. Metric Roy. 8vo. A journal for all social scientists covering sociology, philosophy, anthropology, economics and history. All back numbers available.*

Ethnic and Racial Studies. *Editor – John Stone. Vol. 1 – 1978. Published quarterly.*

Religion. Journal of Religion and Religions. *Chairman of Editorial Board, Ninian Smart. Vol. 1, No. 1, Spring 1971. A journal with an inter-disciplinary approach to the study of the phenomena of religion. All back numbers available.*

Sociological Review. *Chairman of Editorial Board, S. J. Eggleston. New Series. August 1982, Vol. 30, No. 1. Published quarterly.*

Sociology of Health and Illness. *A Journal of Medical Sociology. Editor – Alan Davies; Associate Editor – Ray Jobling. Vol. 1, Spring 1979. Published 3 times per annum.*

Year Book of Social Policy in Britain. *Edited by Kathleen Jones. 1971. Published annually.*

Social and Psychological Aspects of Medical Practice
Editor   Trevor Silverstone

Lader, Malcolm. Psychophysiology of Mental Illness. *280 pp.*

● **Silverstone, Trevor** and **Turner, Paul.** Drug Treatment in Psychiatry. *Third edition. 256 pp.*

Whiteley, J. S. and **Gordon, J.** Group Approaches in Psychiatry. *240 pp.*